Masters, Slaves, and Exchange

This book examines the political economy of the master-slave relation viewed through the lens of consumption and market exchange. What did it mean when human chattel bought commodities, "stole" property, or gave and received gifts? Forgotten exchanges, this study argues, measured the deepest questions of worth and value, shaping an enduring struggle for power between slaves and masters. The slaves' internal economy focused intense paternalist negotiation on a ground where categories of exchange – provision, gift, contraband, and commodity – were in constant flux. At once binding and alienating, these ties endured constant moral stresses and material manipulation by masters and slaves alike, galvanizing conflict and engendering complex new social relations on and off the plantation.

Kathleen M. Hilliard is Assistant Professor in the Department of History at Iowa State University. She received her B.A. from Wake Forest University and her Ph.D. from the University of South Carolina, where she worked under the direction of Mark M. Smith and won the Wienefeld Award for best dissertation in history. Since 2006 she has studied and taught about the Old South, slavery, and the social and cultural contradictions of antebellum America in the decidedly unsouthern climes of the University of Idaho and Iowa State University. Portions of her work have been published in major essay collections and presented in scholarly meetings in the United States, the Netherlands, and the United Kingdom. She has served on the Editorial Board for *Agricultural History* and Gale/Cengage's *Slavery and Anti-Slavery* digital history project.

CAMBRIDGE STUDIES ON THE AMERICAN SOUTH

Series Editors

Mark M. Smith, *University of South Carolina, Columbia*
David Moltke-Hansen, *Center for the Study of the American South, University of North Carolina at Chapel Hill*

Interdisciplinary in its scope and intent, this series builds upon and extends Cambridge University Press's long-standing commitment to studies on the American South. The series will not only offer the best new work on the South's distinctive institutional, social, economic, and cultural history but will also feature works in a national, comparative, and transnational perspective.

Titles in the Series

Robert E. Bonner, *Mastering America: Southern Slaveholders and the Crisis of American Nationhood*

Ras Michael Brown, *African-Atlantic Cultures and the South Carolina Lowcountry*

Christopher Michael Curtis, *Jefferson's Freeholders and the Politics of Ownership in the Old Dominion*

Ari Helo, *Thomas Jefferson's Ethics and the Politics of Human Progress: The Morality of a Slaveholder*

Kathleen M. Hilliard, *Masters, Slaves, and Exchange: Power's Purchase in the Old South*

Scott P. Marler, *The Merchants' Capital: New Orleans and the Political Economy of the Nineteenth-Century South*

Peter McCandless, *Slavery, Disease, and Suffering in the Southern Lowcountry*

Johanna Nicol Shields, *Freedom in a Slave Society: Stories from the Antebellum South*

Brian Steele, *Thomas Jefferson and American Nationhood*

Jonathan Daniel Wells, *Women Writers and Journalists in the Nineteenth-Century South*

To my parents,
Margaret and Anthony Hilliard

Masters, Slaves, and Exchange

Power's Purchase in the Old South

KATHLEEN M. HILLIARD
Iowa State University

CAMBRIDGE
UNIVERSITY PRESS

CAMBRIDGE
UNIVERSITY PRESS

32 Avenue of the Americas, New York, NY 10013-2473, USA

Cambridge University Press is part of the University of Cambridge.

It furthers the University's mission by disseminating knowledge in the pursuit
of education, learning, and research at the highest international levels of excellence.

www.cambridge.org
Information on this title: www.cambridge.org/9781107636644

First published 2014

Printed in the United States of America

A catalog record for this publication is available from the British Library.

Library of Congress Cataloging in Publication data
Hilliard, Kathleen M., 1975– Masters, slaves, and exchange : power's purchase in the Old South /
Kathleen M. Hilliard, Iowa State University, Ames, Iowa.
    pages   cm. – (Cambridge studies on the American South)
Includes bibliographical references and index.
ISBN 978-1-107-04646-7 (hardback) – ISBN 978-1-107-63664-4 (paperback)
1. Slavery – Economic aspects – Southern States – History – 19th century.
2. Slavery – Social aspects – Southern States – History – 19th century.   3. Slaves – Southern
States – Economic conditions – 19th century.   4. Southern States – Economic conditions – 19th
century.   5. Slaveholders – Southern States – History – 19th century.   6. Plantation
owners – Southern States – History – 19th century.   7. Exchange – Social aspects – Southern
States – History – 19th century.   8. Consumer behavior – Social aspects – Southern States –
History – 19th century.   9. Paternalism – Southern States – History – 19th century.   I. Title.
E449.H65   2013
306.3'620975–dc23   2013022112

ISBN 978-1-107-04646-7 Hardback
ISBN 978-1-107-63664-4 Paperback

Contents

Figures and Tables

Acknowledgments

The experience of writing this book, I am chagrined to say, has often seemed to undermine the very argument it strives to make. I have received so many gifts freely bestowed; incurred countless debts graciously forgiven; trespassed without penalty upon the time of archivists, colleagues, and friends; and entered into a wealth of intellectual exchanges without the least concern of short-changing my partners. I guess that goes to show it is still sometimes possible to embrace scholarly exchange and the life of the mind beyond the purview of power and the dash for cash. Lucky me.

Fortunate I was, first off, to wander into Mark Smith's nineteenth-century seminar during my first term of grad school at the University of South Carolina. At that early point in my academic career, I understood little of what graduate education entailed, and Smith's course was a trial-by-fire experience that left me hooked on southern history. As teacher and mentor, his enthusiasm was immeasurable. Yet, Mark knew when to hold back, too. For both careful guidance and the gift of intellectual space to explore my own ideas, I cannot thank him enough. I offer my appreciation as well to Lawrence Glickman, Paul Johnson, Daniel Littlefield, Katherine Grier, Lacy Ford, Thomas Brown, and Walter Edgar. Well into revision, their comments, insights, and wonderfully divergent perspectives on antebellum society and economy helped shape this book.

Graduate peers were tough critics and generous first readers of this project in its earliest form. How lucky I was to share good conversation and scholarly debate with the likes of Aaron Marrs, Kevin Dawson, Rebecca Shrum, Michael Reynolds, Melissa Jane Taylor, and Eric Plaag. Although the plates of pimento cheese fries are long gone, Aaron and Kevin still pepper my inbox with tantalizing leads and obscure citations. I am grateful for their continued generosity. Even before this project began, Rebecca Shrum proved herself a true friend. She brought patience to my ramblings, good humor to my imagined burdens, and great food to my door when deadlines loomed. She remains a trusted colleague, friend, and critic. As her own manuscript goes forward, I hope that I may mirror her collegiality, kindness, and support.

Much of this project's maturation owes to series co-editor David Moltke-Hansen. His patient prodding to explain ideas more fully and unsurpassed understanding of paternalist thought in all its permutations helped transform this book from a narrow discussion of internal economy to a wide-ranging analysis of the master-slave relation. With intellect keen, vision uncommonly clear, and personality *sui generis*, David's good guidance made this book infinitely better. I'm also glad to thank Lewis Bateman, whose solid support and wry humor made working with Cambridge all the more rewarding, and Shaun Vigil, who shepherded this first-time author through the travails of publication and production.

The Southern Historical Association, the Society for Historians of the Early American Republic, the American Historical Association, the Organization of American Historians, the St. George Tucker Society, and the University of Illinois's Southern History Reading Group graciously provided opportunities for sharing my work. I am grateful to commentators and participants for their criticism. Thavolia Glymph, Larry Hudson, Stephen Mihm, James Oakes, Stephen Whitman, and Jeff Forret all provided wise suggestions and thoughtful insights. Over the years, too, Vernon Burton, Peter Coclanis, Charles Joyner, and Peter Kolchin have taken time to read portions of this manuscript. I am thankful for their kind words of encouragement and honest criticism.

The archives in Virginia, Georgia, and the Carolinas are stunningly rich, both in source material and in knowledgeable staff. At the South Caroliniana Library, Henry Fulmer, Graham Duncan, Robin Copp, Brian Cuthrell, and Allen Stokes guided me through the institution's vast resources. I appreciate, too, advice from Frances Pollard and Nelson Lankford at the Virginia Historical Society; Bryan Collars, Richard Harris, Patrick McCawley, and Steven Tuttle at the South Carolina Department of Archives and History; and the helpful professionals at the North Carolina Office of Archives and History, the Southern Historical Collection at the University of North Carolina, the Georgia Archives, the South Carolina Historical Society, the National Archives and Records Administration at College Park, and the Library of Virginia. Thanks especially to Leslie Rowland for taking the time to introduce me to Southern Claims Commission records and the rich files of the Freedmen and Southern Society Project at the University of Maryland.

Financial support from the Virginia Historical Society; the Institute for Southern Studies at the University of South Carolina; the Mayflower Society of South Carolina; the South Carolina Chapter of the Colonial Dames; and the College of Letters, Arts and Social Sciences at the University of Idaho facilitated the research and writing of this book. I am especially grateful to the Department of History and the College of Liberal Arts and Sciences at Iowa State University for their continued support.

Last Christmas, I unwrapped a package of bright pink pencils, my name and academic title embossed upon each. They're the key prop in a running joke within my family: Margaret and Anthony Hilliard have long threatened to show up to conferences and classrooms, passing these out to friends, colleagues, and students, a commodified sign of my labors, and of the close tie between us. Today, the splash of color in my desk drawer reminds me daily of the love, support, and good-humored perspective they have offered over the years, and all the writing I have yet to do. Let this book serve as poor payment for those pencils, and all the wonderful things they stand for. *Masters, Slaves, and Exchange* is dedicated to my parents, with love.

Pencils to sharpen, books to write, archives to plumb, the journey ahead is all the more exciting with Lawrence McDonnell at my side. Larry and I came together in work and love over an awful dinner at a hole-in-the-wall restaurant in Washington, DC's, Chinatown, fates sealed, so the fortune cookie said. Every day since has been a gift. My thanks to him, for everything, knows no bounds.

Archive Abbreviations

DUKE   David M. Rubenstein Rare Book and Manuscript Library, Duke University, Durham, North Carolina

GDAH   Georgia Department of Archives and History, Morrow, Georgia

GHS   Georgia Historical Society, Savannah, Georgia

LVA   Library of Virginia, Richmond, Virginia

NCOAH   North Carolina Office of Archives and History, Raleigh, North Carolina

SCDAH   South Carolina Department of Archives and History, Columbia, South Carolina

SCHS   South Carolina Historical Society, Charleston, South Carolina

SCL   South Caroliniana Library, University of South Carolina, Columbia, South Carolina

SHC   Southern Historical Collection, Louis Round Wilson Special Collections Library, University of North Carolina at Chapel Hill, Chapel Hill, North Carolina

VHS   Virginia Historical Society, Richmond, Virginia

Introduction

There was nothing unusual about the transactions: four sales – tobacco, a fine tooth comb, calico, and sugar – listed in sequence. Others bought more or less that day in early March 1855 – a bunch of twine, an assortment of hats, a box of caps. The clerk who logged the day's business surely recognized the purchasers, as the store's daybook listed their names several times before. Often grouped together in the ledger, they showed up once or twice a week. Elijah, Mattison, Dick, and Giss were regular customers.[1]

Of these men, we know little more. Their names do not appear in census rolls. They left no memoirs. No wills or probate documents explicate their identity or achievements at death. The tattered pages of storekeeper Stephen McCulley's daybook from Anderson, South Carolina, offer the most lasting history of these men's lives. Yet these records hint at key relationships and vital choices enacted both in Anderson and across the Old South. The surnames appearing next to those four transactions did not belong to the buyers of goods. Mr. Bailey, Mr. Boaseman, Mr. McCulley, and Col. Sanders claimed those names and, tragically, the men themselves. Elijah, Mattison, Dick, and Giss were slaves, people called property, discovered here in the undeniably human act of commodity exchange.

What can this ledger tell us of the men and women – black and white, enslaved and free – ensnared in the peculiar institution's web? Interrogating columns of names and numbers impels us to explore the tangled interaction of human value and material worth slavery represented.

Of the bondpeople themselves, we can but wonder:

What did they see as they crossed the store's threshold? Did they know exactly what they wanted or did they survey the counter? Could they wander the store and note an

---

[1] Entry of 3 March 1855, Account ledger, 1854–1856, Store Accounts of Stephen McCulley, SCDAH.

I

item for future purchase? Could they haggle for a better price? Might they have imagined a time when they could realize all their material needs and desires?

We could consider the clerk too:

Acquainted with his customers' usual purchases, did he reach for the bin of tobacco or the barrel of sugar when the men walked through the door or did he await their request? Did he follow their eyes as they scanned the mercantile space or was the banality of the interaction such that he barely glanced their way? Did his tone change when he shifted from white customer to black? Or, did familiar cordiality mark their exchange? Did he transmute into their equal in this moment of market liminality?

Finally, we might contemplate an unseen but perpetually looming presence:

Did masters approve of bondpeople's purchases? Did they monitor transactions? Did they sanction trade? Did they worry the money and goods the men came to possess might weaken their ability to discipline and control? Or, were these moments welcomed as opportunities to meet psychological and material needs that they were unwilling or unable to meet themselves?

The scratched notations only hint at the world behind the numbers, but the questions we ask reveal a singular truth. Such transactions were politics distilled – snapshots of struggle in which slave and master negotiated the limits of each other's power. The fading ink here simultaneously conceals and reveals a world of social contradiction, hurt, and worry, which is the main subject of this book.

Interpreting slavery as political struggle is nothing new. In his masterwork, *Roll, Jordan, Roll,* Eugene Genovese argued that masters and slaves of the Old South were tangled in an organic and reciprocal system of rights, privileges, and responsibilities. The hegemonic regime imposed by masters offered rational order and good government. In return, slaveholders demanded steady labor, faithful service, and most importantly, gratitude. Mastery, however, was not as simple as these dictates suggest. The terms, boundaries, rituals, and customs of this system were forever shifting in contentious dispute, entangling both in a web of endless negotiation and incipient violence.[2]

Genovese saw the relations of master and slave as distinct and different within the hemispheric conflicts over labor of which slavery was the most essential and barbarous. In contrast to Brazil or Cuba, where the violence of the warfare state was the norm, by the 1820s, southern masters had developed an ideology and cultural ethos that declared them fit to rule precisely because of the paternalistic character of slavery developed there. More than this, the reciprocity of rights and duties that paternalism imposed on master and slave

---

[2] Although Genovese asserted his paternalist argument most forcefully in *Roll, Jordan, Roll,* his earlier work on the topic bears close reading as well. Eugene D. Genovese, *Roll, Jordan, Roll: The World the Slaves Made* (New York: Pantheon Books, 1974). For a compilation of Genovese's early essays, see *In Red and Black: Marxian Explorations in Southern and Afro-American History* (New York: Pantheon Books, 1968), esp. pp. 102–157.

was not simply a defensive measure or conservative alibi.[3] At its height, in the last decades of the antebellum era, along the Atlantic seaboard it assumed an aggressive, distinctly anti-capitalist cast.

Genovese's paternalist thesis has attracted praise, criticism, and extraordinary misunderstanding.[4] His interpretation draws heavily on Antonio Gramsci's theory of cultural hegemony, and his fiercest critics are those who find fault with the Italian political philosopher's model of class rule. Ruling classes consolidated their power, Gramsci argued, by imposing their worldview upon dependent and subordinate masses. Rather than the persistent application of force, rulers offered concessions as a means of mitigating and minimizing revolutionary disruptions to their power. Outgunned and overmatched, working people had few choices. They took their struggle onto the terrain of culture to seize concessions – moral, ethical, or political – to rally support and maintain common cause.[5]

Understanding the master-slave relation as hegemonic contest troubles those scholars who wish to see "black kinship and black community life on their own terms."[6] Enslaved people's values, attitudes, and behaviors derived from interactions within the bound community. African culture or, at least a creolized version of it, played a far greater role in shaping slaves' lives than did masters' strictures. Song, dance, personal style, foodways, and family relationships reflected this overtly resistant and insular culture. Slaves rejected their owners' worldview outright, these scholars argue, standing firm against emotional, psychological, and political incursions into the world they scratched out for themselves.[7]

---

[3] See Walter Johnson's retrospective review of *Roll, Jordan, Roll* for the most strident, recent interpretation of paternalism as planter alibi. Walter Johnson, "A Nettlesome Classic Turns Twenty-Five," *Common-Place* 1, no. 4 (2001), http://www.common-place.org/vol-01/no-04/reviews/johnson.shtml.

[4] For a representative example of the tendentiousness of some of this criticism, see James D. Anderson, "Aunt Jemima in Dialectics: Genovese on Slave Culture," *Journal of Negro History* 61 (1976): 99–114.

[5] Genovese, *In Red and Black*, 391–422; Genovese, *Roll, Jordan, Roll*, 25–49, 147–149. Gramsci's ideas are fully articulated in his prison notebooks, written while a political prisoner under Mussolini's fascist regime from 1926 to 1934. See Antonio Gramsci, *Selections from the Prison Notebooks of Antonio Gramsci*, eds. Quintin Hoare and Geoffrey Nowell-Smith (New York: International Publishers, 1971), esp. p. 161.

[6] Dylan C. Penningroth, *The Claims of Kinfolk: African American Property and Community in the Nineteenth-Century South* (Chapel Hill: University of North Carolina Press, 2003), 185.

[7] Scholarly literature advancing this perspective is vast. For representative examples, see John W. Blassingame, *The Slave Community: Plantation Life in the Antebellum South* (New York: Oxford University Press, 1972); Charles Joyner, *Down by the Riverside: A South Carolina Slave Community* (Urbana: University of Illinois Press, 1984); Mechal Sobel, *The World They Made Together: Black and White Values in Eighteenth-Century Virginia* (Princeton: Princeton University Press, 1987); Sterling Stuckey, *Slave Culture: Nationalist Theory and the Foundations of Black America* (New York: Oxford University Press, 1987); John C. Inscoe, "Carolina Slave Names: An Index to Acculturation," *Journal of Southern History* 49 (1983): 527–554; Stephanie

At the heart of such criticism lies debate over the nature of resistance – what it consists of, who it affects, and how it is carried out. In *Roll, Jordan, Roll*, Genovese praised the groundbreaking work of Herbert Aptheker – who famously argued for a "revolutionary tradition" in the American slave community – but maintained that Aptheker's exclusive focus on "overt resistance … did not lay bare the essence of the slave experience." Compared to enslaved populations globally, Genovese argued, "slaves of the United States had always faced hopeless odds" and not surprisingly, he found "little evidence of a revolutionary folk tradition" among them. Seeking to "measure the smoldering resentment of an enslaved people who normally had to find radically different forms of struggle," Genovese challenges our understanding of how subordinate classes show discontent, pointing to "a record of simultaneous accommodation and resistance to slavery."[8] At great cost, he argued, contest surrendered concessions to forestall catastrophic capitulation:

Accommodation itself breathed a critical spirit and disguised subversive actions and often embraced its apparent opposite – resistance. In fact, accommodation might best be understood as a way of accepting what could not be helped without falling prey to the pressures for dehumanization, emasculation, and self-hatred. In particular, the slaves' accommodation to paternalism enabled them to assert rights, which by their very nature not only set limits to their surrender of self but actually constituted an implicit rejection of slavery.[9]

Critics claim that this interpretation minimizes slave agency, painting bondpeople as witless victims and guileless pawns. It diminishes the conscious political power bondpeople directed against their oppressors. The paucity of overt and large-scale insurrection, these scholars argue, stems simply from the vast forces arrayed against them. Instead of launching suicidal uprisings, bondpeople's daily acts of resistance chiseled away at masters' power. Wielding the "weapons of the weak" so imaginatively explored by the likes of James Scott and Robin Kelley, bondpeople engaged in politically-conscious and communally-rooted behavior that fundamentally "recalibrated" the master-slave relation.[10]

M. H. Camp, *Closer to Freedom: Enslaved Women and Everyday Resistance in the Plantation South* (Chapel Hill: University of North Carolina Press, 2004); Shane White and Graham White, *Stylin': African American Expressive Culture, from Its Beginnings to the Zoot Suit* (Ithaca, NY: Cornell University Press, 1998).

[8] Herbert Aptheker, *American Negro Slave Revolts* (New York: Columbia University Press, 1943); Genovese, *Roll, Jordan, Roll*, 587–597.

[9] Genovese, *Roll, Jordan, Roll*, 597–598.

[10] James C. Scott, *Weapons of the Weak: Everyday Forms of Peasant Resistance* (New Haven, CT: Yale University Press, 1985); Robin D. G. Kelley, *Race Rebels: Culture, Politics, and the Black Working Class* (New York: The Free Press, 1994). For an insightful description of the ways in which slaves "recalibrated" power relationships in southern communities, see Anthony E. Kaye's *Joining Places: Slave Neighborhoods in the Old South* (Chapel Hill: University of North Carolina Press, 2007). For specific reference to slaves' efforts to "recalibrate the balance of power in their society," see p. 12.

Beneath all of this criticism lies profound discomfort with the term "paternalism" itself. Genovese's word choice here has perhaps obscured, over the years, much that a close examination of his texts might reveal. In the nearly fifty years since Genovese first described the shift from patriarchal to paternalist relations in the antebellum period, critics have read masterly beneficence into paternalism, assuming that the racism that was so rampant in the work of Ulrich Phillips – whose scholarship Genovese greatly admired – pervades Genovese's own model. Nothing could be further from the truth, Peter Kolchin assures us in a thoughtful 2004 assessment of Genovese's career. Although close examination of *Roll, Jordan, Roll* and *Fatal Self-Deception*, his more recent work co-written with Elizabeth Fox-Genovese, reveal an admiration for southern slaveholders, these works do not point to a defense of them. "Kindness, love, and benevolence did not define paternalism," they reaffirmed in their recent work, reminding us unequivocally that the system "depended on the constant threat and actuality of violence."[11]

Despite the mountains of useful, insightful, and interesting work on slave life and culture that has grown up in at least partial response to Genovese's work, his critics have failed to provide a convincing alternative to the dialectic of accommodation and resistance that Genovese saw in the relation between master and slave. The "moonlight and magnolias" interpretation too often ascribed to Genovese's paternalist South has given way to romanticized and unrealistic assertions – and, indeed, expectations – of community solidarity and resistance among the enslaved. For Genovese, such studies demonstrate precisely what he and Elizabeth Fox-Genovese called the "political crisis of social history." That is, in marshaling all manner of cultural and community behavior to show how slaves wriggled out from under the thumb of oppressive masters, they obscure a central political fact. Regardless of how we complicate the narrative, at the end of the day, slaves remained slaves. The real scholarly problem, the Genoveses famously reminded us, is to explain "who rides whom and how" in the past.[12]

Historians of the internal economy – defined broadly as bondpeople's sale and purchase of goods produced or services rendered during their "off" time – have contributed mightily to these debates. Their work is certainly rich and tells much of the mechanics and larger meaning of the peculiar institution across space and time. Told most often in case study form, these analyses have documented the buying and selling of goods by slaves on and off the plantation in rural and urban environments, in the colonial and antebellum eras, and

[11] Peter Kolchin, "Eugene D. Genovese: Historian of Slavery," *Radical History Review* 88 (2004): 58; Eugene D. Genovese and Elizabeth Fox-Genovese, *Fatal Self-Deception: Slaveholding Paternalism in the Old South* (New York: Cambridge University Press, 2011), 2.
[12] Eugene D. Genovese and Elizabeth Fox-Genovese, "The Political Crisis of Social History: A Marxian Perspective," *Journal of Social History* 10 (1976), 219.

in North American and Caribbean contexts.[13] Property accumulation, scholars have argued, solidified bonds among kin and strengthened communities. Transactions across lines of class and race threatened an already porous southern social order. Most importantly, many historians and anthropologists have maintained, the internal economy affected the master-slave relation, serving as a means of self-expression and resistance to slaveholder rule. Finding full flourish in the 1980s and 1990s, such work has since become an indispensable component of research on slave life, economy, and culture and, significantly, a crucial cudgel in attacks levied against the paternalist thesis.[14]

Overlooked in many of these studies, however, is the simple tragedy of it all. The negotiation or bargain Genovese imagined brings to mind scripture and verse understood by most nineteenth-century Americans. "For what shall

[13] The rich historiography of the internal economy took root with questions posed by Sidney Mintz and Douglas Hall about Jamaican marketing practices and has since become a staple of work by historians, anthropologists, and sociologists in the region. See, in particular, Sidney W. Mintz, "The Jamaican Internal Marketing Pattern: Some Notes and Hypotheses," *Social and Economic Studies* 4 (1955): 95–103; Mintz and Douglas G. Hall, "The Origins of the Jamaican Internal Marketing System," *Yale University Publications in Anthropology* 57 (1960): 3–26. For an overview of Mintz's work, including several essays on internal economy, see Mintz, *Caribbean Transformations* (New York: Columbia University Press, 1974). Other important contributions to the study of Caribbean internal economy include work by Hilary M. Beckles, Woodville K. Marshall, Dale Tomich, and Mary Turner. For an overview of the literature in the Caribbean, see Ira Berlin and Philip D. Morgan, eds., *The Slaves' Economy: Independent Production by Slaves in the Americas* (London: Frank Cass, 1991).

[14] Philip D. Morgan was at the forefront of this movement, authoring two essays exploring the nature of the task system in lowcountry South Carolina and Georgia. See Morgan, "The Ownership of Property by Slaves in the Mid-Nineteenth-Century Lowcountry," *Journal of Southern History* 49 (1983): 399–420 and "Work and Culture: The Task System and the World of Lowcountry Blacks, 1700–1800," *William and Mary Quarterly* 3rd ser., 39 (1982): 563–599. Other important foundational work includes Loren Schweninger, *Black Property Owners in the South, 1790–1915* (Urbana: University of Illinois Press, 1990); Roderick A. McDonald, *The Economy and Material Culture of Slaves: Goods and Chattels on the Sugar Plantations of Jamaica and Louisiana* (Baton Rouge: Louisiana State University Press, 1993); Larry E. Hudson, Jr., "'All That Cash': Work and Status in the Slave Quarters," in *Working Toward Freedom: Slave Society and Domestic Economy in the American South*, ed. Larry E. Hudson, Jr. (Rochester: University of Rochester Press, 1994); Betty Wood, *Women's Work, Men's Work: The Informal Slave Economies of Lowcountry Georgia* (Athens: University of Georgia Press, 1995); Ted Ownby, *American Dreams in Mississippi: Consumers, Poverty, and Culture, 1830–1998* (Chapel Hill: University of North Carolina Press, 1999), esp. ch. 2; Timothy J. Lockley, "Trading Encounters between Non-Elite Whites and African Americans in Savannah, 1790–1860," *Journal of Southern History* 66 (2000): 25–48; Dylan C. Penningroth, *The Claims of Kinfolk: African American Property and Community in the Nineteenth-Century South* (Chapel Hill: University of North Carolina Press, 2003); Jeff Forret, "Slaves, Poor Whites, and the Underground Economy of the Rural Carolinas," *Journal of Southern History* 70 (2004): 783–824. For an overview of scholarship in this area, including essays by John Campbell, John Schlotterbeck, and Roderick A. McDonald, see Ira Berlin and Philip D. Morgan's edited collections, *The Slaves' Economy* and *Cultivation and Culture: Labor and the Shaping of Slave Life in the Americas* (Charlottesville: University Press of Virginia, 1993).

Mehfistohfeles
pronounciation

it profit a man, if he shall gain the whole world, and lose his own soul?" St. Mark asked. So too did Christopher Marlowe in his telling of the "tragical tale" of Dr. Faustus. Seeking godlike power and knowledge properly denied to sinful man, Marlowe tells us, Dr. Faustus summoned the devil before him. Mephistopheles appeared offering worldly plenty – knowledge, magical powers, and riches beyond Faustus's wildest dreams. The benighted scholar had only to promise his soul to the devil twenty-four years hence.[15]

Fallible Faust took the deal Mephistopheles proffered. Masters and slaves did too in their daily struggle for power in plantation communities. But who was the slave and who the devil in the paternalist bargain? The answer is not as clear-cut as historical labels might suggest. Antebellum planters, to be sure, imagined godlike power though, as slaves well understood, that power was often put to hellish purposes. With one hand masters held the whip and with the other they held out riches, demanding that slaves take part in the feast they had set out for them. Time and again, slaves did, risking salvation for more immediate gains. Keeping mind and body sound required recognition of slaveholders' terms but, as we will see, not complete acceptance of them – for slaves could play devil, too. Bondpeople offered tempting riches of their own – the fruits of their labor, certainly – but, more importantly, mastery itself. By holding prating paternalists to their own Faustian bargain, bondpeople measured their masters. Day-to-day resistance and moral judgment meant that slaveholders' power required constant refiguring, refining, readjusting. Peace, security, salvation, mastery – all stood upon sand. Although planters may have won temporary victories, perfect power gleamed just out of reach.

Faustian tragedy, then, fell on all sides. This book explores the paternalist bargain as it played out in one particular area of slaves' lives – the internal economy. Here the seductive riches in Marlowe's story serve as metaphor and reality. The internal economy both offered and required expenditures of capital – economic, political, and social – to and from slaves and masters alike. It simultaneously strengthened and attenuated ties between master and slave. Mechanics of exchange encouraged connections beyond the material world so carefully constructed by masters, yet reduced the impetus to flee it permanently. So it was too with the ideas and values attending these transactions. "Dream worlds" of material possibility invited imagination of a most dangerous sort – bidding slaves both to create fantasies of freedom and to question the very foundations of their owners' power.[16]

But slaveholders could match these challenges with denigrating judgments of their own, using the internal mechanisms of market exchange to cast aspersions

[15] Mark 8:36–37; Christopher Marlowe, *The Tragical History of Doctor Faustus*, in *The Complete Plays*, ed. J. B. Steane (London: Penguin, 1969), 259–339.
[16] The term, "dream worlds," refers to Rosalind H. Williams' discussion of late-nineteenth-century consumption in France. See Williams, *Dream Worlds: Mass Consumption in Late Nineteenth-Century France* (Berkeley: University of California Press, 1982).

gains were
are

They didn't do it on purpose; it was a commodity cultivated by the white man

fight for freedom → into sinful delusions for capital that while led to rebellion also perpetuated this whole idea of morally corrupt

on the selling and especially spending bondpeople engaged in. Daniel Horowitz
has called the value judgments that attend consumer behavior the "morality
of spending," arguing that Americans have long struggled with the ethical
implications of market expansion and material prosperity. That easy wealth
could corrupt a sturdy republican citizenry led commentators and social critics – from de Tocqueville to Veblen to Progressive-era budget managers – to
establish primers for principled purchasing. These guidelines, Horowitz argues,
served less as helpful suggestions for reforming America's moral character than
as weaponry for those who wished to distinguish themselves as social betters.
Appraisals of who, what, and how goods were purchased served to ascertain
social status, personal industry, and moral worth.[17]

Nowhere were these judgments more dangerous and damning than in the
antebellum South. Morals and markets both inside and outside the plantation
were inextricably entwined. Examining the ways that men and women who
lived in this world spent their money has the potential to reveal the mechanisms of accommodation and resistance at paternalism's core.

Lawrence Glickman has noted that the definition of consumer society is an
"essentially contested concept" with historians, anthropologists, and sociologists debating significance and meaning in terms of politics, material wealth,
infrastructure, economy, consciousness, or simple chronology.[18] This project
avoids attaching such a label to plantation communities. But it is useful to
consider a set of general markers or characteristics for evaluating the evolution
of consumer consciousness in society. Elaborating on John Benson's expansive definition,[19] Peter Stearns argues that a consumer society is one in which
a substantive portion of the population can purchase goods and services that
are not "necessities" and has the means, whether cash or access to credit, to be
able to do so. Second, a substantive portion of the population must derive emotional satisfaction from not only the acquisition of goods but also the search
for them, and that the qualities of "yearning" and "striving" necessarily must

[17] Daniel Horowitz, *The Morality of Spending: Attitudes Toward the Consumer Society in America,
1875–1940* (Baltimore: The Johns Hopkins University Press, 1985).

[18] Lawrence B. Glickman, "Born to Shop? Consumer History and American History," in *Consumer
Society in American History: A Reader* ed. Lawrence Glickman (Ithaca, NY: Cornell University
Press, 1999), 10. The historiography of consumerism and consumer societies has grown exponentially over the past thirty years and I cannot do it justice in terms of scope or influence in this
brief introduction. For a comprehensive overview of early work in the field, see Glickman's bibliographical essay in *Consumer Society in American History*, 299–314. For a more recent discussion of historiographic trends, see Frank Trentmann, ed., *Oxford Handbook of the History
of Consumption* (New York: Oxford University Press, 2012).

[19] According to Benson, consumer societies "are those in which choice and credit are readily available, in which social value is defined in terms of purchasing power and material possessions,
and in which there is a desire, above all, for all that which is new, modern, exciting and fashionable." John Benson, *The Rise of Consumer Society in Britain, 1880–1980* (New York: Longman,
1994), 4. Quoted in Peter N. Stearns, "Stages of Consumerism: Recent Work on the Issues of
Periodization," *Journal of Modern History* 69 (1997): 105.

accompany this behavior. Finally, consumer behavior must affect and, more importantly, confuse social structures.[20]

The term "substantive" here is relative and allows for consideration of the development of consumer behavior and its impact across space and time. It also demonstrates the perils of applying anything less than a malleable framework for interpreting the significance of the slaves' internal economy to the bondpeople who participated in it and to the plantation system as a whole. As this project demonstrates, many antebellum slaves purchased goods and services unnecessary for subsistence; many of these enslaved consumers appear to have gained emotional satisfaction (some historians would even argue "empowerment") from not only purchased goods but also the process and choice involved in acquiring them; and finally, as debate in planters' prescriptive literature and legal statutes attest, slaves' ability to acquire goods and services simultaneously enhanced and challenged management strategies to promote slaveholder hegemony. *explain in answer to Q1*

Viewing the internal economy through the lens of consumer studies illuminates the hidden power of material exchange. This book argues that the consumption of goods served as a vehicle through which social relations – and politics – were produced.[21] More than chains bound masters and slaves – shifting webs of exchange entangled both in profitable and perilous contests for power. The hegemonic nature of slaveholder authority compelled battle, even if the anxiety it produced did little to provide lasting security for either. Slaves' acquisition of goods came at costs more than monetary, slaveholders hoped: hopes for freedom became fetishized in goods consumed. As bondpeople grasped opportunities to express themselves and create new relationships, slaves ensured masters paid too, their actions demanding constant assessment and justification of authority. *really ... is that what they were trying to do*

Since the 1970s, economists, anthropologists, and sociologists have sought to uncover and define the structure and mechanics of exchange in a growing global "informal economy." Although these scholars debate terminology (underground, internal, informal, cash-in-hand, gray or black market) or the way economy is delineated, a couple of common principles have come to guide this literature. First, the boundaries of these economies are porous, with economic actors readily slipping between "licit" and "illicit" realms of exchange. And second, this exchange is interwoven and interdependent in the economic, social, political, and cultural life of resource-scarce communities. Attempting to disentangle this Gordian knot of exchange – sorting out the affairs of off-

---

[20] Stearns, "Stages of Consumerism," 105–106, 115–117.

[21] For discussion of the relationship between production and consumption, see Karl Marx, *Grundrisse*, transl. and ed. Martin Nicolaus (New York: Penguin, 1993), 90–94; T. H. Breen, "The Meanings of Things: Interpreting the Consumer Economy in the Eighteenth Century," in *Consumption and the World of Goods*, eds. John Brewer and Roy Porter (New York: Routledge, 1993), 250.

the-books peddlers, vendors, prostitutes, hawkers, tip-earners, haulers, and the like from the overarching political and economic structure that sustains and restricts them – serves only to highlight the deeply embedded, necessary, and adaptive nature of these networks.[22] The "slaves' internal economy" was no different. What was allowed or forbidden, given or bought, stolen or taken, remains maddeningly difficult to discern. This book aims to identify these forms of exchange, certainly, but also to show the ways in which masters and slaves blurred boundaries between them for, when it came to matters of economy, the master-slave relation involved constant manipulation of lines of material transfer.

Sociologist Arjun Appadurai emphasizes this point explicitly in a collection of essays addressing the "social life of things," cautioning scholars against static definitions of commodity exchange. In his view, "the commodity phase of the life history of an object does not exhaust its biography; it is culturally regulated; and its interpretation is open to individual manipulation to some degree."[23] The internal economy engaged the full "biography" Appadurai describes, demonstrating well the liminal qualities of the market sphere. In plantation communities, categories of transfer and acquisition – provision, commodity, contraband, and gift – proved difficult to distinguish. Masters and bondpeople each consciously and unconsciously muddled boundaries, appropriating meanings and materials that suited their needs best. This study embraces such calculated ambiguity, examining the range of ways in which goods flowed in and out of the quarters and thinking about the meaning slaves and masters assigned to each.

I have organized *Masters, Slaves, and Exchange: Power's Purchase in the Old South* with Appadurai's liminal and culturally-regulated "biography" in mind, emphasizing in particular the ways in which masters and slaves took advantage of and were exploited by malleable lines of exchange. Seeking to secure mastery, slaveholders manipulated the internal economy to manage bondpeople more effectively. Slaves' material exchange, they imagined, not only allayed long-term discontent, it potentially bolstered masters' self-perceived roles as models, protectors, and judges of slave spending and acquisition. Although the mechanics of commodity purchase, gift exchange, and provision

---

[22] Interdisciplinary work on so-called "informal economies" is rich, exciting, and expansive. For a thorough overview of early work in the field, see Abol Hassan Danesh, *The Informal Economy: A Research Guide* (New York: Garland, 1991). For thought-provoking recent work – and a book that proved important in my thinking on this topic – see Sudhir Alladi Venkatesh, *Off the Books: The Underground Economy of the Urban Poor* (Cambridge: Harvard University Press, 2006).

[23] Arjun Appadurai, "Introduction: Commodities and the Politics of Value," in *The Social Life of Things: Commodities in Cultural Perspective*, ed. Arjun Appadurai (New York: Cambridge University Press, 1986), 17. Here, Appadurai draws on the work of Igor Kopytoff whose important essay, "The Cultural Biography of Things: Commoditization as Process," is also included in this volume, 64–91.

market transaction

distribution necessarily differed, in masters' eyes, they served a singular purpose: to strengthen the tie between master and slave. Hence the lines between these categories of exchange were blurred – often deliberately – by masters looking to solidify paternalist bonds.

But bondpeople whom slaveholders struggled to master could not be bought so easily, for slaves' motivations and behavior were just as complex as those of plotting paternalists. Internal economies provided opportunity for the enslaved to support their families and supplement meager rations, to be sure. More importantly, slaves might buy clothing, food, or "luxuries" to distinguish themselves from provisioned masses, to acquire, if not freedom outright, then at least markers of it. For such opportunities, slaves pushed masters to alter management strategies, wrenching concessions and compelling masters to recognize them as economic actors.

Market transactions, black market trade, and gift exchange complicated these contests for power. Formal venues of consumption like small stores and shops brought interests of masters, slaves, and merchants into conflict. Each side had much to gain – and lose – from slave spending. Slaveholders hoped to enlist merchants in their bid to control bondpeople through consumer prospects, but worried that goods purveyed might threaten discipline on the plantation. Merchants desired profits from slave and slaveholder alike, but risked legal sanction when they met desires for goods not permitted by masters. Slaves might reap the bounty of market exchange in these venues but, time and again, they found that their chattel status mitigated the otherwise leveling influence of the market. Market exchange required constant strategizing and recognition of the tangled economic and political ties that bound southern communities.

Theft, too, inspired conflicting interpretations. Universally lamented by slaveholders, "stealing" by slaves depleted their stores and caused trouble in the larger white community. "Taking" what they felt belonged to them and adjusting purchasing strategies to mitigate risks inherent in the consumption of black market goods, slaves forced grumbling and often anxious adjustments to masters' management prescriptions. E. P. Thompson's arguments on moral economy only partially – and somewhat romantically – explain the significance of black market transactions. The bigger the wrench "thieving" slaves threw into planters' plans, the more justified slaveholders felt in imposing them. Viewed realistically as both slave resistance and pretext for planter control, theft and black market consumption further ensnared slave and slaveholder in a deeply unsatisfying paternalist web.

Seen superficially, gifts suited planters' political aspirations perfectly. As sociologists and anthropologists have taken pains to explain, gift-giving is an act demanding reciprocity, tying giver and taker, and creating obligations to bestow, receive, and return. For this reason, planters imbued all sorts of transactions with gift-giving characteristics. Through a carefully-scripted set of singularizing rituals and performances, slaveholders painted provisioning, market transactions, and even wage payment with the brush of largesse and generosity. Slaves accepted these presents gratefully but imposed payment terms slave-holders had no choice but to accept through gritted teeth. The ties planters wove required constant tending, and gifts given raised expectations that – in good times and bad – had to be met. To do less signified failure, mastery lost.

The twisted logic of paternalism revealed itself most starkly in transactions involving that most precious commodity – or, more properly, good – freedom. Most slaves struggled to carve out bits of independence and power within the plantation system, but others sought to break the legal chains that bound them to their masters. Whether by purchase, theft, or bequest, these men and women adapted strategies honed in daily transactions of a less precious sort. The costs were high, slaves found out, and not just in monetary terms. Slaves who stole or took themselves through absconding risked all, and found that the use or display of their own bodies required constant caution. Even those slaves who earned the gift of manumission paid a price by going to "extraordinary" efforts to singularize themselves in their masters' eyes. Ironically, only those slaves who did their duty best, thus assuring their masters of the seemingly indissoluble paternalist bonds between them, earned the right to sever masters' legal claims.

In the end, then, the economic, social, and political promises that the internal economy seemed to hold failed to meet the lofty expectations of most who engaged in it. Imagining opportunity to subdue bondpeople and enhance claims to mastery, slaveholders embraced opportunities to judge, protect, and model consumer behavior. Slaves imposed their own moralism on the spending choices of masters and forced constant adjustments to slaveholder prescriptions, but opportunities to gain material comfort and distinction muted ambitions to promote more drastic – and potentially violent – forms of resistance. Neither drew lasting comfort from this most tragic of Faustian bargains. Bound together in constant contest, the struggle for power in plantation communities was constant, corrosive, and deeply worrisome to all involved.

Although this study focuses frequently on close analysis of particular details of discreet, minor, and long-forgotten economic transactions, it never aims merely at history of those quid pro quos.[24] Slaves and masters exchanged goods all across the plantation South, and there are scads of daybooks, diaries, and legal and personal manuscript sources chronicling such transactions scattered in archives from Arkansas to Florida. This study, though, focuses on the seaboard states from Virginia to Georgia, both to mine their superb, abundant,

---

[24] This "thick description" at the heart of so much recent historical analysis of the politics of cultural relations has been underutilized by scholars focusing upon the economic life of working people. See Clifford Geertz, "Thick Description: Toward an Interpretive Theory of Culture," in *The Interpretation of Cultures* (New York: Basic Books, 1973), 3–32; Lynn Hunt, ed., *The New Cultural History* (Berkeley: University of California Press, 1989), especially Aletta Biersack's essay, "Local Knowledge, Local History: Geertz and Beyond," 72–96.

> caution us against
> seeing something in
> everything

and well-organized documentary record and to make a larger analytic point. It was in the coastal states especially that the ideology of paternalism first took root in the early decades of the nineteenth century, where planters strove most ingeniously to reshape the terms of the master-slave relation and bondpeople pushed back hardest to redefine the paternalist bargain on their own terms. To that end, this book provides no year-by-year or county-by-county study of the internal economy; rather, it conceives of economic relations as political, best interpreted in broad stages. For that reason, it considers the period 1815 to 1860 as a single unit inasmuch as this was the heyday of paternalism as a political strategy.[25]

This period, too, was a time of intense economic growth and market expansion, as planters and farmers shifted from subsistence farming and became increasingly enmeshed in systems of credit and debt. Such connections brought new goods, but also new worries into southern communities, which found themselves increasingly destabilized by outside economic entanglements. Ranks of modernizationist scholars have chronicled this transformation, pitting their interpretations at paternalism's antagonistic pole, arguing that profits and progress ranked highest among slaveholders' concerns. Much of this useful and interesting work remains descriptive, however, unfolding markers of historical change – the growth of cities, the expansion of markets, internal and agricultural improvements – across a surprisingly progressive antebellum southern narrative. But in doing so, modernizationists often obscure the story of conflict and struggle dynamizing the master-slave relation, indeed all class relations, in the midst of drastic change. This project hardly denies or argues against the expansive market growth that came to characterize southern communities during this time period; rather, it embraces and enlarges upon it, just as slaveholders and slaves did as they negotiated the limits of each other's power. How these men and women, enslaved and free, exploited a developing South's opportunities and navigated attendant risks informs much of the exploration of paternalism I present here.[26]

---

[25] For a recent extended discussion of the periodization of paternalism, see Lacy K. Ford, *Deliver Us From Evil: The Slavery Question in the Old South* (New York: Oxford University Press, 2009), 7–10.

[26] In *The Political Economy of Slavery*, Genovese argued that "Southern ideals constituted a rejection of the crass, vulgar, inhumane elements of capitalist society." In later work, he clarified his assessment, arguing that slaveholders accommodated economic changes confronting their world, but on their own terms and in such a way as to maintain social order. This project largely holds to that view. See Genovese, *The Political Economy of Slavery: Studies in the Economy and Society of the Slave South*, 2nd ed. (Middletown, CT: Wesleyan University Press, 1989), 30; Genovese, *The Slaveholders' Dilemma: Freedom and Progress in Southern Conservative Thought, 1820–1860* (Columbia: University of South Carolina Press, 1991). Although plenty of historians have advanced capitalist narratives in response to Genovese's work, his most notable adversaries have been James Oakes, Robert Fogel, and Stanley Engerman. See, in particular, James Oakes, *The Ruling Race: A History of American Slaveholders* (New York: Alfred A. Knopf, 1982); James Oakes, *Slavery and Freedom: An Interpretation of the Old South* (New

Given the nature of evidence so often used to gauge the economic, political, and social life of the peculiar institution, measuring how change affected the master-slave relation in precise chronological terms is difficult. The retrospective nature of many of these sources – antebellum published slave narratives, Reconstruction-era petitions from the Southern Claims Commission, late nineteenth- and early twentieth-century plantation memoirs, depression-era WPA (Works Progress Administration) narratives – make year-by-year or even decade-by-decade assessment of these adjustments empirically impossible. To be sure, the United States broadly and the South specifically underwent many of the changes so thoroughly described by modernizationist scholars. These necessarily affected the ways in which planters imposed their rule and the means by which enslaved people attempted to undermine them. This project presents a broad array of risks and strategies, recognizing that change occurred in fits and starts, and that risks and challenges faced in some communities necessarily differed from others. However fast or slow this change, I argue, market growth amplified struggle, making political decisions on all sides all the more critical, upping rewards and magnifying peril. By drawing together disparate events and conflicts across a wide range of communities and years, we can more easily delineate the contours of political struggle as focused in the liminal sphere of the marketplace. Here then is the site where, in its sharpest, most complex, and revolutionary forms, masters and slaves struggled over slavery's meanings and freedom's measures in the decades leading up to the Civil War.

This book is a meditation, too, on the relationship between freedom and consumption. White masters who longed for the authority, power, and control that, they hoped, wealth might buy found it diminished by the troublesome property they so readily consumed and cultivated. So too, men and women who desperately did not want to be seen as things just as desperately yearned for order, security, and the meaning that we still pursue even more heedlessly in the contemporary marketplace. Coins, cloth, drams of liquor, battered top hats: these were the weapons by which black and white men and women pursued slavery and freedom. As my argument shows, they found them both in full measure.

York: Alfred A. Knopf, 1990); and Robert William Fogel and Stanley L. Engerman, *Time on the Cross: The Economics of American Negro Slavery* (Boston: Little, Brown, 1974). For an excellent overview of more recent work in this area, see L. Diane Barnes, Brian Schoen, and Frank Towers, eds., *The Old South's Modern Worlds: Slavery, Region, and Nation in the Age of Progress* (New York: Oxford University Press, 2011).

I

Money and Moralism

What do slaves want with money? What good can it possibly do them?

So asked a contributor to the *Southern Cultivator* in April 1860. With
Republicans ascendant and secession agitation reaching fever pitch, the author,
A. T. Goodloe, struggled to maintain some semblance of order on his plantation. He feared his slaves, with cash in hand, would wander "wherever their
inclination may lead them" and that money would end up in the hands of
proprietors of local dram shops, "road-side groceries," and other "filthy institutions." Anxious to maintain a productive, obedient, and healthy workforce,
Goodloe viewed these venues of consumption as dangerous temptations and
sought to remove opportunities for their patronage. Yet, despite these fears,
Goodloe remained cognizant of the needs and, more importantly, material
desires of his bondpeople. Bestowing extra goods was a way to allay long-term
discontent and keep his people close to home.[1]

But what, exactly, did his slaves want? How could he be sure he was fulfilling their material desires so as to prevent them from seeking opportunities outside of his control? Goodloe shared his solution with readers of the *Southern
Cultivator.* He urged the slaveholder to "[t]ake his negroes to the nearest dry
goods store, or send the overseer with them (do not let them go alone) and let
them select such things as suit their fancies, within a certain limit, and pay for
the goods himself; always rewarding more liberally those that have performed
their duty best."[2] Even though slaveholders differed in their management techniques and many likely scoffed at Goodloe's liberality, the struggle to maintain an obedient workforce was universal and one often addressed through a
process of negotiation and manipulation of slaves' material wants, needs, and

---

[1] A. T. Goodloe, "Management of Negroes," *Southern Cultivator* 18 (1860): 130.
[2] Goodloe, "Management of Negroes," 130–131.

desires. Slaveholders' journals and prescriptive literature are filled with thoughtful and often anxious considerations about material exchange between master and slave. Slaveholders across the South united in defense of their mastery, but they differed widely on the best way to achieve it, particularly with regard to maximizing workforce efficiency in political economic terms. Beginning in the 1820s, articles on agricultural management and reform filled the pages of widely-read periodicals like the *Southern Planter, Southern Cultivator, Southern Agriculturist*, and *De Bow's Review*. Far from describing a monolithic ideal of slave management, these ruminations present the tip of the iceberg of vigorous debate that surrounded issues of mastery and subservience. Slaveholders argued endlessly about whether bondpeople should be granted small plots or patches to farm and the liberty to trade. They debated the quantity, quality, and variety of rations slaves should be given. They bragged about the "luxuries" or "trifles" they gave their people as gifts or rewards. These varying themes introduced seemingly clashing categories of political economy – commodity exchange and wage payment, material provisions that straddled the line of obligation between that payment and paternalist responsibility, and outright beneficence shaped by *dicta* of moral economy.

Market transactions could strain the bonds between master and slave. Douglas Egerton has recently argued as much, situating "entrepreneurial bondmen" at the vanguard of Atlantic rebellion, insisting that cash economies brought hope to the enslaved and made resistance more tenable – and desirable.[3] With few exceptions, the historiography of the internal economy leans in this direction – labeling opportunities for market activity a form of empowerment, if not outright resistance.[4] Although providing valuable contributions to our collective understanding of the peculiar institution, such accounts reflect the eagerness of social historians to engage in debates about working-class agency and identity, yet turn a blind eye to the political relations and power structures that shaped life and labor in the Old South.

The internal economy played a vital role in this unending process. If some slaves sought to trade their way to better – and potentially freer – lives, masters, too, seized on the dynamics of market exchange as a superb mechanism for aggressively enlarging the dimension of their hegemony. Slaves' spending was an opportunity for slaveholders, not simply to tie bondpeople to

---

[3] Douglas R. Egerton, "Slaves to the Marketplace: Economic Liberty and Black Rebelliousness in the Atlantic World," *Journal of the Early Republic* 26 (2006): 636.

[4] Lawrence T. McDonnell has made a strong – and convincing – critique of this position, arguing that market exchange instead undergirded individualism and conflict within the slave community. See Lawrence T. McDonnell, "Money Knows No Master: Market Relations and the American Slave Community," in *Developing Dixie: Modernization in a Traditional Society*, eds. Winfred B. Moore, Jr., Joseph F. Tripp, and Lyon G. Tyler (Westport, CT: Greenwood Press, 1988), 31–44 and "Work, Culture, and Society in the Slave South, 1790–1861," in *Black and White Cultural Interaction in the Antebellum South*, ed. Ted Ownby (Jackson: University Press of Mississippi, 1993), 125–148.

property and plantation, but to serve as models, protectors, and judges of their choices in the marketplace. Doing so, they imagined, strengthened claims to mastery, squaring the circle between paternalist dreams and market realities. Commodity exchange, they understood, was a double-edged sword, one that could sever the very bonds they sought to strengthen. Yet, they took that risk. To use it effectively required slaveholders to confront fundamental questions of agency, choice, and control. The answers they supplied varied widely and formed the constantly shifting framework of management and moralism that marked slaves' political and economic lives. Capricious and uncertain, to be sure, but always aggressively pursued and manipulated, policies regarding material exchange reflected the political and economic strategies of the master class. "What good can [money] possibly do them?" A. T. Goodloe asked in April 1860, but more truly he schemed, "What good does a slave with money do me?"

Presumably, the enslaved men and women living on A. T. Goodloe's plantation would have sought to acquire goods provided in insufficient quantities by their master, although Goodloe's strict monitoring likely hindered their ability to fulfill material desires in a truly substantial and satisfying manner. Other bondpeople, though they earned purchasing ability through overwork, could more fully engage in the consumer process. They, too, faced limits and restrictions not encountered by their free and white brethren. In either case, these restrictions formed a consumer framework in which white southerners expected enslaved men and women to operate.[5]

The first pillar of this framework was slave provisioning, the quantity and quality of which has been hotly debated by historians. Ulrich Phillips argued that a paternal relationship existed between master and slave, that slaves were docile and content, and that slave life was no more difficult than the lives of other nineteenth-century laborers. "Crude comfort was the rule," according to Phillips, and he attributed the "winsome" nature of plantation babies to the fact that their "parents, free of expense and anxiety for their sustenance, could hardly have more of them than they wanted." Nearly forty years later, Kenneth Stampp responded to Phillips's assessment, agreeing on some matters of substance, but differing substantially in tone. Stampp conceded that food rationing was of "sufficient bulk but improper balance," although this lack was due

---

[5] This chapter does not assume that conditions prescribed by slaveholders were a true depiction of life and labor in southern communities. Rather, it examines the dialectic of slave management, arguing that the constantly shifting strategies of management and moralism presented an uncertain framework in which slaves had to function. Likewise, the language and attitudes expressed in the prescriptive literature described here are often degrading and patronizing, rife with race and class stereotypes, and generally reprehensible. Parsing these stereotypes is crucial to understanding the world in which bondpeople lived; they are not the views of this author. For a more detailed discussion of racial stereotypes in the antebellum era, see George M. Fredrickson, *The Black Image in the White Mind: The Debate on Afro-American Character and Destiny, 1817–1914* (New York: Harper and Row, 1971).

less to penuriousness of the slaveholder and more to dietetic ignorance. Slaves' clothing and housing insufficiencies, on the other hand, were more often the result of "carelessness, indifference, and economy."[6]

Stampp situated his assessment within a framework of scientific knowledge available to slaveholders at the time. Dissatisfied with Stampp's anecdotal evidence and analysis, Robert Fogel and Stanley Engerman brought the "cliometric revolution" to bear on the issue of slave provisioning. Their book, *Time on the Cross*, argued that slaves were indeed exploited, but denied that enslaved men and women were "demoralized" or the black family reduced to "cultural chaos." The authors' statistical analysis of slaves' diet, food, and shelter argued against such presumptions. They contended that average slave diets exceeded even modern (1964) standards for recommended daily levels of nutrients and protein. Although their information on housing quality was sparse, they concluded that slave cabins were not crowded, at least compared to northern urban tenements. Slave clothing received little analysis in the book. Even though Fogel and Engerman admitted that clothing allowances were insufficient, they argued that slaves could supplement their wardrobes with articles of their own purchase.[7]

Historians heaped savage criticism on *Time on the Cross*. In the view of many scholars, Fogel and Engerman's use of evidence and statistics was methodologically suspect, their presumptions about incentives and slaves' work ethic skewed, and their assumptions about the economic rationality of slaveholders lacking evidentiary support. Fogel and Engerman's discussion of provisioning received particular criticism. In the words of Richard Sutch, "[t]he prevailing view of the slave ration as monotonous, crude, and nutritionally suspect has not been upset by Fogel and Engerman's cliometrics." Sutch further argued that housing was "commensurate with absolute necessity" and that Fogel and Engerman's estimate of clothing allowances was overstated.[8]

---

[6] Ulrich B. Phillips, *American Negro Slavery: A Survey of the Supply, Employment and Control of Negro Labor As Determined by the Plantation Regime* (1918; Baton Rouge: Louisiana State University Press, 1966), 296, 298; Kenneth M. Stampp, *The Peculiar Institution: Slavery in the Ante-bellum South* (New York: Vintage Books, 1956), 279–295, quotations, 282, 289.

[7] Robert William Fogel and Stanley L. Engerman, *Time on the Cross: The Economics of American Negro Slavery* (Boston: Little, Brown, 1974), 107–117, quotations, 108–109. Through the use of statistical analysis, Fogel and Engerman hoped to counter the "myth of black incompetence," a stereotype they thought was promoted by the exaggeration of slaves' physical hardships and the assumptions of the resulting psychological toll that such hardships took on the enslaved. Cf., Stanley M. Elkins, *Slavery: A Problem in American Institutional and Intellectual Life*, rev. 3rd ed. (Chicago: University of Chicago Press, 1976), 81–139. For descriptive information on southern foodways and slave provisioning, see Sam Bowers Hilliard, *Hog Meat and Hoecake: Food Supply in the Old South, 1840–1860* (Carbondale: Southern Illinois University Press, 1972).

[8] Richard Sutch, "The Care and Feeding of Slaves," in *Reckoning with Slavery: A Critical Study in the Quantitative History of American Negro Slavery*, ed. Paul A. David, *et al.* (New York: Oxford University Press, 1976), 231–301, quotations, 281, 298.

Sutch admitted, however, that insufficiency of evidence prevented him or any other historian from properly analyzing the provisioning of the average slave. In many respects, this inability complicates consideration of bondpeople's spending. After all, it is difficult to assess the needs, wants, and motives of the enslaved buyer if the adequacy of his or her basic life provisions cannot be determined. What we can ascertain, however, are slaveholders' and slaves' differing conceptions of acceptable quantities and qualities of provisioning. Neither slaves nor masters made economic choices based on complex quantifications of recommended daily allowances of vitamins and minerals or per capita occupancy rates. Rather, they decided to spend their money to fulfill material needs, wants, and desires, intangibles that economic analysis simply cannot identify. Accordingly, we must take a different approach to the issue of slave provisioning, one flexible enough to accommodate the differing viewpoints and assessments of not only masters and slaves but also the variety of individuals within each of these groups.[9]

Ironically, Phillips's characterization of "crude comfort" might best suit such a discussion. Ideas of "comfort" are historically subjective, changing across time and circumstance. Concerned as they were with maintaining order and discipline, binding bondpeople to the home place, and increasing profits, slaveholders bragged about both the comforts they provided for their bondpeople and the amount of energy they spent in providing them. Virginian Letitia Burwell remembered that her mother and grandmother were "almost always talking over the wants of the negroes ... the principal object of their lives seeming to be in providing these comforts" while another slaveholder, more concerned with his own interests, noted that "it behooves us ... to make them [slave laborers] as comfortable as possible." Overseers were urged to see that "everything has been attended to which conduces to their comfort and happiness" and to check the cabins to see that "all are comfortable."[10]

Mere paeans to comfort rarely suited the slaveholder looking to maximize the efficiency of his laborers, and discussions of just what "comfort" meant consumed pages of prescriptive literature. At the very least, conceptions of early nineteenth-century comforts included attention to basic notions of hygiene, raiment, food, and shelter. A popular 1852 plantation guide and instruction book urged slaveholders to "[s]ee that their [slaves'] necessities be supplied; that their food and clothing be good and sufficient; their houses comfortable; and be kind and attentive to them in sickness and in old age."[11] The mainstays

---

[9] Sutch, "Care and Feeding of Slaves," 281.

[10] Letitia M. Burwell, *A Girl's Life in Virginia Before the War* (New York: Frederick A. Stokes, 1895), 7; A Southron, "Hints in Relation to the Dwellings and Clothing of Slaves," *Farmers' Register* 2 (1836): 703; "Overseers' Rules," *Southern Planter* 18 (1858): 411; "Management of Cotton Estates," *De Bow's Review* 26 (1859): 579.

[11] A Southern Planter, *Plantation and Farm: Instruction, Regulation, Record, Inventory, and Account Book* (Richmond: J. W. Randolph, 1852), 5. See, in particular, Richard Eppes Diary, 1858, Section 43, Eppes Family Papers, VHS. Slaveholders and prescriptive authors issued these

of such comforts were fairly standard, reflecting the reformist nature of many agricultural journals of the time. "Suitable bedding" and "a proper outfit," paternalists argued, would add "greatly to the comfort and health of the slave." Others asserted that slaves should be well-clothed, sleep on "comfortable mattresses," and have food variety, as "healthy as it is pleasant." Quality, according to the literature, was as important as quantity, with contributors opining that "none but provisions of the best quality" should be issued along with "the best clothes" and even such necessaries as "combs and razors."[12]

Historian John Crowley has argued that sympathy shapes material culture and that, in the late eighteenth and early nineteenth centuries, this sentiment undergirded reform movements in the United States and Britain.[13] A standard of abolitionist critiques and reform literature, such sentimental appeals reached the eyes and ears of nineteenth-century slaveholders as well. Whether as a response to abolitionist pressure or simply as a means of promoting their own interests, some called for fellow planters to reevaluate conceptions of comfort and to assess honestly whether the needs and wants of their charges were being met. Consider the exhortation of Georgia slaveholder Thomas Clay in 1833:

> Masters do not sufficiently acquaint themselves with the wants of their negroes. They are too prone to think them well supplied, when they have received their clothes and allowance, particularly if the pint of salt once a month is not forgotten. To know what is wanting to the comfort of his negro, let him visit his house during a hard shower, and stand just where it leaks, – or call in on a pleasant day, and take a seat on his bench, hang his hat on the nail, or place it on the table or dresser, drink water from his pail and calabash, – see if he has plates and spoons, and look where he sleeps – send to purchase his eggs and poultry, and ask what he wishes in return.[14]

Clay asked fellow slaveholders to consider far more than slaves' basic dietary and raiment needs – he wanted them to evaluate bondpeople's physical surroundings within the context of slaveholders' own notions of comfort and discomfort. The estimation of a sympathetic master, he argued, would ensure a suitable standard of living for the average slave, one that would completely satisfy him or her. After all, slaveholders maintained, "negro" tastes were simple

---

guidelines to their overseers and reprinted them in any number of publications. See, for example, "Rules in the Management of a Southern Estate," *De Bow's Review* 22 (1857): 376 and "Rules for Plantation Management on a Cotton Estate, 1857," in *Plantation and Frontier, 1649–1863*, ed. Ulrich B. Phillips (1909; New York: Burt Franklin, 1969), I: 113.

12 Robert Collins, "Essay on the Management of Slaves," *Southern Cultivator* 12 (1854): 205; H[olland] N. McTyeire, "Plantation Life – Duties and Responsibilities," *De Bow's Review* 29 (1860): 358, 359; P[lowden] C. [J.] Weston, "Management of a Southern Plantation," *De Bow's Review* 22 (1857): 38; "Notions on the Management of Negroes, &c.," *Farmers' Register* 4 (1837): 494.

13 John E. Crowley, *The Invention of Comfort: Sensibilities and Design in Early Modern Britain and Early America* (Baltimore: The Johns Hopkins University Press, 2001), 166–169.

14 Thomas S. Clay, *Detail of a Plan for the Moral Improvement of Negroes on Plantations* (n.p.: Georgia Presbytery, 1833), 20.

and a slave's motivation to acquire more sophisticated material comforts was low. In providing for the comfort of their slaves, slaveholders were imposing a level of "civilized" living that many enslaved, it was thought, were just barely capable of understanding. One Virginia farmer desponded that, "[t]hey [slaves] only want to support life: they will not work for anything more; and in this country it would be hard to prevent their getting that." Further, as a group of fellow Virginians noted, "the motives of cleanliness, comfort, and independence are seldom, if ever, strong enough to prevail upon the negro to labour; and that no inducements sufficiently strong can be found excepting necessity and compulsion." In short, to "be well fed and clothed for life," as determined by an informed and sympathetic master, ensured that the slave would "regard himself as the happiest of mortals."[15]

To simplify slave tastes to sufficient dietary, clothing, and housing comforts may have proven satisfactory to some slaveholders, but others offered more sophisticated plans for slave provisioning – management strategies that distinguished providing bondpeople with goods that could be considered "comforts" and those that might be considered "luxuries." The distinction is important for a number of reasons. First, the issuance of luxuries reflected more than simple reformist humanitarianism. Such provisions implied beneficence that could have the effect of elevating slaveholders' status in the eyes of not only their slaves but also white neighbors.[16] But, again, the definition of luxury was

---

[15] Frederick Law Olmsted, *The Cotton Kingdom: A Traveller's Observations on Cotton and Slavery in the American Slave States, 1853–1861* (1953; New York: Da Capo Press, 1996), 78; Charles A. Murray, *Travels in North America during the years 1834, 1835, and 1836, including a summer residence with the Pawnee tribe of Indians in the remote prairies of the Missouri, and a visit to Cuba and the Azore Islands* (London: Richard Bentley, 1839), I: 165; Robert J. Turnbull, "Communication," in *A Refutation of the Calumnies Circulated against the Southern and Western States Respecting the Institution and Existence of Slavery Among Them. To which is added, a Minute and Particular Account of the Actual State and Condition of the Negro Population. Together with Historical Notices of All the Insurrections that Have Taken Place Since the Settlement of the Country*, ed. A South-Carolinian [Edwin C. Holland] (Charleston: A. E. Miller, 1822), 55. Sociologist Elizabeth Shove has recently observed that historical studies of comfort can highlight "considerations of equity and justice," that is, issues of power. Such study emerges as particularly important, she rightly argues, "once we detach comfort from human biology and attend to the wider politics of where and how notions of physical well being are reproduced, how they circulate and with what consequence for the forms of consumption associated with them." Though Shove – and Crowley – emphasize the way "discourses of comfort cut across social hierarchies," it is worth noting that not all slaveholders were willing to universalize comfort sentiment, instead using nineteenth-century discourse over comfort to reinforce the disparate sensibilities race and class brought to bear on the master-slave relation. Elizabeth Shove, "Comfort and Convenience: Temporality and Practice," in *The Oxford Handbook of the History of Consumption*, ed. Frank Trentmann (New York: Oxford University Press, 2012), 296.

[16] Thorstein Veblen explored the phenomenon of "vicarious consumption," arguing that servants, retainers, and courtiers relayed their dependence on an obviously wealthy and generous patron through ostentatious and carefully-crafted display. Despite his wide-ranging application of the term, Veblen took care to distinguish those in direct menial service of the patron (servants, for

subject to diverse opinion. What some slaveholders considered crucial for comfort, others deemed superfluous luxury. In some cases, luxury implied a higher quality of provisions or unnecessary extras that would add flavor or variety to slave diets. One slaveholder argued that "nothing has a greater tendency to inspire cheerfulness and industry, than to look forward to the prospect of a good meal" and it was "a source of pleasing reflection to the master, to afford the additional happiness which such luxuries never fail to yield." Others were more specific. The addition of molasses to the slave's diet, for example, would "be but a trifle" to the average slaveholder, but "the negro will esteem it as a great luxury." Provisions occasionally included "fresh meat," as well as "molasses, sugar, coffee, and flour," with one slaveholder "generally laying out about $10 per hand for such luxuries."[17] Clothing, too, could fall under the category of luxury, with the furnishing of "coarse fabrics for working use" and comfort and "Sunday or holiday attire" provided as a luxury designed to keep "alive among servants a proper self-respect."[18]

Yet the provision of luxuries could be problematic and, not surprisingly, was a subject of debate among planters. Even for white men and women, luxurious living could draw suspicion, calling to mind an air of aristocracy seemingly antithetic to a republican way of life. Levying criticism on residents of the "meridian of Georgia, where, for a series of years, so much time and money have been consumed by the indulgence of luxurious habits," the editors of the *Southern Cultivator* printed an 1843 oration calling on farmers to "get rid of our luxurious habits; abandon the fashionable follies of the day; lay off all unnecessary expenses, and return to the plain, unsophisticated customs of our forefathers."[19] And while southerners almost universally condemned superfluous luxury, the debate itself was, as Timothy Breen terms it, "quicksand." Breen makes the useful point that moral condemnations of "luxury" were couched in

example) and those who profited from a benefactor's patronage. Many slaveholders viewed their slaves as symbols of their wealth and their prowess as masters and, consequently, took care to provide at least a façade of more than sufficient (if not luxurious) living for their charges. James Buckingham made an explicit comparison between the southern slaveholder and the English gentry, noting that "the master and mistress of a family, and all the younger members of it, feel as natural a pride in having their personal attendants to look well in person and in dress, when slaves, as they do when their servants are free; for the same reason as ladies or gentlemen in England like to have their livery servants handsome and well-dressed." Nehemiah Adams noted this same awareness of slaves' appearance, explaining that "the pride we have in the respectable appearance of children is felt by southern mistresses with regard to their servants." See Thorstein Veblen, *The Theory of the Leisure Class* (1899; Mineola, NY: Dover Publications, 1994), 43–62; J[ames] S. Buckingham, *The Slave States of America* (London: Fisher, Son, 1842), I: 131; Nehemiah Adams, *A South-Side View of Slavery; or, Three Months at the South, in 1854* (Boston: T. R. Marvin and B. B. Mussey, 1854), 32.

17 "Management of Slaves, &c.," *Farmers' Register* 5 (1837): 32; Agricola, "Management of Negroes," *Southern Cultivator* 13 (1855): 171; A Small Farmer, "Management of Negroes," *De Bow's Review* 11 (1851): 372.

18 McTyeire, "Plantation Life – Duties and Responsibilities," 358–359.

19 "Good Advice," *Southern Cultivator* 1 (1843): 55.

terms of "otherness." That is, those who preached against the consumption of luxurious indulgences rarely included themselves in their criticism. Slaveholders' justifications were typical of the attitude Breen describes. Although they, too, had likely consumed the new goods and services that growing American markets proffered, their spending was controlled and "temperate," their purchases respectable and restrained complements to mundane necessities. Those of the lower orders, slaveholders argued, be they Irish laborers in the North or black slaves in the South, lacked the refined ability to spend money wisely.[20]

It was just this paradox that made the provision of luxuries a contentious but ultimately useful dialectic for southern planters.[21] On the one hand, slaves possessing luxuries were symbols of slaveholders' own wealth and beneficence, serving both to impress white neighbors and appease otherwise recalcitrant slaves. On the other hand, masters might use slaves' consumption of luxuries to validate stereotypes of black intemperance and improvidence, especially if slaves were permitted to buy these luxuries themselves. Bondpeople could trade in an extra bag of corn for "calico or tobacco," sell fowl or eggs to buy sugar or coffee, or use the profits from patches to purchase "some little comforts, luxuries or finery" – goods rarely provided and considered unnecessary for the subsistence of the average slave. Others bought "fine" clothing, in some cases spurring outrage from whites who felt they were dressing beyond the means set for them. A contributor to the *Southern Cultivator* complained that "[t]he *town* negroes of this State are the b'hoys of the South, sporting their fine Havanas and twirling their fancy canes on the side walks – who but they! No

---

[20] T. H. Breen, *The Marketplace of Revolution: How Consumer Politics Shaped American Independence* (New York: Oxford University Press, 2004), 184–187; Crowley, *The Invention of Comfort*, 162–166. Such concerns weighed heavily on the minds of ruling classes in the North too. Though, in these instances, slaveholders judged consumer ability according to race, it is worth noting that such judgments were often class-based as well. See Michael Zakim, "The Business Clerk as Social Revolutionary; or, a Labor History of the Nonproducing Classes," *Journal of the Early Republic* 26 (2006): 587.

[21] Economic and social theorists have long struggled to define "luxury." Most counterpose luxury to necessity in some way, though theorists like Jean Baudrillard and Werner Sombart have complicated this definitional spectrum. More appropriate for this study is, again, the work of Arjun Appadurai, who examines luxury in terms of power, arguing, "[t]he necessity to which [luxuries] respond is fundamentally political." A more explicit iteration of this argument comes to us from French cultural theorist Pierre Bourdieu. His path-breaking study, *Distinction: A Social Critique of the Judgement of Taste*, explains, "[t]he true basis of the differences found in the area of consumption ... is the opposition between the tastes of luxury (or freedom) and the tastes of necessity." Classes seeking distinction from social inferiors, then, impose protocols and, importantly, judgment on appropriate use of goods and proper execution in choosing, acquiring, or displaying them. In other words, distinguishing between luxury and necessity is a political act, one slaveholders exploited whenever possible to validate their rule. Arjun Appadurai, "Introduction: Commodities and the Politics of Value," in *The Social Life of Things: Commodities in Cultural Perspective*, ed. Arjun Appadurai (New York: Cambridge University Press, 1986), 38 and Pierre Bourdieu, *Distinction: A Social Critique of the Judgement of Taste*, trans. Richard Nice (Cambridge: Harvard University Press, 1984), 177–178, 246–249.

southern cities, save those of Alabama, allow them such luxuries as parading the principal thoroughfares of the city, and acting Beau Brummel to perfection." More often, commentary on slaves' spending habits took the form of resigned and sometimes smug moralism. Because slaveholders imagined that all of their slaves' comforts were provided for, the extra money they earned through overwork or patches necessarily went to "luxuries of food and dress that the 'peasantry of England' sigh after in vain." Traveler Almira Coffin commented on such marketing opportunities in the South Carolina lowcountry, remarking that the slaves would not eat the eggs and poultry that they raised, that instead, "they always want finery in exchange or some luxury to eat, as a sufficient quantity of useful food & clothing is provided without buying." Moreover, while whites would often "deny themselves many a common indulgence, that the negroes may not be denied any of their usual comforts," the enslaved could enjoy lives that were not only "abundant, but if they choose, luxurious."[22]

With the ability to earn cash, the enslaved could engage in more intemperate pleasures. Among the worst of these, slaveholders imagined, was alcohol, potentially the most dangerous consumable a slave could buy. "Negro men," white southerners argued, "were notoriously weak in that direction. The most honest could not resist the sight and smell of liquor. The failing would seem to be racial." Hence, planters worried that slaves would go to extraordinary lengths to "gratify their passion for liquor." Worse, they lamented, this desire was so strong that slaves settled for "poisonous liquors – chiefly the worst whiskey, much watered and made stupefying by an infusion of tobacco." Any number of white and black members of free society were willing to enable these moral inadequacies, serving as "itinerant venders of circulating poison, which they introduce into all the veins and arteries of society, stopping at every

---

[22] Robert Q. Mallard, *Plantation Life before Emancipation* (Richmond, VA: Whittet and Shepperson, 1892), 32; H. C., "On the Management of Negroes," *Farmers' Register* 1 (1834): 565; "Seeing is believing," *Raleigh Register, and North-Carolina Gazette*, 9 August 1836, reprinted from "Leaves from the South-west and Cuba: or, Familiar Passages from the Journal of a Valetudinarian," *The Knickerbocker, or New-York Monthly Magazine* 8 (1836): 51; "Discipline Among Negroes," *Southern Cultivator* 14 (1856), 192; [Patrick H. Mell], *Slavery. A Treatise Showing that Slavery is Neither a Moral, Political, Nor Social Evil* (Penfield, GA: Benjamin Brantley, 1844), 40; Almira Coffin to M. H. Osgood, 9 May 1851, Almira Coffin Letters, SCHS; David Brown, *The Planter: or, Thirteen Years in the South* (Philadelphia: H. Hooker, 1853), 55. In their comprehensive history of African-American style and expressive culture, Shane White and Graham White argue "slaveholders used clothing as a means of reinforcing paternalism." Their interpretation of paternalism, however, differs significantly from the one I offer here. Whereas White and White astutely note that slaveholders incorporated clothing choice and purchase into their system of management, I push the argument further. Slaveholders not only allowed the internal economy to persist, but actively held slaves' choices as consumers against them, thereby confirming their mastery. See *Stylin: African American Expressive Culture from Its Beginnings to the Zoot Suit* (Ithaca, NY: Cornell University Press, 1998), 30.

crossroad and every gathering, stopping man, boy and slave, selling them in every quantity from gallons to drams."[23]

The lengths to which some slaves would go to acquire money to satisfy their thirst exacerbated the perceived problem of "negro intemperance." Theft was a constant concern and will be discussed further in Chapter 4. The sale or "waste" of weekly provisions was another. A slave in Bryan County, Georgia, told Thomas Clay that he could not keep provisions in his house, that "mine and my children's were sold to buy rum." Others were "always found ready to barter away their whole weekly allowance to some neighboring dram shop, for a gallon of whiskey, or a pound or two of tobacco, or bread." Another planter argued that "[n]othing is more common than for them to sell their food, and in fact any thing upon which they can lay their hands, for the purpose of procuring grog and tobacco." He further warned that "[e]very planter, who has provisions served out in a raw state, may be positively assured, a portion at least, will find its way to some place, where a market can be had for *any thing*, – from a tenpenny nail to a gold lever watch."[24]

Many white southerners considered the inability to resist alcohol, and the resulting lack of discipline when confronted with it, an innate failing of black character. They viewed the combination of such foibles as intemperance and the weaknesses of improvidence and laziness as hallmarks of those of African descent. Although southern whites would admit that some free blacks were "frugal, provident, and thrifty," most agreed with Edmund Ruffin that these men and women were exceptional. Most, they argued, were "a nuisance, and noted for ignorance, laziness, improvidence, and vicious habits." In particular, many believed that "negroes" were "careless and slothful" and characterized by "idleness." Lest one imagine that such characteristics had been incubated by the system of slavery, others were quick to point out that "[l]aziness is one of the great characteristics of the negro – as a race, it has been said, that is caused

---

[23] Marion Harland, *Marion Harland's Autobiography: The Story of a Long Life* (New York: Harper and Brothers Publishers, 1910), 112; William H. Harrison, "Stoves for Negroes' Dwellings," *Farmers' Register* 8 (1840): 212; Olmsted, *Cotton Kingdom*, 195; Petition of 16 January 1857, Wake County, North Carolina (PAR# 11285706), in Loren Schweninger, ed., *Race, Slavery and Free Blacks: Series 1, Petitions to Southern Legislatures, 1777–1867* (Bethesda, MD: University Publications of America, 1998) [hereafter cited as *Legislative Petitions*]. PAR#s refer to the Petition Analysis Record, an organization system internal to Schweninger's Race and Slavery Petitions Project. The definitive work on alcohol consumption in the United States remains W. J. Rorabaugh's *The Alcoholic Republic: An American Tradition* (New York: Oxford University Press, 1979). Although both monographs on southern temperance and synthetic studies on slave life and culture have necessarily broached the topic, surprisingly there is no focused work on alcohol in the slave community.

[24] Clay, *Detail of a Plan*, 11; "Notions on the Management of Negroes," *Farmers' Register* 4 (1836): 495; "Dieting &c. of Negroes," *Southern Agriculturist, and Register of Rural Affairs* 9 (1836): 518.

by slavery, but this is not the case, for we find in the Northern States of our country, where slavery does not exist, that this characteristic is the same."[25]

If the traits of laziness and idleness most often characterized black people's failings as producers, slaveholders argued, an inability to plan and provide for future needs marked their weaknesses as consumers. Planters and "[a]ll who are acquainted with negroes" knew them to be "an improvident race" that both "must be made to do what is for their own good" and, if left alone, would "sink to the state of savage barbarism." "A negro," another explained, "has no idea of providing for the future ... [his] thoughts are limited to the present." A group of South Carolina citizens cited such characteristics in their petition to return free persons of color to a "happy State of bondage" in 1859. Claiming to "understand the Negroe character," they explained that blacks were inherently "indelent [sic], Lazy, improvident, destitute of forethought, & totally incapable of self government." As such, they were incapable of managing themselves and needed a careful white master to "arouse their dormant energies" and monitor consumption of subsistence goods. South Carolina planter Edward Spann Hammond embraced this stereotype, adjusting management techniques accordingly. Hammond issued provisions once a week rather than once a month, because "[n]egroes are improvident and three out of four will have consumed, wasted or bartered away their allowances long before the month closes, and must commit thefts, or have insufficient and unwholesome food, during a portion of the time." Those of like mind pointed to other anecdotes confirming this stereotype. Frederick Law Olmsted told the story of a "respectable-looking, orderly, and quiet-mannered mulatto" from the rice districts of South Carolina. His master recognized his keen intellect and had him trained as an engineer and machinist, allowing him to hire his time and spend his wages for himself. Unfortunately, the slave was "acquiring dissipated habits, and wasting his earnings," and

---

[25] Edmund Ruffin, *The Political Economy of Slavery; or the Institution Considered in Regard to its Influence on Public Wealth and the General Welfare* (Washington, DC: L. Towers, 1857), 15–16; John M. Turner, "Plantation Hygiene," *Southern Cultivator* 15 (1857): 141; "Hiring Negroes," *Southern Planter* 12 (1852): 376; W. G. Ramsay, "The Physiological Differences between the European (or White Man) and the Negro," *Southern Agriculturist, and Register of Rural Affairs* 12 (1839): 293. Patrick Rael has recently explored the discourse of thrift as it relates to slavery during the early national and antebellum eras, demonstrating the ways that abolitionists and pro-slavery advocates alike used "thrift" as a gauge of the peculiar institution's material and moral soundness. Slaveholders pointed to the supposed thriftlessness of those of African descent. Defenders of slavery, he argues, "tempered thrift with benevolence," thereby simultaneously justifying their rule and distinguishing themselves from the "avarice that made market society so hellish for free laborers." This project takes Rael's argument further, arguing that slaveholders used the discourse of thrift not only to deflect abolitionist criticism, but to shape management policy as well. Patrick Rael, "African Americans, Slavery, and Thrift from the Revolution to the Civil War," in *Thrift and Thriving in America: Capitalism and Moral Order from the Puritans to the Present*, eds. Joshua J. Yates and James Davison Hunter (New York: Oxford University Press, 2011).

the slaveholder brought him back to the plantation where he "soon became contented." Traveler John Ballard relayed a similar incident in 1844. In a letter to his friend William Harrison, he told of a couple of stage drivers, both bondmen, who attempted to transport him to Richmond. The first requested money from him, explaining that he needed a drink. Ballard gave him 12 ½ cents with which he bought "two scrapes of Brandy" and became too drunk to drive the stage. Another driver stepped forward to take his place but he too stopped the stage, asking for money for a drink. In a short time, he was also drunk, and the party stopped for the night. On arrival at the hotel, he granted the slave 50 cents to replace the whip he had lost while drunk, 75 cents for the man's breakfast, 75 cents to feed the horse, and 50 cents to pay the toll. Shortly after, the slave returned, saying he needed even more money. Ballard gave him 50 cents and told him that he "hoped [he] might never see him again." Whether Ballard was simply an overindulgent enabler of intemperate weakness or a victim of calculated cunning and artifice is difficult to determine. The exasperated Ballard likely did not care but his story, probably told over and over as he completed his journey, confirmed what many white southerners already believed: "negroes" could handle neither their liquor nor their money.[26]

White southerners used stories like these to justify their mastery. Clearly, left to their own devices, slaveholders argued, bondpeople could not care for themselves. Even if they could motivate themselves to work beyond the bare minimum for subsistence, their improvident natures prevented them from engaging in anything other than frivolous spending in the form of intemperate drinking, illicit gambling, and outlandish finery. In the view of many southern whites, the guidance of a wise master was the only chance these men and women had for comfort and survival. Agricultural journals assured readers that black men and women, especially, "plantation negroes," were "much more ignorant than most persons suppose" and required a man "qualified to act as their guardian, to give them necessary directions." Traveler James Buckingham found this belief pervasive among slaveholders, recounting the assumption that the enslaved were "wholly unable to maintain and protect themselves" and that slaveholders' efforts to preserve the institution of slavery were in the interests of "pure humanity towards the race."[27]

---

[26] "Dieting &c. of Negroes," 518; A. S. D., "On Raising Negroes," *Southern Agriculturist, and Register of Rural Affairs* 11 (1838): 79; Whitemarsh B. Seabrook, "On the Causes of the General Unsuccessfulness of the Sea-Island Planters," *Southern Agriculturist, and Register of Rural Affairs* 7 (1834): 178; *Legislative Petitions*, Abbeville District, South Carolina, ca. 1859 (PAR# 11385909); "Agriculture," [n.d.], in vol. entitled "Views on Agriculture, 1857–1858," p. 24, Edward Spann Hammond Papers, SCL; Olmsted, *Cotton Kingdom*, 186–187; John Ballard to William Harrison, 14 February 1844, Harrison Family Papers, VHS.

[27] FOBY, "Management of Servants," *Southern Cultivator* 11 (1853): 227; Buckingham, *The Slave States of America*, 1: 65. See also A PRACTICAL PLANTER, "Observations on the Management of Negroes," *Southern Agriculturist, and Register of Rural Affairs* 5 (1832): 181–184.

Slaveholding contributors to southern agricultural journals heartily submitted that "[n]egroes have very inferior minds and brains," "act from feeling and impulse more than from reason," and were therefore "entirely incapable of exercising a correct judgment, as to what would be for their interest and happiness." So judging, some used "science" to justify both the institution of slavery and their management techniques. Samuel Cartwright of Louisiana emphasized black physiology, arguing that sensuality, impulse, and desire ruled the negro race at the expense of intellect. Unaided, the "negro" was prone to *dysaesthesia ethiopica* or "hebetude of mind and obtuse sensibility of body," commonly known by planters as "rascality." The infected slave, "[w]hen aroused from his sloth by the stimulus of hunger ... takes anything he can lay his hands on, and tramples on the rights, as well as on the property of others, with perfect indifference as to consequences." Without proper oversight, slaves ate too much improper food and not enough bread and vegetables. Worse, "the black blood distributed to the brain chains the mind to ignorance, superstition, and barbarism, and bolts the door against civilization, moral culture and religious truth." What caused this wretched disease? "Negro liberty," fostered by permissive masters. According to Cartwright, "[s]laves are not subject to this disease, unless they are permitted to live like free negroes, in idleness and filth – to eat improper food or to indulge in spirituous liquors." Only the "compulsory power" of the white man could save the slave from his innate self.[28]

Cartwright's expositions reveal some of the central conflicts among slaveholding southerners. The issue of dependence loomed large in planter discourse and was, according to Olmsted, the central dilemma of the master class. The issue with which slaveholders struggled most was "[h]ow, without quite destroying the capabilities of the negro for any work at all, to prevent him from learning how to take care of himself" (Figure 1.1). The ability to earn and, notably, to accumulate, spend, and save money wisely was a hallmark of rational economic thought. Presumably, if a slave could be convinced to merge his or her self interest with that of the master, he or she would work more efficiently and increase the productivity of the plantation. In a system where men and women were denied the fruits of their labor, this was surely a difficult task

[28] "Hints on the Management of Slaves," *Southern Agriculturist, Horticulturist, and Register of Rural Affairs* 2 (1842): 534; Samuel A. Cartwright, "Diseases and Peculiarities of the Negro Race," *De Bow's Review* 11 (1851): 333–336. For a more extensive discussion of what Cartwright called, "Slavery in the Light of Ethnology," see his essay in *Cotton is King, and Pro-Slavery Arguments*, ed. E. N. Elliott (Augusta, GA: Pritchard, Abbott, and Loomis, 1860), 691–728; Josiah Clark Nott et al., *Types of Mankind: Or, Ethnological Researches, based upon the Ancient Monuments, Paintings, Sculptures, and Crania of Races, and upon their Natural, Geographical, Philological, and Biblical History* (Philadelphia: Lippincott, Grambo, 1854). For secondary works on the subject, see James Denny Guillory, "The Pro-Slavery Arguments of Dr. Samuel A. Cartwright," *Louisiana History* 9 (1968): 209–227; William Stanton, *The Leopard's Spots: Scientific Attitudes toward Race in America, 1815–1859* (Chicago: University of Chicago Press, 1960) and Fredrickson, *Black Image in the White Mind*, 71–96.

FIGURE 1.1 Antislavery men and women mocked the hypocrisy of slaveholders' central dilemma.

Source: American Anti-Slavery Society. *The American Anti-Slavery Almanac, for 1840.* New York and Boston: Published for the American Anti-Slavery Society, 1839. Courtesy of the Division of Rare and Manuscript Collections, Cornell University Library.

and was recognized as such by the region's slaveholders. "To moralize and induce the slave to assimilate with the master and his interest, has been and is the great desideratum aimed at," explained one planter, but he had "long since desponded in the completion of this task." The enslaved of the antebellum South lacked "the motive of self-interest," a condition that both "stimulate[d] his evil passions" and negated any motives toward productivity, diligence, and carefulness.[29] How, then, could slaveholders imbue a "Protestant work ethic" and a desire for accumulation in the minds and bodies of their slaves?

The internal economy provided a viable, albeit risky, opportunity to instill these values. A contributor to the *Southern Agriculturist* rationalized that, "if industrious for themselves, they will be so for their masters, and no Negro, with a well stocked poultry house, a small crop advancing, a canoe partly finished, or a few tubs unsold, all of which he calculates soon to enjoy, will ever run away." His own slaves had become more productive, he explained, since he had "impress[ed] upon their minds the advantage of holding property." Prescription met reality in some parts of the lowcountry. James Ritchie Sparkman explained to fellow planter Robert F. W. Allston that "the custom prevails with most of

---

[29] Olmsted, *Cotton Kingdom*, 48; B. McBride, "Directions for Cultivating the various Crops Grown at Hickory Hill," *Southern Agriculturist, and Register of Rural Affairs* 3 (1830): 238; John A. Calhoun, E. E. DuBose, and Virgil Bobo, "Management of Slaves," *Southern Cultivator* 4 (1846): 114; Floyd, "Management of Servants," *Southern Cultivator* 11 (1853): 301. See also Achates [Thomas Pinckney], *Reflections, Occasioned by the Late Disturbances in Charleston* (Charleston: A. E. Miller, 1822): 21.

my neighbors of supplying all reasonable demands by exchange." Even though the mechanics of such transactions differed from plantation to plantation, the benefits to master and slave were obvious. "The point established," he emphasized, "is that by reasonable industry and ordinary providence, our people all have it in their power to add materially to their comforts and indulgencies, and that their owners very wisely and humanely offer every encouragement to this effort." Thomas Clay illuminated further this particular form of slaveholder sagacity, arguing that "[t]he possession and increase of personal and domestic comforts, are the safest pledge that the slave will be faithful to the interests of his master." Moreover, he emphasized the means by which the slave should accumulate property. According to Clay, accumulated goods meant more when acquired with the "kind assistance of his master – I say *assistance*, for he will value them more if they are partly the fruit of his own exertion: neither would it be expedient to furnish him with these comforts, before he had made some effort to obtain them; for, if given before he wants them; they will be destroyed by neglect and abuse. These favors, however trifling they may appear to us, will exert a happy influence on the negro." Clearly, Clay recognized and encouraged a desire for labor's just reward within the enslaved and advised slaveholders to offer opportunities for both production and consumption as a means of satisfying it.[30]

Other planters were more mindful of the risks that attended spending opportunities, some even arguing that trafficking worked against masters' interests. In the view of an 1834 contributor to the *Farmers' Register*, "[i]t renders the slave independent in a great measure of his master, thoughtless of, and careless in the performance of every duty, inattentive to, and even destructive of every interest of his owner, and only attentive to the means of carrying on his traffic, spending his nights in toilsome roving, and in debauchery." A slave with the ability to carry on trade of his or her own embraced feelings of independence, thus making masters' generous provisions of "rude comforts" less meaningful and, worse, less necessary. Instead of instilling feelings of empowerment and capability in the slave, some argued that the planter should "provide for him yourself, and by that means create in him a habit of perfect dependence on you. Allow it once to be understood by a negro, that he is to provide for himself, and you that moment give him an undeniable claim on you for a portion of his time to make his provision; and should you from necessity, or any other cause, encroach upon his time, disappointment and discontent are seriously felt."[31]

[30] R[ufus] King, Jr., "On the Management of the BUTLER Estate, and the Cultivation of the Sugar Cane," *Southern Agriculturist, and Register of Rural Affairs* 1 (1828): 525; James R. Sparkman to Benjamin Allston, 10 March 1858, in *The South Carolina Rice Plantation as Revealed in the Papers of Robert F. W. Allston*, ed. J. H. Easterby (Columbia: University of South Carolina Press, 2004), 350; Clay, *Detail of a Plan*, 20.

[31] Charles Woodson, "On the Management of Slaves," *Farmers' Register* 2 (1834): 248; "Management of Slaves," *Southern Cultivator* 4 (1846): 44.

But it was not just the fear of the feelings of independence such opportunities inspired. The possession of money itself, and what slaves might spend it on, worried planters. Slaveholders asked, "What is money worth to one whose common sense and self-discipline are so little developed that it is used to patronize extravagance and strengthen vice and crime?" Quite a bit, some feared. In the wake of the Denmark Vesey crisis, Thomas Pinckney addressed the causes of the purported insurrection. Among the more dangerous contributing factors was "the possession of much money" in the hands of the region's slaves. Cash "spent in drunkenness and debauchery" transformed them into "willing instruments of any delusive plan of mischief." On the eve of an even greater upheaval thirty-eight years later, Carolina planter David Gavin recoiled with similar fear. "[N]o person can be honest and carry on illicit trafick [sic] with negroes," he railed in 1859, "I consider them worse than a thief." The fall of 1860 found both his apprehension and his anger amplified. A cry of alarm pierced the October night, awakening his lowcountry neighborhood. Worried about insurrection, local slaveholders sent out patrols to search plantation quarters. "Nothing more destructive was found amongst the negroes than spirits," Gavin recorded. His anger far from allayed, he surmised that the spirits had been "no doubt bought of mean democratic white men who are no better than abolitionists." Seething, he continued: "[O]ur democratic alias mob-o-crat-ic government allows it and is defended and supported by demagogues who pretend to be in favour of the South and slavery." Bluster of this sort was not just relegated to private journals. Members of the St. Helena Agricultural Society fell into "quite a row" in February 1857, lowcountry planter Thomas Chaplin reported, "originating from some remarks of Mr. Edgar Fripp, about some one or more members trading with Negroes." The "hard words" passed among anxious men threatened the long-standing club – in existence since 1826 – with dissolution. "I do not think the society will meet again," Chaplin worried, "and if it does, it will be with greatly reduced numbers." Reading through his diary years later, Chaplin found his comments disturbingly prescient, noting, "In about 3 years after, they were all scattered." Less paranoid, perhaps, but equally concerned, one slaveholder explained to readers of the *Southern Cultivator* risks inherent in the cash trade. He allowed patches and provision grounds on his plantation but not the growing of corn or cotton, "believing ... that the possession of too much money is calculated to generate bad habits, and produce disorder, where sobriety, good feeling and happiness should prevail."[32] A group of citizens articulated both of these fears to the South Carolina

---

[32] Daniel Lee, "A Lecture on Labor," *Southern Cultivator* 15 (1857): 74; Achates, *Reflections, Occasioned by the Late Disturbances in Charleston*, 9; Entries of 11 February 1859 and 29 October 1860, David Gavin Diary, SHC; Theodore Rosengarten, ed., *Tombee: Portrait of a Cotton Planter* (New York: William Morrow, 1986), 686; FOBY, "Management of Servants," 227. Interestingly, a reader wrote a scathing response to FOBY, chastising him not just for allowing his slaves to spend freely, but for allowing them to trade on Sundays, insisting "[t]here is as little, I should say less probability of having their morals corrupted by the free use of money,

legislature in 1840, explaining, "[g]ive the slave money or property which is its Equivalent" and "you place it in his power at once to place himself beyond the reach of servitude." After all, they warned, "'money is power,' & none need live in Servitude who can command it."[33]

Clearly, unchecked economic power by slaves gave pause to the master class. But the benefits of the internal economy to slaveholders proved difficult to overlook. How could they reap the benefits of the internal economy while maintaining mastery? Letters to agricultural journals proposed varied management policies, techniques that would allow slaves to earn and spend money in ways that provided for comfort and happiness without risking serious disciplinary problems. Even though his own motives differed from those of antebellum slaveholders, Olmsted was keenly interested in this problem. Economic opportunities engendered by the task system impressed Olmsted, inspiring him to propose a project of gradual emancipation that would remove the burden of slavery from the United States while educating a new class of American citizens. Imparting consumer skills served as the basis for his plan. He explained:

Let, for instance, any slave be provided with all things he will demand, as far as practicable, and charge him for them at certain prices – honest, market prices for his necessities, higher prices for harmless luxuries, and excessive, but not absolutely prohibitory, prices for everything likely to do him harm. Credit him, at a fixed price, for every day's work he does, and for all above a certain easily accomplished task in a day, at an increased price, so that his reward will be in an increasing ratio to his perseverance. Let the prices of provisions be so proportioned to the price of task-work, that it will be about as easy as it is now for him to obtain a bare subsistence. When he has no food and shelter due to him, let him be confined in solitude, or otherwise punished, until he asks for opportunity to earn exemption from punishment by labor.

When he desires to marry, and can persuade any woman to marry him, let the two be dealt with as in partnership. Thus, a young man or young woman will be attractive somewhat in proportion to his or her reputation for industry and providence. Thus industry and providence will become fashionable. Oblige them to purchase food for their children, and let them have the benefit of their children's labour, and they will be careful to teach their children to avoid waste, and to honour labour.[34]

Roundly criticized by most southerners, Olmsted would find few supporters of his consumer-based reform proposal in toto. It is worth noting, however, that some did incorporate elements of this approach. Georgia planter James Towns set up a system in which his slaves received "payment" for good behavior at the end of the year. Although he used to give crops, he found that an annual settlement of cash worked to both of their advantages. He explained:

than by suffering them thus to profane the Sabbath." Agricola, "Management of Servants – Strictures on Foby's Article," *Southern Cultivator* 11 (1853): 301.
[33] *Legislative Petitions*, South Carolina, Union District, 12 November 1840 (PAR# 11384005).
[34] Olmsted, *Cotton Kingdom*, 198–199.

I furnish any extra clothing that any of them may want during the year; they are charged with it, and at pay day, as they call it, it is brought up against them; it makes them much more careful with their clothes, for they are very proud to go off with a pocket full of silver, and I always pay them in silver. It is a day of settlement with one for all offences during the year; I now bring up in judgment their misdeeds, and they feel the effect, the only way that many persons can feel – their purse is touched.[35]

"Pay days," like those anticipated by Towns's bondpeople occurred throughout the South and, as the Georgian's blunt explanation of managerial scheming reveals, played a crucial role in plantation discipline. Plantation books and prescriptive literature alike indicate that many planters worried far more about how the enslaved acquired goods to sell – fearing theft – than about what slaves did with their money. Consequently, planters often went out of their way to place money in the hands of their bondpeople. Richard Eppes prohibited trafficking on his Virginia plantations but allowed his slaves $5 per year for cutting four cords of wood in addition to the $1 per year they could earn for good behavior.[36] South Carolinian Ben Sparkman, too, paid for wood cutting, while fellow Palmetto planter, Edward Spann Hammond, as an incentive to marriage, gave each new couple "a bounty of 5$, to be invested in household articles." Michael Gramling paid "Old Joan" $2 for staying with a fellow slave during childbirth while, in the midst of a particularly wet winter, Virginia planter Lewis Mason issued to each slave a new coat and "to all of them money so as to secure them having warm clothes & little things besides their allowance which they may require."[37]

Other planters arranged for the exchange of fowl, swine, and crops, doling out funds at regular intervals throughout the year. Savannah River planter Charles Manigault, for example, explicitly barred overseers from raising chickens, instead reserving poultry-keeping for his slaves "because this is the only thing my people can raise for themselves ... which enable[s] them to procure some little extra Comforts for themselves, & which tends to attach them to their homes." William Elliott bought fowls and chickens from slaves Love and Kate for 75 cents and 56 ¼ cents respectively in 1848, while Dorothea A. Richardson regularly kept accounts with ten to twenty slaves per year for

---

[35] James M. Towns, "Management of Negroes," *Southern Cultivator* 9 (1851): 86.

[36] "Code of Laws for Island Plantation" and "Rules & Regulations for Island Plantation," Section 69, Eppes Family Papers, VHS. For reproductions of these documents, see Michael L. Nicholls, "'In the Light of Human Beings': Richard Eppes and His Island Plantation Code of Laws," *Virginia Magazine of History and Biography* 89 (1981): 67–78. Though these documents are undated, Nicholls argues that Eppes's set of "Rules and Regulations" can be dated between 1852 and 1854.

[37] Entry of November 1848, Ben Sparkman Plantation Journal, SHC; "Agriculture" [n.d.] in vol. entitled "Views on Agriculture, 1857–1858," p. 35, Edward Spann Hammond Papers, SCL; Entry of 26 June 1850, Michael Gramling Plantation Book, SCL; Lewis Edmunds Mason to Mary Anne (Fort) Mason, December, n.d., Section 35, Mason Family Papers, VHS. See also, Agricola, "Management of Negroes," *Southern Cultivator* 13 (1855): 171; "Management of Negroes – Bathing Feet, Remark," *Southern Cultivator* 11 (1853): 302.

chickens, ducks, hens, gobblers, roosters, and geese from 1850 to 1860. Swine, too, increased slaves' spending power. James Ritchie Sparkman regularly bought hogs from slaves between 1850 and 1859. He paid 5 cents per pound, for example, for hogs in 1858. At 254 pounds, Martha's hog earned most, the bondwoman taking $12.70 for her husbandry. The year 1859 proved less profitable for slaves. Whereas over thirty bondpeople earned cash for swine in 1858, less than ten did so in 1859 with neighbor Shaffer's Ben earning most for his two hogs (240 pounds and 122 pounds respectively), an impressive $18.10 for his coffers. Perhaps most common, slaveholders transacted crops with their slaves, often maintaining extensive accounts for cotton, corn, and/or fodder. Plantation books record complex transactions. Carolina planter Francis Withers, for example, bought several bushels of corn "of the People" in 1847 while George Kollock regularly exchanged cash for fodder.[38]

In each of these cases, planters provided means for slaves to earn money. What bondpeople bought with this money was their choice – with significant restrictions, of course. Although many planters recognized and encouraged slaves' abilities as consumers, surveillance and monitoring of slave spending was necessary, if not for slaveholders' protection, then for protection of slaves themselves. Masters envisioned themselves as models of moral and, notably, consumer behavior; bondpeople, they argued, were lucky to be in a state of "apprenticeship of civilization." Some planters took this responsibility quite seriously, well aware that their own behavior could serve as example to impressionable and weaker-minded charges. A Georgia slaveholder explained that the master "must respect the rights of property in the smallest matters, and cherish among his people a love of property honestly acquired: it will help them to become honest, and possibly teach him to control a passion – the love of accumulation – that may be too strong in his own bosom." "Philom" likewise urged readers of the *Southern Cultivator* to "be just and generous towards them, and not be too covetous of riches – for 'the love of money is the root of all evil.'" Bondpeople absorbed the moral of greed and its attendant dangers although their masters likely did not serve as quite the positive models they imagined themselves to be.[39]

---

[38] Charles Manigault to James Haynes, 1 March 1847, in *Life and Labor on Argyle Island: Letters and Documents of a Savannah River Rice Plantation, 1833–1867*, ed. James M. Clifton (Savannah: The Beehive Press, 1978), 49; "Poultry raised at Pon Pon in 1848," William Elliott Plantation Book for Pon Pon, 1840–1851, Elliott and Gonzales Family Papers, SHC; Dorothea A. Richardson, Poultry Books, 1850–1860, James Burchell Richardson Papers, Duke; "Hogs Purchased, November 1858" and "Hogs Nov. 1859," Birdfield and Dirleton Memorandum Book, 1857–1859, James Ritchie Sparkman Papers, SCL; Entry of 9 September 1847, Francis Withers, Springfield Plantation Journal, SCHS; Entry of 23 March 1842, Plantation Book, Rosedew Plantation, 1842–1843, p. 66, George J. Kollock Plantation Journals, SHC. For examples of this sort of accounting, see Daina Ramey Berry, *Swing the Sickle for the Harvest is Ripe: Gender and Slavery in Antebellum Georgia* (Urbana: University of Illinois Press, 2007), appendices C and D.

[39] "What is to be done with the Negro?" *Southern Cultivator* 16 (1858): 378; *Proceedings of the Meeting in Charleston, S. C., May 13–15, 1845 on the Religious Instruction of the Negroes,*

Slaveholders could impart more concrete lessons as well. Northern proslavery apologist Reverend Nehemiah Adams described the fine quality of bondpeople's Sabbath dress, noting that "[i]t was a pleasant paradox to find that where the colored people are not free, they have in many things the most liberty, and among them the liberty to dress handsomely, and be respected in it." But this "liberty" was not without significant guidance and direction. Noting that one did not see the "tawdriness of color" and "violations of taste" that one would often see among free northern blacks, Adams explained that enslaved women were lucky enough to "each have a mistress, a matron, or young lady, to advise and direct them." Likewise, a contributor to the *Southern Planter* urged overseers to repress the urge to deride slaves who "dress themselves in the ridiculous finery which they sometimes display" and "encourage [rather] than repress their taste in dress." Why? "It aids very materially in giving them self-respect." Another argued that slaves "should always be aided and encouraged in dressing, and their own particular fancies indulged to a reasonable extent."[40]

General surveillance was key to ensuring proper consumer behavior. Lucky slaves, southerners argued, could "add to their common welfare not only the comforts, but many of the luxuries of life" while protected from the "vice of intemperance" that plagued northern free-laboring brethren. Nehemiah Adams pushed this comparison farther, arguing that "the wholesome restraint laid upon the colored population" prevented the wild debauchery seen in poor white elements of the population. He explained further that many a slave had come to appreciate the master's oversight and eagerly embraced the opportunity to consume and acquire goods cooperatively with him. He painted a rosy, if not completely realistic, picture of "the master and servant, chatting side by side, counting their net profits, discussing the state of the markets, inventing new commodities, the master stepping in at the Savings Bank, on the way home, and entering nine or ten dollars more in Joe's pass-book, which already shows several hundred dollars." White oversight, paternalists argued, tempered perceived black inclinations toward careless spending, allowing desired values of providence and thriftiness to pass from master to slave. Other masters claimed that slaves benefited materially from white market savvy and consumer skills. Arguing that "negroes" were "not capable of managing," a planter handled the marketing of his slaves' corn crops, explaining that "more justice will be done them than if disposed of by themselves." So too prated another concerned slaveholder: "I hardly ever go to town without having commissions to execute for some of them," the Virginian explained, "and think they prefer to employ me, from a belief that, if their money should not quite hold out, I would add a

---

Together with the Report of the Committee, and the Address to the Public (Charleston: B. Jenkins, 1845), 58; Philom, "Moral Management of Negroes," *Southern Cultivator* 7 (1849): 105.

[40] Adams, *A South-Side View of Slavery*, 31; "Overseers," *Southern Planter* 16 (1856): 148; Collins, "Essay on the Management of Slaves," 206.

little to it; which I not unfrequently do, in order to get a better article." Some
of his neighbors preferred "paying in *Money* and allowing them [their slaves]
to trade for themselves," but James Sparkman more closely monitored spending. He preferred to buy goods "for" his slaves "which are ordinarily only to
be obtained through shop keepers, and retailing to them in exchange for their
poultry." Dismissing concerns that such a policy might lead to abuse, he touted
the clear benefit slaves gained with his assistance and oversight. "They frequently ask me to become *Treasurer* of their little funds," he explained. "I have
become satisfied that they get better bargains than can be made by themselves
with the shop keepers. I hold now in this way upwards of $70, which will be
called for in dimes and quarters, through the current year."[41]

Payment passed from hand to hand served the master well, but, in the Old
South, hard cash was dear, especially in the weeks and months before factors'
checks made their way back to the plantation at harvest's end. Cash earned
meant cash owed and planters' records note the complicated web of credit
and debt that linked masters and slaves, neighbors and kin. Master or mistress often presided over transactions, channeling money into the system and,
importantly, controlling where it went. Georgia widow Martha Jackson, for
example, gave "prizes" of between 8 cents and 70 cents for six days' cotton
picking in 1851. Her records not only reveal careful accounting of her own
funds but also the entrenched system of credit exchange on the plantation over
which she presided. On October 18th, for example, Bob was credited with
1136 pounds of cotton, earning 70 cents. In recording the payment, however,
Jackson noted that he "gave his balance to Harriet." On September 30th, Mary
netted 1023 pounds of cotton, earning 60 cents, but apparently "[lent] Eliza
her balance," still owing Jackson "10 cts." Slaves and mistress alike counted
on harvest prizes, records reveal. Not only were debts among slaves paid, so
were debts to Jackson herself. For 740 pounds picked from October 31st until
November 5th, for example, Ms. Jackson paid Harriet "40 cents on Dress
bought on my account" at a local mercantile establishment. That same week,
the slave Martha picked 751 pounds and made a similar arrangement, though
Jackson noted that she still owed $1.60 for her dress. Lowcountry planter
Alexander Lawton followed suit. In 1837, for example, he bought nine hogs of
"Big Brister." The hogs weighed 1150 pounds, earning the slave $69. Of Dick,
he bought a 159-pound hog for his "Negroes Bacon for 1840." From the $9.54
he owed his slave, Lawton deducted $7.50 and applied the remaining $2.04 to

[41] J. P. C., letter to the editor, *South-Carolina Temperance Advocate and Register of Agriculture
and General Literature* [hereafter *South-Carolina Temperance Advocate*] (Columbia, SC), 28
November 1844; Adams, *South-Side View of Slavery*, 26, 36; A Practical Planter, "Observations
on the Management of Negroes," *Southern Agriculturist, and Register of Rural Affairs* 5 (1832):
183; J. K. Paulding, "Extract from *Slavery in the United States* – by J[ames] K. PAULDING:
being a letter to the author from a farmer of lower Virginia," *Farmers' Register* 4 (1836):
181; James R. Sparkman to Benjamin Allston, 10 March 1858, in *The South Carolina Rice
Plantation*, 350.

an "old Debt." Little Martin, too, owed Lawton for a coat and shoes that year, applying the $11.34 he earned from hog raising to his account.[42]

But it was not just debts to each other slaves called in when the money started to roll. Once harvest came, masters' debts were due as well. Custom and contract both mandated that the master pay his due at year's end. We can see such policies play out on both large and small scales. In Rowan County, North Carolina, planter William Spruce Macay's plantation book recorded an 1837 register of money "Due to the Negroes for their crops." The nearly illegible list of single-entry accounts – items crossed out as Macay paid his debts – listed payments for bushels of oats and corn ranging from 50 cents to $5. Farther south, in December 1857, St. Helena Island planter John Edwin Fripp paid Daniel $2 for a hog, noting that he still owed the slave $3. He was in arrears with Miley, too, having paid her only $1 of the $10 he owed her. Margaret Armstrong Wylly engaged in similar transactions on another island plantation. Taking over their St. Simon's estate after her husband's death in 1833, Wylly maintained a corn account for the plantation's slaves. In the fall of 1834, she bought over twenty-nine bushels of corn from eight slaves, paying them off six days after receiving $200 from Savannah's Younge and Sons "by letter."[43]

Historian John Campbell has written extensively on slaves' participation in the cotton market, arguing that the sale and production of cotton stuffs both offered material benefit and opened new opportunities for slaves to assert "control over their own affairs." Slaves on three upcountry South Carolina plantations, he argues, found opportunities both to perform waged overwork and, increasingly, to grow Mexican short-staple cotton. Such opportunities came at the price of increased debt and monitoring, however. Few slaves sold cotton without oversight, and perhaps more significantly, Campbell argues, the "[t]he long arm of the master ... shaped the way slaves spent their earnings." By paying slaves with credit, slaveholders retained control over slaves' material worlds. In the end, Campbell concludes that the internal economy was Janus-faced. Market exchange benefited the slave materially, to be sure, but at the expense of independence they might have hoped to gain.[44]

But even slaves on the plantations Campbell examines had occasional access to cash and, like their fellows throughout the South, looked for ways to escape

---

[42] Entries of 16 and 30 September 1851, 10 and 18 October 1851, 5 November 1851, Plantation Day Book, 1851, Jackson and Prince Family Papers, SHC; Entry of 23 November 1837, Plantation Journal [Alexander James Lawton], 1810–1840, Alexander Robert Lawton Papers, SHC.

[43] "Due to Negroes for their Crops, 1837," William Spruce Macay Account Book, 1834–1846, Macay and McNeely Family Papers, SHC; Entry of 23 December 1857, Diary, 1857–1858, John Edwin Fripp Papers, SHC; Entries of September–November 1834, Margaret Armstrong Wylly Diary, Couper and Wylly Family Papers, GHS.

[44] John Campbell, "'As a Kind of Freeman'?: Slaves' Market-Related Activities in the South Carolina Up Country, 1800–1860," in *Cultivation and Culture: Labor and the Shaping of Slave Life in the Americas*, eds. Ira Berlin and Philip D. Morgan (Charlottesville: University Press of Virginia, 1993), 243–274.

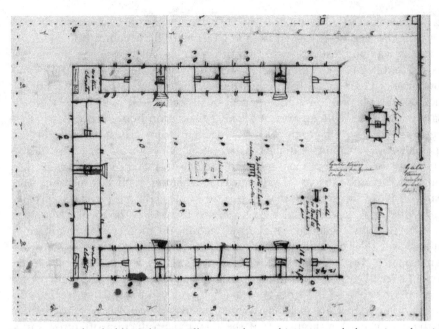

FIGURE 1.2 Slaveholder John B. Miller turned to architecture and plantation planning to curb nighttime trading and pilfering.
Source: John B. Miller to unknown and enclosure [1846], Miller-Furman-Dabbs Papers, SCL. Courtesy of the South Caroliniana Library, University of South Carolina.

oversight. Planters lamented the problem, searching for solutions both on and off the plantation. So concerned was South Carolina slaveholder John Miller about "the evils that result from the illicit trade that is carried on between the free Blacks & Shop Keepers at night" that he incorporated market surveillance into plantation design. In 1846, he drew up a set of architectural plans aimed to contain the threat. "The plan of their houses," he explained, "is to have them all enclosed, so as to prevent egress to them but at the gate." At night, a watch appointed by the driver would monitor the compound's only entrance, making sure "no person attempted to go out or come in." Noting that "this plan was adopted on the Island of Cuba," Miller hoped to shut out material exchange that threatened his hold on slaves' economic lives (Figure 1.2).[45]

[45] John B. Miller to unknown and enclosure, [1846], Miller-Furman-Dabbs Papers, SCL. Miller likely referred to nineteenth-century Cuban *barracón de patio*. Historical archaeologist Theresa Singleton describes the structure as a "rectangular-shaped building usually constructed of *mampostería* that surrounded a *patio*, an open yard-like area located in the center." Described as both "notorious" and "prison-like," such housing was not commonly used by slaveholders in the nineteenth-century American South. Further, there is no evidence that John Miller built such a structure for his own slaves. His interest in doing so, however, reveals the threat the internal economy posed. Theresa A. Singleton, "Slavery and Spatial Dialectics on Cuban Coffee Plantations," *World Archaeology* 33 (2001): 102.

When not directly supervising their bondpeople, slaveholders placed what might best be described as a tempered trust in their slaves' spending habits. An 1839 slave pass illustrates this ambivalence. A proprietor issued a pass for a group of slaves to visit their home in Franklin, Virginia. According to the document, ten men and women were permitted to travel alone and had been "furnished with funds to pay for what they may need," with the *caveat*, "should proper economy be used." What was considered "proper economy" was left to white readers' discretion. Other planters displayed ambivalence toward slaves' consumer capacities through the imposition of restrictions on when and where purchasing could take place. Edward Spann Hammond allowed his slaves to raise crops but strictly monitored their sale, allowing "ten fellows" to go to Augusta every Thursday to trade "but no other time unless sent." Another planter permitted, on Sundays, "two and only two boys ... to visit town for the purpose of trading," provided they returned home "duly sober."[46]

Despite their best efforts, planters simply could not maintain constant surveillance over bondpeople and, much to their disappointment, sometimes found that the trust they placed in slaves was ill-founded. In lieu of monitoring the behavior of slaves, some sought to regulate the venues of consumption where slaves were known to spend their money. General stores were the focus of much slaveholder ire and will be discussed in detail in Chapter 3. Roving salesmen posed an even greater threat. In 1842, a group of Botetourt County planters complained to the Virginia legislature of

a swarm of foot peddlers, who travel the country in every direction; dealing in goods of the most inferior and deceptive kinds; resorting to every species of cunning, and misrepresentation, to aid them in perpetrating frauds; seeking opportunities when the heads of families are absent; to take advantage of those who know nothing either of the quality or price of goods; and not content in annoying us in this way, they visit our negro cabins and not only excite the slaves by their intercourse, and the inducements they hold out to purchase, to dishonesty, but discontent with their situation.[47]

Other petitioners voiced concerns about peddlers who hawked "tinsel-merchandise," taking advantage of the "ignorance & credulity" of the country people and cheating them out of the "hard-earned fruits of honest industry." Newspapers across the South echoed these complaints, warning readers of shady traders who overcharged their customers, sold inferior products, passed counterfeit currency, and even spread disease.[48] That peddlers hawked wares

[46] Slave pass, 24 August 1839, Holland Family Papers, VHS; "Rules of a Plantation," [n.d.], plantation diary, 1856, Edward Spann Hammond Papers, SCL; FOBY, "Management of Servants," 227.

[47] *Legislative Petitions*, Virginia, Botetourt County, 8 January 1842 (PAR# 11684202).

[48] *Legislative Petitions*, North Carolina, New Hanover County, 20 December 1831 (PAR# 11283101). For examples of peddlers carrying diseases like smallpox and yellow fever, see "How Yellow Fever is Propagated," *Daily Morning News* (Savannah, GA), 15 June 1859; "Small Pox," *Raleigh Register, and North-Carolina Gazette*, 17 December 1841; "From Dr. Reese's Medical Gazette," *Charleston (SC) Mercury*, 11 June 1859.

"generally imperfect" and "impos[ed] faulty goods on the ignorant" – gilt watches passed as gold, chalk- and soda-tainted molasses sold as "northern strained honey" – was a given.[49] The popular image of the "Yankee peddler" humbugging the unwitting was a common one. Fictional accounts of wily itinerant traders, among them clock peddler Sam Slick, captured Americans' imaginations, animating discussion of commerce. David Jaffee's study of economic change in the rural North argues that the "peddler combined the roles of market analyst, entertainer, and trickster," breaking down rural resistance to market expansion and whetting rough tastes for consumer goods.[50] This interpretation fits the South too – but with some modification. More than in the North, peddlers' tricks served less to entertain than to threaten a precarious social order.

Thomas Haliburton's Sam Slick tales were advertised widely through the South, but resonated more ominously in public discourse.[51] Time and again, southerners lobbed the name as aspersion at shady and conniving northern interlopers. That hawkers interacted with their slaves was troubling, but even here, masters found opportunity to reinforce their right – their responsibility – to rule. Paternalist editors of the Augusta *Daily Chronicle and Sentinel* warned of "Jew peddlers" prowling the country on Sundays. Vigilance was needed, they argued, to protect the enslaved lest they "fall into the hands of these heartless sharpers." Raleigh readers found no better confirmation of "negro's" inferior consumer acumen than an article that appeared in 1830. A peddler with a counterfeit bill allegedly duped a slave. The editor assured readers that "no mercantile man" would think to accept such a check, "badly executed" as it was but urged his readers "to have eye" out for such articles. The slave, like many "ignorant, honest men in the community" was clearly not discerning enough to protect his own interests. The paternalists of southern society would worry for them.[52] Transient traders preyed upon the gullible, the intemperate, and the improvident, causing discord among elements of society that white planters could ill afford to excite. As a venue of consumption, then, peddlers were especially worrisome because slaveholders could exert no control over

---

[49] "All is Not Gold that Glistens," *Raleigh Register, and North-Carolina Gazette*, 13 June 1843; "Pedlars," *Raleigh Register, and North-Carolina Gazette*, 8 October 1819; "Yankee Ingenuity," *Camden (SC) Commercial Courier*, 13 May 1837.

[50] David Jaffee, "Peddlers of Progress and the Transformation of the Rural North, 1760–1860," *Journal of American History* 78 (1991): 528. See also Jaffee, *A New Nation of Goods: The Material Culture of Early America* (Philadelphia: University of Pennsylvania Press, 2010).

[51] Advertisements for Thomas Haliburton's 1836 *The Clockmaker: or, the Sayings and Doings of Samuel Slick, of Slickville* appeared in newspapers throughout the South including the *Daily Morning News* (Savannah, GA), the *Charleston (SC) Courier*, the *Charleston (SC) Mercury*, among many others.

[52] "Larceny, Peddling, &c.," *Daily Chronicle and Sentinel* (Augusta, GA), 3 March 1855; "Counterfeit Check," *Raleigh Register, and North-Carolina Gazette*, 25 November 1830.

when, where, and how slaves spent their money. Peddlers rearranged planter control over time and space, rendering both independent of the master.

Attempts to restrict the purchase of liquor by slaves most clearly reflected efforts and strategies to regulate venues of consumption in the antebellum South. Even though Joseph Leconte remembered that "prohibition laws" in Liberty County, Georgia, were "enacted and strictly enforced," others fretted about the many opportunities slaves had for purchasing alcohol. Teetotalers sought to rectify this problem by arguing for the prohibition of liquor altogether. Citizens in Prince Edward County, Virginia, complained in an 1839 petition that there was "a large population of coloured people who give way to the temptation to drunkenness when ever it is presented" and, for their sake, asked that liquor traffic be prohibited.[53]

For other concerned citizens, prohibition was unnecessary – and undesirable. After all, as one teetotaler noted sarcastically, "WE WANT A DROP OR TWO FOR OUR OWN COMFORT. WE CAN USE IT THE RIGHT WAY. WE MUST LET WHITE MEN TO BUY, SELL, AND DRINK WHISKEY, THOUGH IT WOULD BE TOO VILE FOR OUR NEGROES TO DO EITHER!"[54] For most, such hypocrisy rang hollow – the editor's commentary reflected exactly their attitude toward drink in southern communities. How, then, could they satisfy their own modest and controlled desire for spirits while limiting slave access? Southerners pitched a number of solutions. There was already legislation prohibiting the sale of alcohol to slaves, some argued; authorities simply needed to enforce the law – increased fines and even public whippings of white sellers, if needed.[55] Others sought to extend the law's reach. In 1848, for example, a group of Accomack County planters appealed to the Virginia legislature, asking that the state not only enforce the prohibition of liquor sales to slaves but extend that restriction to free blacks as well. According to the petition, "[w]e highly approve the law which prohibits the sale of intoxicating liquors to slaves; we regard it as extremely beneficial in design, but as almost, if not entirely useless in effect, so long as the same restriction does not extend

[53] Joseph Leconte, *The Autobiography of Joseph Leconte*, ed. William D. Armes (New York: D. Appleton, 1903), 13; *Legislative Petitions*, Virginia, Prince Edward County, 8 January 1839 (PAR# 11683906). For an overview of southern temperance efforts, see Ian R. Tyrrell, "Drink and Temperance in the Antebellum South: An Overview and Interpretation," *Journal of Southern History* 48 (1982): 485–510; John W. Quist, *Restless Visionaries: The Social Roots of Antebellum Reform in Alabama and Michigan* (Baton Rouge: Louisiana State University Press, 1998).
[54] "What does it Mean?" *South-Carolina Temperance Advocate* (Columbia, SC), 23 July 1846.
[55] For examples of discussions regarding physical punishment of whites convicted of trading with slaves, see "The Elections," *Fayetteville (NC) Observer*, 18 October 1858; "Abstract of Col. Owens' Remarks in the Debate between him and Gen. Ayer, at Barnwell, on the 5th instant, on the subject of their Constituencies," *Charleston (SC) Mercury*, 15 September 1859; "To His Honor, the Mayor," *Charleston (SC) Mercury*, 9 November 1859; Whitemarsh B. Seabrook, "Governor's Message," *Mountaineer* (Greenville, SC), 14 December 1849.

to free-negroes; for it is a well-known fact that, through them as agents, the slaves are as capable of purchasing as if there were no legal restraint upon them."[56] Peddlers, too, received blame and petitioners demanded regulation. Complaining that "scores of whiskey hucksters" were doing "demoralizing work among the negroes and others when we are asleep," a FARMER urged readers of the *South-Carolina Temperance Advocate* to let itinerant vendors know "they are watched and regarded as enemies by us." In Virginia, frustrated residents moaned, "[T]he law does not prohibit hucksters or cartmen from selling cakes candies &c. in the main roads or on the lands of persons who give the privilege, and under the guise of this privilege, they frequently sell spirits." These hawkers, frequently black men and women, "profess to be engaged in what they call the innocent business of buying and selling mellons [sic] Cakes &c. but in that situation it is easy to introduce spirits which we know often to be done." Commerce, southerners knew, masked all sorts of temptations and threats, of which liquor was only a part.[57]

Clearly white and black possessors of alcohol required oversight and regulation. How could slaveholders best govern their activities? From the 1830s through the Civil War, citizens advocated and legislatures sought to monitor and limit opportunities for liquor purchase by imposing taxes or licensing fees on vendors of alcohol, especially those who sold liquor in small amounts. The addition of a tax – and, notably, an oath pledging not to sell to slaves – would prevent those of questionable moral judgment and in need of slave cash from participating in the commercial sphere.[58] Licensing, too, became an intense subject of debate. In Duplin County, North Carolina, citizens argued for the institution of a graduated permit. Those who wished to sell ardent spirits in quantities less than one quart would pay the highest fee of $20, those who sold in volumes from one quart to one gallon would pay $10, and those who wished to vend amounts above one gallon per customer paid the lowest fee of $5. The idea was to discourage the sale of alcohol in quantities and for prices that the average slave (or poor) consumer could purchase.[59] To regulate these vendors, however, shops had to be located within a locus of surveillance. In at least one North Carolina county, this became an issue of much dispute. Some residents

[56] *Legislative Petitions*, Virginia, Accomack County, 2 March 1848 (PAR# 11684812). See also *Legislative Petitions*: Virginia, Northumberland County, 26 February 1836 (PAR# 11683612); North Carolina, Washington County, 27 December 1850 (PAR# 11285005).

[57] A FARMER, "Whiskey Wagons," *South-Carolina Temperance Advocate* (Columbia, SC), 10 June 1841; *Legislative Petitions*, Virginia, Culpepper County, 26 January 1846 (PAR# 11684602).

[58] For examples of discussion regarding peddler taxes, see "Virginia," *Daily Morning News* (Savannah, GA), 21 March 1850; *Mountaineer* (Greenville, SC), 14 January 1832; "Spiritous Liquors and the 'Tiger,'" *Fayetteville (NC) Observer*, 16 February 1857 and 15 July 1858; *Columbia (SC) Telescope*, 20 December 1831.

[59] *Legislative Petitions*, North Carolina, Duplin County, 1830 (PAR# 11283002). See also *Legislative Petitions*: North Carolina, Warren County, ca. 1854 (PAR#11285411); North Carolina, Rowan County, 29 January 1857 (PAR# 11285703); North Carolina, Pasquotank County, 23 December 1848 (PAR# 11284803).

hoped to prohibit sales of liquor within two miles of Rockingham while others, in a petition filed with war and possible slave revolt looming, argued that it was wise to locate vendors within the village limits, the better to monitor slaves' purchases.[60] This vigorous debate over licensing – who sold what and where, how much, and at what cost – animated communities throughout the South and mirrored larger discussions of the role of internal economy in slave management.

Perhaps the best way to provide for the material needs and desires of slaves while maintaining some degree of control over purchases was through the operation of a plantation store or shop. An 1836 contributor to the *Southern Agriculturist* exhorted fellow planters to keep "a store of such articles as his slaves usually purchase elsewhere. These can be dealt out to them for their corn and such things as they have to sell." The benefits to the master were many, argued the planter, namely, "your negroes will be better and more cheaply provided; and be put out of the way of the temptation to roguery." Editors for the *Southern Cabinet* observed this technique in action in St. John's Parish, South Carolina. "Many if not all" of the slaveholders there purchased "in large quantities, such groceries and other articles as are most likely to be in request among the negroes, which they let them have at cost, and which secures it to them at wholesale prices." Thomas Clay once again provided readers with one of the most explicit justifications for this management technique. He argued that his policy served not only to allay discontent but also as a means of promoting "habits of industry, economy, honesty and temperance." Clay urged planters to maintain a shop, "keeping on hand for their trade, all, or most of the articles which they wish to purchase." He explained both the parameters and the importance of such a measure: "Each master should confine his trade to his own negroes, and have stated times at which his people may come and buy. How much their comfort is promoted by the facility with which they may thus exchange their surplus provisions, poultry, &c. need not be stated. It removes, too, a great temptation to visit dram shops, and affords the master an excellent opportunity of judging of the thrift of each negro."[61]

Clay's desire not just to monitor his slaves, but to "judge" them reveals a great deal about not only his fastidious nature but also the complex amalgam of management and moralism that served as the white framework for the internal economy. Malleable definitions of comfort and luxury informed slaveholders' provisioning decisions. Stereotypes about "negro" physiology and character shaped conceptions of bondpeople's abilities as producers and consumers.

---

[60] *Legislative Petitions*, North Carolina, Richmond County, ca. 1861 (PAR# 11286108). See also "A Few Plain Thoughts for both Sides," *Raleigh Register, and North-Carolina Gazette*, 6 January 1846.

[61] "On the Conduct and Management of Overseers, Drivers, and Slaves," *Southern Agriculturist, and Register of Rural Affairs* 9 (1836): 230; "Agricultural Survey of the Parish of St. Matthews," *Southern Cabinet* 1 (1840): 202; Clay, *Detail of a Plan*, 21–22.

Tempered and ambivalent faith in the bounds of their own mastery affected planters' management techniques and strategy. Agricultural journals, newspapers, and prescriptive literature embraced this multifaceted dialectic but, as we have seen, complete agreement on the resolution of these issues was rare – with one major exception. The internal economy, specifically opportunities granted to black slaves to act as consumers, served as a powerful component of the proslavery argument and, as such, rang out in response to northern abolitionist critiques. Their argument was simple. In the South, benevolent white masters provided for the comfortable subsistence of the enslaved, thus freeing earnings from overwork or patches for gratuitous spending. An editor for the *Southern Cultivator* scoffed at the "'tom-foolery' and nonsense about the 'poor oppressed slaves'" perpetrated by northern abolitionists, citing instances in which planters had paid out $156, $600, and $300 respectively for corn and cotton from slave patches. Others compared free but poor laborers of the North with their own enslaved. "Our negroes are better off than those in the non-slaveholding States, *in pecuniary condition*," one apologist explained. "Our servants are sure of food, raiment, and shelter, as long as they live," many of them "amass considerable money, and most of them, by a little industry, are enabled to afford luxuries of food and dress." Another argued further that "there is not an adult male slave in the entire South, provided he possess the necessary energy, who can not lay up more ready money in a twelvemonth than most day-laborers in the North or elsewhere, and at least double as much as the poor Coolies can at their ... pay." Again and again, white southerners pointed out the "clear gain" some slaves were able to obtain, crowing that northern free laborers were hard-pressed to realize such advantages. Sally Baxter Hampton, a northern woman who married a South Carolina planter, mocked Yankee abolitionists. Having described the $500 that her plantation slaves would be paid and the "luxuries" on which they would likely spend their money, she asked, "[t]his looks like 'a gigantic system of wickedness & iniquity' does it not – Alas! Alas! 'they know not what they do' nor say."[62]

The consumer component of the proslavery argument resonated with southerners eager to justify their mastery. Yet tempered faith in the bounds of their hegemony shaped planters' management techniques at every step. Agricultural journals embraced multifaceted strategies but, as we have seen, lasting resolution, complete agreement on these issues, proved impossible. The constantly shifting terrain of this running battle placed enslaved consumers in a political double bind. Hewing to the consumptive prescriptions of masters lashed them to the plantation but to stray did them no better, at least in the eyes of their

---

[62] "The 'Poor Slave,'" *Southern Cultivator* 18 (1860): 101; [Mell], *Slavery. A Treatise Showing that Slavery is Neither a Moral, Political, Nor Social Evil*, 40; Daniel R. Hundley, *Social Relations in our Southern States* (New York: Henry B. Price, 1860), 355; Sally Baxter Hampton to George Baxter, 22 December 1860, in *A Divided Heart: Letters of Sally Baxter Hampton, 1853–1862*, ed. Ann Fripp Hampton (Spartanburg, SC: Reprint Company, 1980), 79.

moralizing masters, to whom this served instead as paternalistic justification of the peculiar institution itself. By posing as models of consumptive propriety, protectors of their people's economic interests, and judges of their spending, slaveholders transformed the alienating aspects of the market into an ideal which slaves could neither fully realize nor abandon.

Slaves and Spending

One Saturday night in May 1851, a group of slaves gathered in a cabin on Simpson's plantation in Anderson District, South Carolina. Eager to earn some extra cash, Joe planned to steal, then sell, a few turkeys from James Gray's farm and tried to enlist his fellow slaves to go along with him. Despite concerns by Leah and Henry that the would-be thieves would "get into a scrape," Sam agreed to join Joe in the heist. As they watched the two men slip into the woods, Henry turned to Leah and asked, "Joe loves money don't he?"

Why wouldn't Joe love money? Having property and cash presented Joe with opportunities ostensibly denied to slaves of the antebellum South. He could purchase food and tobacco as supplement to weekly rations, drink and gamble, or participate in a wider consumer market, purchasing manufactured goods such as hats, dresses, umbrellas, and watches. Joe may have even derived a sense of empowerment from the jingle of silver in his pocket and the sight and feel of banknotes held securely in his own pocketbook. Leah, however, interpreted the situation differently. In response to Henry's assessment of Joe, she commented, "Joe is like the rest ... but that he was not to be depended on." Even though Leah probably had benefited materially from the availability of cash among her fellows, her remark reveals a mindful ambivalence toward the role of the market and the availability of cash within the slave community. Perhaps she was wary of temptations and tensions that market activity could engender or, maybe, Joe's desire for money served as an all too stark reminder of her master's own avarice, a characteristic that could only find fulfillment through the exploitation of the labor of, or equity in, her and her family.[1]

---

[1] Anderson/Pendleton District, Magistrate and Freeholders Court, Trial Papers (hereafter Anderson Trial Papers): *State v. Joe, Henry*, 5 May 1851, SCDAH.

Such was the nature of the internal economy. Even though the enslaved of the antebellum South appreciated purchasing opportunities proffered by market expansion, their attitude toward their roles and abilities as consumers was as complex and variegated as masters' strategies of management and control. Certainly, the reality of slave spending differed significantly from the idyllic landscape of luxury and gratuitous spending that apologists painted. But this reality did not reflect a simple survival strategy to stave off nutritional deprivation or physical exposure brought about by inadequate food, shelter, and clothing provision either. Bondpeople brought to the consumer process a set of values informed by community cultural norms, but also their own experience as chattel property, principles that both contested the boundaries that separated black from white and were challenged by the limiting influences of their own enslavement.

Provisioning again serves as the framework for understanding slave taste and spending. Bondpeople often abhorred the very qualities masters valued in provisioned items. Ideally, slaveholders provided food and clothing of sufficient quantity to satisfy basic necessities of nutrition and raiment. The issue of quality, however, was subject to interpretation and was one on which slaveholder and slave rarely agreed. As a means of sustaining a healthy and efficient workforce, slaveholders provided food and clothing that they considered hearty and durable. Sarah Byrd bitterly recalled that her mistress never gave her anything but "the coarsest foods" and only gave families milk after it had soured. Even though many ex-slaves interviewed for the WPA claimed that the quantity of food they received was sufficient, several made a point of noting that daily provisions were "plain," and not at all "fancy."[2]

When applied to clothing, the term "durable," translated to "coarse" or "rough" and was resented by bondpeople. Tina Johnson remembered that she and her family "ain't had nothin' but de coarsest food an' clothes" and Willie McCullough explained that slaves were provided with plenty of food and clothing but that these provisions were "rough." With regard to clothing in particular, slaveholders bragged about the coarseness of provided cloaks, shirts, and pantaloons, arguing that the long-term durability of these items was indicative of their high quality. Bondpeople, too, noted the coarseness of material, but rarely couched commentary in such glowing terms. Tempe Pitts remembered that the clothes provided to slaves were "good, do' tough." Booker T. Washington described his clothing provisions in more detail. The tow shirt given by his master was "stiff and coarse ... as if a thousand needle points were pricking his flesh" and would remain that way for a good six weeks until the fabric had become worn. Writing in 1901, Washington still cringed at the sight of a "new" shirt. Rachel Adams made a similar comment with regard to

---

[2] George P. Rawick, ed., *The American Slave: A Composite Autobiography*, 41 vols. (Westport, CT: Greenwood Press, 1972–1978), 12, pt. 1: 169; *Ibid.*, Suppl. ser. 1, 4, pt. 2: 490; *Ibid.*, Suppl. ser. 1, 3, pt. 1: 244.

provided bedding, explaining that it was "so coarse det it scratched us little chillun most to death, it seemed lak to us in dem days."[3]

Shoes warranted particular criticism. Although some slaves would have been happy to have shoes to wear at all, especially during the winter months, few bondpeople recalled them with affection.[4] They were indeed durable, but this sturdiness came at the expense of comfort. Mom Ryer Emmanuel complained that "dey never didn' have nothin 'cept dem old coarse shoes widout no linin." More specifically, George Eason explained that he suffered blisters as a result of the hard leather from which the shoes were made, and Amanda Jackson noted that her shoes "wuz made out o' cowhide an' wuz very stiff." Not only did these shoes cause discomfort, bondpeople argued, they were impractical as well. One ex-slave complained that "you couldn' hardly walk in 'em" and another explained that "you couldn't run in them a-tall" and "just had to stomp along!" The inflexible wooden soles of brogans merited comment, with ex-slaves noting they "*had* to wear wooden bottom shoes," complaining that they made the shoes "sorta stiff" and they had "no spring to them."[5]

Enslaved men and women begrudged provisions not simply because of the goods' absolute quality but because, in many cases, the slaves saw the fruits of their labor spent more luxuriously – by and for masters and their families. The distinction between "negro" and "white" quality was stark and provoked significant commentary. Some ex-slaves insisted that they "et jess whut our white folks had," but others qualified their remarks, noting that their fare lacked the "fancy trimmins" enjoyed by their masters. Sally Brown vividly recalled salivating over the waffles she served to her master's family – she and her kin "wuzn't 'lowed to eat at all the different kinds of victuals the white folks et." Patsy Mitchner remembered not waffles but biscuits, bitterly commenting, "No

---

[3] Rawick, ed., *American Slave*, 15, pt. 2: 21; *Ibid.*, 15, pt. 2: 77; *Ibid.*, 15, pt. 2: 174; Booker T. Washington and Frank Beard, *An Autobiography: The Story of My Life and Work* (Toronto: J. L. Nichols, 1901), 16–17. Travelers commented on the coarseness of slave clothing as well. Abolitionist James Redpath remarked that the shirts worn by rural slaves were "a cross between 'a gent's under-garment' and an ordinary potato bag," noting that the cloth was "*very* coarse." James Redpath, *The Roving Editor, or Talks with Slaves in the Southern States*, ed. John McKivigan (1859; reprint, University Park: Pennsylvania State University Press, 1996), 119. See also Frederick Law Olmsted, *The Cotton Kingdom: A Traveller's Observations on Cotton and Slavery in the American Slave States, 1853–1861* (1953; New York: Da Capo Press, 1996), 37; Silas Xavier Floyd, *Life of Charles T. Walker, D.D. ("The Black Spurgeon.") Pastor Mt. Olivet Baptist Church, New York City* (Nashville: National Baptist Publishing Board, 1902), 26. For more on slave clothing, including complaints about the coarseness of provisioned raiment, see Shane White and Graham White, *Stylin': African American Expressive Culture, from Its Beginnings to the Zoot Suit* (Ithaca, NY: Cornell University Press, 1998), 5–36.

[4] Rawick, *American Slave*, 12, pt. 1: 137.

[5] Rawick, *American Slave*, 2, pt. 2: 23; *Ibid.*, 12, pt. 1: 301; *Ibid.*,12, pt. 2: 291; *Ibid.*, 12, pt. 1: 115; *Ibid.*,15, pt. 2: 247; *Ibid.*,16, Virginia Narratives: 15; *Ibid.*, 3, pt. 1: 147; *Ibid.*, 3, pt. 1: 195. For other references to coarse, stiff, crude, and/or wooden-bottomed shoes, see Rawick, *American Slave*, 14, pt. 1: 153, 160, 316, 434–435; *Ibid.*, 15, pt. 2: 120, 313, 415; *Ibid.*,13, pt. 3: 72–73, 151, 179; *Ibid.*, 3, pt. 3: 172–173.

biscuit wus seen in de slave houses. No sir, dat dey wus not. No biscuit for niggers at marsters." The reason for the lack of biscuits in the slave quarters was simple. Slaves made their bread out of "shorts," while the "first grade was always used in the master's house." Raiment revealed this distinction even more starkly. The prickly clothing worn by slaves was made of "nigger cloth," the flax used to weave plantation clothing, "separated into two grades; fine for the white folks, and coarse for the Negroes." Similarly, coarse shoes were given the appellation "nigger brogans." "White folks' shoes," on the other hand, "were made from soft calf leather." Rebecca Grant, too, noted distinctions between herself and her master's family, commenting that only war could bring white folks' material world in line with their own. "[D]e white folks had to use de cloth woven by hand, themselves," she noted. We can but wonder what impact this visual and tactile leveling had upon the relation her master had so carefully created and distinguished.[6]

So wide was the disparity between slaves' and masters' material worlds that some slaves hinted at internalizing the distinctions. Englishwoman Fanny Kemble recounted a conversation with a slave near Darien, Georgia. With disgust, she asked the passing cook what he was going to do with some "revolting-looking 'raw material,'" the innards, she supposed, of a drum fish. He replied that "colored people eat it." When asked why he specified "colored people," he replied, "Because, missis, white people won't touch what we too glad of." Kemble assured the man that the distinction was attributable to his poverty not his color but the man left unpersuaded. Escaped slave Henry Brown relayed a similar incident. Although provided with good quality clothes by his current master, Brown was curious about the condition of his brethren on other plantations, knowing that his fortunes could change at a moment's notice. Upon visiting a grain mill, Brown came across "a number of forlorn-looking beings … dressed with shirts made of coarse bagging." Unlike himself, these men possessed no hats, shoes, or vests. Brown's own appearance was a curiosity to them, as they "had never seen negroes dressed in that way before."[7]

---

[6] Rawick, *American Slave*, 13, pt. 4: 32; *Ibid.*, 12, pt. 1: 87; *Ibid.*, Suppl. ser. 1, 3, pt. 1: 101; *Ibid.*,15, pt. 2: 120; *Ibid.*,12, pt. 2: 297; *Ibid.*, 13, pt. 4: 139; *Ibid.*, 2, pt. 2: 75; *Ibid.*, 12, pt. 2: 149; *Ibid.*, 2, pt. 2: 183–184.

[7] Frances Anne Kemble, *Journal of a Residence on a Georgian Plantation in 1838–1839* (New York: Harper and Brothers, 1863), 265; Henry Box Brown and Charles Stearns, *Narrative of Henry Box Brown, Who Escaped from Slavery, Enclosed in a Box 3 Feet Long and 2 Wide. Written from a Statement of Facts Made by Himself. With Remarks Upon the Remedy for Slavery* (Boston: Brown and Stearns, 1849), 21–22. Stanley Elkins's infamous slavery-as-concentration-camp metaphor attracted criticism from historians. Character types like the passive and deferential "Sambo," Elkins argued, stemmed from deep internalization of the traumas of life in bondage. Although his interpretation perhaps granted too little import to enslaved life, family, and culture, the idea that some slaves may have suffered from lifelong feelings of inadequacy bears consideration and further study. Stanley M. Elkins, *Slavery: A Problem in American Institutional and Intellectual Life*, rev. 3rd ed. (Chicago: University of Chicago Press, 1976), 81–139. For a more recent discussion of the psychological trauma of slavery, see Nell Irvin

But not all slaves internalized the inferior quality of their material world – others highlighted the distinctions, railing against what they saw as slave-funded white avarice and oppression. Escaped slave John Quincy Adams condemned the "style" that masters "put on off of the poor slave." Remembering the lavish parties he witnessed while down South, he described how his masters "appeared in all their grandeur and splendor," noting that they purchased this "style" with "the poor slave's labor." Escaped slave Charles Ball explained bondpeople's frustration in more detail: "The slave sees his master residing in a spacious mansion, riding in a fine carriage, and dressed in costly clothes, and attributes the possession of all these enjoyments to his own labour; whilst he who is the cause of so much gratification and pleasure to another, is himself deprived of even the necessary accommodations of human life." Runaway William Craft echoed this sentiment, ruefully maintaining that bondpeople could not help but be frustrated that they "had to give up [their] hard earnings to a tyrant, to enable him to live in idleness and luxury." Masters, these men argued, stripped away the fruits of slaves' labor, purchasing luxuries for themselves and leaving bondpeople to scrap for material comforts.[8]

The dialectic of "comfort" and "luxury" so extensively debated in agricultural journals had parallels in the slave community. Bondpeople, too, lamented intemperate and improvident expenditures of money on "luxuries," but they directed judgments, not against fellow enslaved, but against masters. For slaves far more than their masters, the consequences of improper spending were dire. As property subject to handling and shuffling, slaves could suffer at the hands of an improvident master. The fact that masters spent the money *they* had earned made slaveholders' perceived pecuniary indiscretions even more egregious. It is worth noting that their concerns were not without basis. Even though planters were loathe to admit it, poor accounting – of both money and behavior – endangered slaves' well-being. Thomas Chaplin was unusually blunt in his self-assessment following the sale of ten of his slaves in 1845. "I can't express my feelings on seeing so many faithful Negroes going away from me forever," he wrote, "not for any fault of their own but for my extravagance." Although he assured himself that "they may see their children again in time," the experience was, he thought, "a dearly bought lesson."[9]

Painter, *Creating Black Americans: African-American History and Its Meanings, 1619 to the Present* (New York: Oxford University Press, 2006), esp. 91–93.

[8] John Quincy Adams, *Narrative of the Life of John Quincy Adams, When in Slavery, and Now as a Freeman* (Harrisburg, PA: Sieg, 1872), 20–21; Charles Ball, *Slavery in the United States. A Narrative of the Life and Adventures of Charles Ball, a Black Man, Who Lived Forty Years in Maryland, South Carolina and Georgia, as a Slave Under Various Masters, and was One Year in the Navy with Commodore Barney, During the Late War* (New York: John S. Taylor, 1837), 299; William Craft, *Running a Thousand Miles for Freedom; or, the Escape of William and Ellen Craft from Slavery* (London: William Tweedie, 1860), 1.

[9] Theodore Rosengarten, ed., *Tombee: Portrait of a Cotton Planter* (New York: William Morrow, 1986), 348.

Just like their masters, bondpeople found alcohol among the most abhorrent indicators of consumptive impropriety, associating excessive drinking with laziness and, worse, violence. Ex-slave Jacob Manson maintained that his master "did not do any work but drank a lot of whiskey, went dressed up all de time an had niggers to wash his feet an comb his hair." Another accused his master of being "a rang tang" who loved his liquor and his "colored women." South Carolina ex-slave Jacob Stroyer issued more explicit warnings about the physical effects of alcohol consumption. According to Stroyer, a local planter, Mr. Young, was known to "draunk [sic] so hard, that he used to go into a crazy fit." Stroyer did not specify whether or not bondpeople suffered as a result of his actions, but other slaves detailed the physical manifestation of such "fits" upon themselves and fellow enslaved. Dinah, for example, explained that when her master drank, "which he very often did, his language was of the coarsest, and his acts of the most brutal description," while Ellen Trell explained that when her master "was in his cups he was mighty rough, and any slaves who displeased him at these times were liable to get a beating."[10]

Gambling posed particular risks and bondpeople were keen observers of the fortunes of their masters. Mary Frances Brown remembered "happy time back dere" on her master's Marlboro District, South Carolina, plantation, noting that her master "spend plenty money on horse race." Likewise Herndon Bogan remembered seeing "cocks fightin'" in pits and heaps o' horse racin'." Food and dancing followed a lucky outing for his master but, Bogan equivocated, "if he lost, oh!" Ex-slave Peter Randolph was even more explicit, describing the depraved gambling and drinking at "Cabin Point," a small group of stores gathered at a crossroads in Surrey County, Virginia. Overseers, he ruefully remembered, made "the backs of the outraged Negroes pay the bills" for debauched evening excesses. Masters chalked slaves' gambling to improvidence, lack of discipline, and general intemperance – further proof that bondpeople lacked the ability to use money wisely. Gambling, they argued, led to violence and disorder. Such behavior concerned the enslaved as well but, again, their commentary reflected much deeper concerns about masters' spending. Escaped slave Moses Grandy condemned the white man to whom he was hired out, recounting many nights in which he was forced to "wait on the gambling table" and, grimly detailing the one occasion he was beaten for "nodding for want of sleep." But for some bondpeople, physical abuse was the least of their

[10] Rawick, *American Slave*, 15, pt. 2: 97; *Ibid.*, 15, pt. 2: 208; Jacob Stroyer, *My Life in the South* (Salem, MA: Salem Observer Book and Job Print, 1885), 29; John Hawkins Simpson, *Horrors of the Virginian Slave Trade and of the Slave-Rearing Plantations. The True Story of Dinah, an Escaped Virginian Slave, Now in London, on Whose Body Are Eleven Scars Left by Tortures Which Were Inflicted by Her Master, Her Own Father. Together with Extracts from the Laws of Virginia, Showing That Against These Barbarities the Law Gives Not the Smallest Protection to the Slave, But the Reverse* (London: A. W. Bennett, 1863), 6; Rawick, *American Slave*, 15, pt. 2: 361. See also *Ibid.*, 15, pt. 2: 388; Ball, *Slavery in the United States*, 328; Redpath, *Roving Editor*, 110–111, 135.

worries. As property themselves, the consequences of an unlucky night could
have tragic consequences. Austin Steward, for example, described his master
as a man who "was not only a sportsman, but a gamester, and was in the
habit of playing cards, and sometimes betting very high and losing accordingly." During one particularly bad outing, he lost two horses, a slave, and his
wife's gold watch. His master's proclivity for horse racing also placed slaves at
constant risk. Steward described the grand racecourse and fine horses found
on his master's plantation. He disdainfully noted that all of this "grand out-
lay" served both to satisfy the "pleasure and gratification of witnessing the
speed of a fine horse" and the "vanity of prejudging concerning it." Although
Steward appreciated the beauty of the animals so carefully husbanded on the
northern Virginia plantation, he and his fellow enslaved were acutely aware of
the risks associated with his master's behavior – after all, on his fortunes rested
their own (Figure 2.1). Frances Fedric recounted a similar experience, providing an important perspective on not only the physical, but the psychological
effect a gambling master had on the slave community. Fedric and his fellow
bondpeople lamented their young master's deplorable gambling habit, noting
that increasing debts caused him to drink and become more violent. Worse,
to pay these debts, he sold his slaves, who were "in general the first property
parted with." Fedric recalled the consternation that pervaded the quarters of a
debtor's plantation, with slaves constantly asking, "Is it me? Is it me? Who'll
go next?"[11]

Just as masters judged slaves' consumer skills, so too did slaves judge masters. In many cases, bondpeople charged slaveholders with the same qualities
of laziness, intemperance, and improvidence that southern whites held as evidence of inferior "negro character." Whereas masters lamented the inefficiency

[11] Rawick, *American Slave*, 2, pt. 1: 135; *Ibid.*, 14, pt. 1: 126; Peter Randolph, *From Slave Cabin
to the Pulpit. The Autobiography of Rev. Peter Randolph: The Southern Question Illustrated
and Sketches of Slave Life* (Boston: James H. Earle, 1893), 173; Moses Grandy, *Narrative of
the Life of Moses Grandy; Late a Slave in the United States of America* (London: C. Gilpin,
1843), 12; Austin Steward, *Twenty-Two Years a Slave, and Forty Years a Freeman; Embracing
a Correspondence of Several Years, While President of Wilberforce Colony, London, Canada
West* (Rochester, NY: William Alling, 1857), 22–23, 41; Frances Fedric, *Slave Life in Virginia
and Kentucky; or, Fifty Years of Slavery in the Southern States of America* (London: Wertheim,
Macintosh, and Hunt, 1863), 41–42. See also Rawick, *American Slave*, 15, pt. 2: 307–308;
Ibid., 15, pt. 2: 233. Citing Clifford Geertz's seminal treatise on "deep play" in Balinese cock-
fighting as a model, Timothy Breen argues that colonial planters "preserved class cohesion"
through elite, high-stakes "gaming relationships." Gambling – on horseracing, specifically –
among Virginia elites, "helped persuade subordinate white groups that gentry culture was
desirable, something worth emulating." Breen has little to say about slaves, noting only that
they too probably made wagers. As the evidence here shows, this overlooked perspective is
indeed important. Subordinated not just by race but by class and title to their bodies, slaves
more acutely understood the risks attending such activity. Breen, "Horses and Gentlemen: The
Cultural Significance of Gambling among the Gentry of Virginia," *William and Mary Quarterly*,
3rd Series, 34 (1977): 239–257. See also Clifford Geertz, "Deep Play: Notes on the Balinese
Cockfight," in *The Interpretation of Cultures* (New York: Basic Books, 1973), 412–453.

"Away they go, sweeping round the course with lightning speed, while every spectator's eye is strained, and every countenance flushed with intense anxiety."

page 41.

FIGURE 2.1 Enslaved Virginian Austin Steward – and chattel like him – knew too well the risks associated with masters' gambling.

Source: Austin Steward, *Twenty-Two Years a Slave, and Forty Years a Freeman; Embracing a Correspondence of Several Years, While President of Wilberforce Colony, London, Canada West*. Rochester, NY: William Alling, 1857. Courtesy of Documenting the American South, The University of North Carolina at Chapel Hill Libraries.

and disorder created by slaves' inability to handle money, enslaved persons feared, judged, and often suffered the consequences of masters' financial indiscretions. This improvidence particularly rankled those bondpeople who felt that masters had wasted money that they and fellow enslaved had earned. Masters, of course, argued that slaves received "pay" for the labor they completed through comfortable, quality provisions. Even though some bondpeople acknowledged this arrangement, the rationalization rarely proved satisfactory. It was true that most slaves did not have to spend money to pay for basic food and raiment. Masters appropriated the fruits of their labor and allotted provisions accordingly, a responsibility, slaveholders argued, that simple-minded bondpeople could not handle. Removing the responsibility and privilege of choice from the hands of the enslaved, a master could create the slave as he imagined, making him or her easily identifiable even without regard to skin color. Dull, shapeless clothing and red shoes were visual markers of slave status (red, because coarse leather shoes often remained untanned).[12] To the touch, these articles of raiment were coarse and rough. Likewise, slaves and their clothing could sometimes be identified by a smell that one traveler described as "negro funk," explained by ex-slave John Andrew Jackson by the fact that they have "but only one suit for the summer, and the perspiration is so great that they smell rank." Even the sound of the slave was distinct. Wooden-soled shoes "would make a loud noise" when slammed flat on the floor, making "sich a sound as they made when the folks walked 'round with 'em on."[13]

The internal economy complicated this image, blurring distinctions between black and white, slave and free, and challenging stereotypes so often attributed to those of African descent. Moreover, it allowed slaves a domain in which they could reap the fruits of their labor and, more importantly, spend the profits as they saw fit. In this realm, masters relinquished choice to slaves who, in turn, created a material world starkly different from the one allocated to them by their owners. Ex-slaves highlighted this vital component of the consuming process. Georgia ex-slave "Uncle Willis" recalled the money he and his fellow bondpeople made by selling patch-grown cotton. According to Uncle Willis, "You could take dat money and spend it any way you wanted to." Petitioners to the Southern Claims Commission likewise emphasized choice in personal economic affairs. Stephen Graham explained that his master allowed him "the liberty to buy different articles – in fact anything I wanted." Prince Stewart indicated that his master allowed slaves "a chance," explaining that those who

[12] See Rawick, *American Slave*, 12, pt. 2: 141, 214; *Ibid.*, 13, pt. 4: 184; *Ibid.*, Suppl. ser. 1, 4, pt. 2: 645.

[13] William Thomson, *A Tradesman's Travels, in the United States and Canada, in the Years 1840, 41, and 42* (Edinburgh: Oliver and Boyd, 1842), 189; John Andrew Jackson, *The Experience of a Slave in South Carolina* (London: Passmore and Alabaster, 1862), 23; Rawick, *American Slave*, Suppl. ser. 1, 11: 64; *Ibid.*, 12, pt. 2: 275. For a more thorough discussion of slavery and the senses see Mark M. Smith, *How Race is Made: Slavery, Segregation, and the Senses* (Chapel Hill: University of North Carolina Press, 2006), esp. 21–36.

took advantage of that chance would use it "to get what they wanted" and "buy what we pleased." Other slaves were more specific about what, exactly, a "chance" entailed. Hercules Lecounte testified that task work allowed him to accumulate time that he, in turn, transformed into cash. The result? According to Lecounte, "I ... could buy such things as I wanted."[14]

Clearly the process by which bondpeople made their choices was as important as the acquisition of property itself. Selecting and paying for merchandise held appeal to men and women whose material world had been defined by masters' notions of necessity, comfort, luxury, and profitability. Accordingly, slaves developed a set of consumer skills that allowed them to derive the most benefit from economic transactions. Among the most important skills was a basic understanding of numeracy and pricing. Numeracy in the slave community has received no attention from scholars, even those who have focused on literacy and other overt and covert learning opportunities available to bondpeople. According to historian Patricia Cline Cohen, Americans considered the ability to perform basic arithmetic unnecessary until the turn of the nineteenth century when market expansion made such skills a crucial part of everyday life. But was the ability to count, to add and subtract, and to calculate value a skill understood and used by enslaved people? Ex-slave Amy Penny explained to a WPA interviewer that she "never could learn to make a number correct," while Bill Williams reported that "In them days I couldn't count up to a hundred." Other ex-slaves provide evidence to the contrary, however. Paul Jenkins insisted that his father "learn[ed] to read, write, and cipher." Lavinia Hayward made the same claim about her mother. In the slave quarters, as in the white community, such skills were learned – but from whom? Sam Aleckson credited his mistresses, "three maiden ladies (sisters)," with teaching bondpeople in their Charleston household "to read, write, and cipher, too." More specifically, Aleckson "got an idea of grammar, of weights and measures, etc." Runaway Harriet Jacobs's young son Benny learned to count from his Uncle William. Held in a jail cell until he or his relatives would reveal the runaway Jacobs's whereabouts, Benny calculated the length of his imprisonment, telling a relative, "Uncle Will taught me to count. I have made a mark for every day I have been here, and it is sixty days."[15]

[14] Rawick, *American Slave*, 13, pt. 4: 170; Claim of Stephen Graham, Catawba County, NC, Case Files, Southern Claims Commission, Records of the 3rd Auditor, Allowed Case Files, Records of the U.S. General Accounting Office, Record Group 217, National Records and Archives Administration, College Park, MD (hereafter SCC); Claim of Prince Stewart, Liberty County, GA, SCC; Hercules Lecounte, Liberty County, GA, SCC. See also testimony of Ann Witcher in claim of Allen Witcher, Floyd County, GA, SCC; Testimony of Pulaski Baker in claim of Scipio King, Liberty County, GA, SCC; Claim of Adam Lecounte, Liberty County, GA, SCC; Testimony of Peter Winn in claim of Samuel Harris, Liberty County, GA, SCC; Deposition of Linda Jones in claim of Caesar Jones and Linda Jones, Liberty County, GA, SCC.
[15] Patricia Cline Cohen, *A Calculating People: The Spread of Numeracy in Early America* (1982; New York: Routledge, 1999); Rawick, *American Slave*, 15, pt. 2: 160; *Ibid.*, 3, pt. 2: 199; *Ibid.*, 3, pt. 1: 32; *Ibid.*, 2, pt. 2: 277; Sam Aleckson, *Before the War, and After the Union. An*

Where and how slaves learned to count and perform basic arithmetic remains open to question. That slaves incorporated these skills into their daily lives is not. Queried by WPA interviewers, ex-slaves hinted at numeracy in descriptions of money possession and handling. Although some ex-slaves scoffed at the suggestion that they might have had money, many others recalled, at the very least, receiving dimes and quarters as children either as payment for small tasks or as gifts given by their masters.[16] Ransom Sidney Taylor, for example, explained that "our marsters gave us some money five and ten cents at a time" and Elizabeth Sparks remembered that "sometimes the white folks give yer 'bout ten cents to spend." Other bondpeople earned money by making baskets, clearing fields, sewing clothing, polishing shoes, performing overwork, and selling produce from their patches. As North Carolina ex-slave Squire Dowd reported, "We had money."[17]

But it was not enough for slaves to have money and be able to count it; the careful consumer needed to understand market value and pricing. As children, ex-slaves interviewed by the WPA remembered receiving money for the first time and plotting exactly how they would spend it. Neal Upson recalled that he had grand plans for the first dime he received, telling the interviewer, "I was all sot to buy myself a hat, a sto-bought suit of clothes, and some shoes that what warn't brogans." Upson learned his first lesson in consumerism that day, coming home with only "gingercake and a nickel's wuth of candy."[18] As Upson grew older, he likely participated in many other transactions, in so doing learning exactly what his money could and could not buy. Records ranging from WPA slave narratives to transcripts from slave courts in the South Carolina upcountry indicate that enslaved people recognized a rough standardization of pricing and fully understood the value of the money they possessed. For example, ex-slaves Isaac Johnson, Edna Blalock, and George Rogers of North Carolina remembered whiskey selling for 10 cents a quart. Robert Kimbrough

---

Autobiography (Boston: Gold Mind, 1929), 20, 26; Harriet Jacobs, *Incidents in the Life of a Slave Girl. Written by Herself*, ed. Lydia Maria Francis Child (Boston: Printed for Author, 1861), 161.

[16] For examples of ex-slaves claiming they never possessed money, see Rawick, *American Slave*,14, pt. 1: 412; *Ibid.*, 12, pt. 1: 107; *Ibid.*, 3, pt. 1: 56, 58, 80, 210, 233; *Ibid.*, 3, pt. 2: 164.

[17] Rawick, *American Slave*, 15, pt. 2: 339; *Ibid.*, 16, Virginia Narratives: 53; *Ibid.*, 14, pt. 1: 266. The politics of gift-giving will be discussed in more detail in Chapter 5. My purpose here is not to prove that slaves had money or to detail the ways in which they earned it – the canon of internal economy scholarship has already provided detailed descriptions of the production side of slaves' economic transactions across space and time. Rather, I have provided examples of cash possession as evidence of basic patterns of numeracy of many enslaved. For a concise yet thorough overview of the many ways in which enslaved people were able to earn money through the internal economy, see Dylan C. Penningroth, *Claims of Kinfolk: African American Property and Community in the Nineteenth-Century South* (Chapel Hill: University of North Carolina Press, 2003), 45–78.

[18] Rawick, *American Slave*, 13, pt. 4: 54. For other recollections of "first money," see Rawick, *American Slave*, 2, pt. 2: 43, 76; Brown, *Narrative of Henry Box Brown*, 26.

recalled brandy in Talbot County, Georgia, selling for a bit higher – "$1.00 a gallon at the 'stills'" and "50 cents a quart" when retailed at groceries. Clothing and other material goods also possessed rough values recognized by bondpeople. Aaron Ford, for example, remembered buying "cloth dat cost 12 ½ cents a yard" with the first money he earned. In a South Carolina court, an enslaved woman testified with even more monetary specificity. In August 1843, Aaron Vanderer's Polly complained to her master that she had lost several hanks of cotton cloth and suspected that Brummer, property of John McFall, had stolen them. Fully aware of the value of these items, she quantified, with some precision, her loss in market terms, stating that as a result of this theft she had lost "5 cents in Blue hank worth 25 cents – 4 cents in white hank worth 12 ½ cents." Clothing and personal accoutrements, recalled bondpeople, could range in price from the 62 cents Alfred paid for a pair of shoes in 1850 to the $1 Cato handed over for a hat in 1849 to the $10 Henry spent on a stolen watch in September 1851.[19]

Even though slaves clearly earned, possessed, and understood the value of cash, hard money and banknotes were not always available for exchange. Hence, many enslaved engaged in sophisticated systems of debt and credit to acquire desired provisions or property. Beaufort District, South Carolina, slave William Drayton testified to the Southern Claims Commission that he paid $200 for a mule, making "payments at three different times." Drayton described the transaction in detail. "I paid One hundred dollars in gold and silver at first payment. At second payment I paid Fifty dollars all in silver. At third payment I paid Fifty dollars in State Bank bills." Records from the South Carolina Court of Magistrates and Freeholders reveal similar patterns of debt and credit, although on a smaller scale. John Snoddy's Isaiah, for example, sought to repay a debt to David Smith's Lesel in October 1853, telling a bystander that "he wanted to see him as he was owing him and he wanted to pay him." The common occurrence of debts logically indicates that potential sellers were willing to extend credit to slaves desirous of purchasing their goods. In July 1838, Phil "contracted" with Joe for a fiddle. According to Dave, a witness to the transaction, "Phil was to give Joe a Dollar down, & Seventy five cents on a credit." A more complicated transaction took place at Dr. Webb's Anderson District plantation in August 1855. According to Jerry, he had "sold the watch to Bob for $15 to a pair of shoes in part pay at $1.25, & Bob was some time this week 3 Dollars & the balance." Credit could be costly, however. In January 1852, three upcountry South Carolina slaves sorted out a set of tangled transactions involving stolen shoes and a year-old debt. Edmond testified to the magistrates that Amos had "sold [shoes] to Ned for 75 cents if he paid cash or $1.00 on credit." The

19 Rawick, *American Slave*, 15, pt. 2: 18; *Ibid.*, 14, pt. 1: 106; *Ibid.*, 15, pt. 2: 221–222; *Ibid.*, Suppl. ser. 1, 4, pt. 2: 358; *Ibid.*, 2, pt. 2: 76; Anderson Trial Papers: *State v. Brummer*, 12 August 1843; *State v. Joe*, 30 October 1850; *State v. Cato*, 16 March 1849; *State v. Dick*, 6 September 1851, SCDAH.

complicated nature of the transactions not only indicates that slaves were well-versed in market trade and negotiation, but also that they were willing to go to some lengths to acquire the goods they desired.[20]

Learned consumer skills – numeracy, market pricing, and debt and credit negotiation – not only facilitated property acquisition but also contradicted fundamental stereotypes about slaves' purchasing abilities. In contrast to the image of the improvident and intemperate spendthrifts painted by slavehold-ers, many enslaved people acted judiciously, saving their money and earning reputations for thrift and industry. Ex-slave Caroline Ates insisted that "if we wuz smart an' made a good crop, we had mo' money than the lazy ones did," while Squire Dowd explained that the "negroes who were thrifty had nice well-kept homes." Testimony made on behalf of claimants to the Southern Claims Commission is particularly revealing on this score. Burdened with not only proving that their property had been lost during the Civil War, but also that they possessed the ability to purchase the property in the first place, enslaved people and the black and white witnesses who testified on their behalf refuted white stereotypes of black laziness and improvidence. In particular, claimants and witnesses attributed property purchase and accumulation to a slave's sense of "thriftiness." Simon Walthour testified to the Commission that Paris James was "as thrifty a man as there was in Liberty County." Others expanded on the theme of economical management. A fellow former slave described James McQueen as a "steady, sober, and industrious man" while another witness described William Anderson as a "thrifty, industrious man very economical & prudent."[21]

Characteristics of thriftiness, prudence, and temperance were most evident in discussions of slaves' ability to save and accumulate money. Traveler Fredrika Bremer noted, with some surprise, that slaves in the South Carolina lowcountry

---

[20] Claim of William Drayton, Beaufort District, SC, SCC; Spartanburg District, Magistrates and Freeholders Court, Trial Papers, SCDAH (hereafter Spartanburg Trial Papers): *State v. Leslie, Martha, Isaiah*, 22 October 1853, SCDAH; Anderson Trial Papers: *State v. Phil*, 21 July 1838; *State v. Bob*, 14 August 1855; *State v. Amos*, 15 January 1852, SCADH. See also Spartanburg Trial Papers: *State v. Titus, John*, 11 October 1855, SCDAH.

[21] Rawick, *American Slave*, Suppl. ser. 1, 3, pt. 1: 27; *Ibid.*, 14, pt. 1: 265; Testimony of Simon Walthour in claim of Paris James, Liberty County, GA, SCC; Testimony of Benjamin Morris in claim of James McQueen, Marlborough District, SC, SCC; Testimony of George Cope in claim of William Anderson, Chatham County, GA, SCC. For other claims and testimony describ-ing ex-slaves as "sober," "industrious," or "thrifty," see claim of Harriet Dallas, Chatham, GA, SCC; Commissioner's Report on claim of Toney Elliott, Liberty County, GA, SCC; Testimony of William Bass and Emily Bass in claim of Silas Cook, Marlborough District, SC, SCC. For ex-tensive discussion of working people's strategies for making the most of scarce and irregular in-come – and exploration of bourgeois criticism of their spending – see Paul Johnson, *Saving and Spending: The Working Class Economy in Britain, 1870–1939* (New York: Oxford University Press, 1985). See also Lendol Calder, "Saving and Spending," in *The Oxford Handbook of the History of Consumption*, ed. Frank Trentmann (New York: Oxford University Press, 2012), 348–375.

"often lay by money, and I have often heard of slaves possessing several hundred dollars." According to Bremer, the slaves she saw "invested" money "with interest" with their master. Accounts of such formal saving measures are rare, but testimony from the WPA and the Claims Commission indicates that enslaved people rarely spent money in the indiscriminate fashion portrayed in white stereotypes of black behavior. Harriet Dallas, for example, described her husband as a "hard working man and careful" who "did not spend any money foolishly," while South Carolina ex-slave Mack Duff Williams was described as "careful with his money." Accumulated savings drew particular notice on the part of witnesses and served as a point of pride for petitioners to the Southern Claims Commission. A witness testified that Jacob Allman was a "shifty, smart fellow and saved all he could," and a neighbor described Jacob Quarterman as a "real providing kind of man and saved what he got." Quarterman himself added to this testimony: "I labored for the money, as we are doing now. I laid it aside, same as we are doing now." To save required discipline, a trait not all people possessed, especially as children. Elisha Doc Garey sheepishly explained to a WPA interviewer, "I might have saved more of my money if I hadn't loved dat store boughten pep'mint candy so good." Other children, however, were able to resist the temptation of immediate gratification. Ex-slave Anderson Furr took all of the extra money he earned and "turned it over to my Ma," claiming that children "warn't 'lowed to spend money den lak dey does now." Gable Locklier saved his money too – though he never felt any compulsion by his parents to do so. His mother gave him "a needle en thread en little sack en I sew my 10 cents in it. Put it in de rafter en it stay dere till next Christmas." He eagerly pulled the money down when a man came by selling tobacco – he bought a piece and gave it to his father.[22]

As youngsters, Furr and Locklier learned the value of saving money, a process in which many would engage later in life as they participated more fully in the internal economy. Although trinkets and candy and, as they got older, liquor and tobacco, offered immediate pleasure, some enslaved people proved that limiting daily spending could lead to greater future rewards. Larry Williams, for example, characterized himself as a "simple man," a trait that allowed him to "save." As a result, he "accumulated in this way, a good deal." Mack Taylor was more explicit, explaining to a WPA interviewer that he "pinched and saved and didn't throw my money away on liquor, or put it into de palms of every Jezebel hussy dat slant her eye at me," a lesson he heeded throughout his life. Likewise, Sandy Small attributed his substantial property holdings to the fact

---

[22] Fredrika Bremer, *America of the Fifties: Letters of Fredrika Bremer*, ed. Adolph B. Benson (New York: American-Scandinavian Foundation, 1924), 111; Claim of Harriet Dallas, Chatham County, GA, SCC; Testimony of David Brown in claim of Mack Duff Williams, Charleston District, SC, SCC; Testimony of Alex Quick in claim of Jacob Allman, Marlborough District, SC, SCC; Testimony of Edward Quarterman in/and claim of Jacob Quarterman, Liberty County, Georgia, SCC; Rawick, *American Slave*, 12, pt. 2: 3; *Ibid.*, 12, pt. 1: 346; *Ibid.*, 3, pt. 1: 114–115.

that he "worked part of the time day and night and saved my money," adding
that he "did not drink."[23]

Bondpeople saved their money as a means of providing simple security for
future needs, but others saved with a specific property goal in mind. Andy
Brice remembered seeing his master "twistin' de ears on a fiddle and rosinin' de
bow." Hearing the music and watching his master play for the first time, Brice
decided then and there to "save and buy me a fiddle." He purchased one the following Christmas "and been playin' de fiddle ever since." Even more than the
interviews of the WPA, the records of the Southern Claims Commission reveal
a process of accumulation based on careful planning, investing, and spending.
Ex-slave Joseph Jones explained to commissioners that he "commenced buying
& raising when I as a young man till I was married & then after that kept on
buying & raising & increasing all the time my stock, this & being industrious
was the way I got my property." Primus Wilson provided even more detail on
this process. According to Wilson,

I had been working and owning property for 25 or 30 years ... I first raised some corn
and other truck, sold, got some money and bought me a sow-pig, then I raised from
her and kept increasing my stock of hogs, I raised Poultry too and kept selling till I got
money enough to buy a yearling heifer and from her I raised cows and so I kept on till I
bought a young mare colt, and raised horses I think I bought the first colt 20 or 25 years
before the raid – in that way I came in possession of the property the Yankees took from
me by the increasing of stock.

Other slaves recounted a similar process of accumulation, moving up a met-
aphorical ladder of property ownership, buying and selling crops, then fowl,
then pigs or goats, and then – if they were particularly prosperous – a horse
and/or buggy.[24]

Did all slaves spend their money wisely? Did all bondpeople sacrifice immediate desires in order to save for long-term goals of security or major purchases? Of course not. But the traits of thrift, prudence, and self-discipline
present in so many bondpeople repudiate stereotypes about black character.
Slaves' consumer behavior was as complex and varied as masters', with most
spending occurring outside the realm of formal market venues. Hence, it is
difficult to characterize patterns of slave consumption across space and time
definitively. Evidence culled from Southern Claims Commission records, WPA
interviews, published narratives, and court testimony reveal a set of general

[23] Claim of Larry Williams, Chatham County, Georgia, SCC; Rawick, *American Slave*, 3, pt. 4:
157; Claim of Sandy Small, Chatham County, Georgia, SCC.
[24] Rawick, *American Slave*, 2, pt. 1: 76; Claim of Joseph James, Liberty County, GA, SCC; Claim of
Primus Wilson, Chatham County, GA, SCC. For other examples of this process of property ac-
cumulation see claim of Scipio King, Liberty County, GA, SCC; Claim of John Lecounte, Liberty
County, GA, SCC; Claim of Prince Maxwell, Liberty County, GA, SCC; Claim of Windsor
Stevens, Liberty County, GA, SCC; Claim of Toney Elliott, Liberty County, GA, SCC; Claim of
John Bacon, Liberty County, GA, SCC; Claim of James Miller, Liberty County, GA, SCC.

consumer values, however, that are suggestive of a desire to choose for themselves and to construct a material world different from the one provided by the slaveholding class.

Even though their masters found comfort in belief to the contrary, slaves possessed complicated tastes and eagerly pursued means to satisfy them. Northern visitors to Port Royal during the early 1860s reported a population of willing and knowledgeable consumers. Austa French observed that both the landscape and the population of Port Royal were ripe for development, explaining that the "Colored, in freedom, will not hoard, but spend money. They will dress, and ride, in good style. The table and house, will be secondary, usually. Imagine the trade set in motion the moment they get wages. What a brisk market for everything conceivable." James McKim also reported eager spending by the newly freed in the South Carolina lowcountry, explaining that freedpeople possessed not only a "Yankee turn for traffic," but a real desire for money and manufactured goods. By way of example, he told of the $300 and $800 respectively he and a colleague had earned by selling goods to freedpeople, arguing that both could have sold more had they had a more extensive stock. In particular, he commented on "a quantity of very small, low-priced looking glasses, and a half dozen iron pots and pans." Each of these goods sold readily; the demand for pots and pans, however, vastly exceeded his supply, causing quite a "scramble." Noting that many of the lowcountry enslaved already possessed some property, he speculated that "as soon as these people become free, their wants increase" and that an "*enlarged market for Northern manufactures ... will be created by an enlarged area of freedom*." To be sure, French and McKim accepted stereotypes about black spending but within their commentary was recognition that freedpeople's past lives as enslaved consumers had prepared them to take full advantage of all that a free market could offer.[25]

Given an eagerness to spend money, what exactly did slaves buy? Different sources suggest slightly different patterns of consumption. As most men and women interviewed by the WPA were children during slavery, their spending reflected juvenile desires. Ex-slave Anna Parks explained, "All a piece of money meant to me in dem days, wuz candy, and den mo' candy." Gus Feaster agreed, saying, "I bought candy wit de money; people was crazy 'bout candy den. Dat's de reason I ain't got no toofies now." Sara Crocker recalled buying ginger cakes while Richard Jones remembered he and his young pals purchasing "fish hooks, barlows, juice harps, and marbles."[26]

---

[25] Austa Malinda French, *Slavery in South Carolina and the Ex-Slaves; or, The Port Royal Mission* (New York: Winchell M. French, 1862), 308; James Miller McKim, *The Freedmen of South Carolina: An Address Delivered by J. Miller M'Kim, in Sanson Hall, July 9th, 1862; Together with a Letter from the Same to Stephen Colwell, Esq., Chairman of the Port Royal Relief Committee* (Philadelphia: Willis P. Hazard, 1862), 20–22.

[26] Rawick, *American Slave*, 13, pt. 3: 155; *Ibid.*, 2, pt. 2: 43; *Ibid.*, Suppl. ser. 1, 3, pt. 1: 226; *Ibid.*, 3, pt. 3: 66.

As bondpeople grew older, their tastes changed. Southern apologist Daniel R. Hundley noted that slaves exchanged provisions for "nick nacks more to their liking." Prince Stevens explained that "we 'colored peoples' used to sell our little things for gold & silver and put it down – for extras," while Judy Rose told claims commissioners that she bought "things" from time to time. The dialectic of comfort and luxury often informed discussion about what exactly these "things" were. Harriet Dallas explained to claims commissioners that her husband worked hard to ensure that they could "live comfortably," while an attorney for ex-slave Samuel Fuller testified to commissioners that the ability to sell produce from provision grounds allowed Fuller and his neighbors to live "fully as comfortable when slaves, as they are now." A witness testified that a slave woman possessed "comfortable furniture I do not say it was the nicest but good enough," while another bondperson's home was "well supplied with things comfortable."[27]

Escaped slave Charles Ball illuminated more fully the tension between comfort and luxury as perceived by the enslaved consumer. Ball explained that slaves often bought Sunday clothes or "purchased salt and some other articles of convenience" whenever they earned money. More specifically, Ball outlined a rough budget for his readers, explaining that earned money was

laid out by the slaves in purchasing such little articles of necessity or luxury, as it enables them to procure. A part is disbursed in payment for sugar, molasses, and sometimes a few pounds of coffee, for the use of the family; another part is laid out for clothes for winter; and no inconsiderable portion of his pittance is squandered away by the misguided slave for tobacco, and an occasional bottle of rum. Tobacco is deemed so indispensable to comfort, nay to existence, that hunger and nakedness are patiently endured, to enable the slave to indulge in this highest of enjoyments.

Ball's assessment indicates that slaves spent money on basic items of nutrition and raiment but that definitions of "necessity," "convenience," and "luxury" overlapped. Each of these types of purchases contributed to the creation of a "comfortable" life, one that could only be formed through participation in the internal economy.[28]

Clothing, in particular, was the object of significant expenditure. Ex-slave Henry Ryan remembered buying "clothes and things we had to have" with money he occasionally received from his master. Fannie Fulcher explained that slaveholders "give 'um evy-day work clothes ... but dey bought de res'

[27] Daniel R. Hundley, *Social Relations in our Southern States* (New York: Henry B. Price, 1860), 341; Claim of Prince Stevens, Liberty County, GA, SCC; Claim of Judy Rose, Chatham County, GA, SCC; Claim of Harriet Dallas, Chatham County, GA, SCC; Testimony of C. W. Dudley in claim of Samuel Fuller, Marlborough District, SC, SCC; Testimony of John Wilson in claim of Charlotte Thompson, Chatham County, GA, SCC; Testimony of Jacob Quarterman in claim of Pompey Bacon, Liberty County, GA, SCC.
[28] Charles Ball, *Fifty Years in Chains; or, the Life of an American Slave* (New York: H. Dayton, 1859), 129.

themselves" while Sam Osgood testified to the Claims Commission that he used his own money to "buy things clothes and such like that our master would not give." Escaped slave Allen Parker expounded on this distinction. Parker assured readers that among slaves, "the love of dress was just as strong as those more fortunate with funds." With money from overwork, many men and women supplemented their wardrobes, usually in the form of a suit of clothes "a little better than the clothes they wore every day" so that they could dress well while visiting or attending meeting. Olmsted more clearly delineated this distinction, noting that slaves "purchase[d] clothing for themselves" and that on "Sundays and holidays they usually look very smart," as opposed to during the work week when they wore the "ragged and slovenly" attire provided by their master. As ex-slave Tom Singleton explained, "Wid de money dey paid me I bought Sunday shoes and a Sunday coat and sich lak, cause I wuz a Nigger what always did lak to look good on Sunday."[29]

Distinctions between Sunday and holiday clothing bought by slaves and rough articles of raiment provisioned by masters apply to all categories of slave possessions and hinged on a set of values defined by variety and quality. For example, unlike the "coarse and rough" shoes provided by their master, Susan McIntosh remembered that slaves bought "calico, muslin, and good shoes, pants, coats and other nice things for their Sunday clothes." Likewise, Charles Ball noted bondpeople often spent money earned through overwork on "better food than was allowed by the overseer." To the Southern Claims Commission, in particular, ex-slaves made special note of the distinctive nature of their holdings, often using the terms "fine," "sound," or "nice" to distinguish purchased goods from provisions. Jacob Dryer complained to the commission that he had lost "a good sum of clothes that master bought for me," but assured officials that "all the good ones I bought for myself." Frances Brown lost three "fine dresses" to roving Yankees. Aside from clothing, Paris James claimed a "very fine leather saddle" while Jordan Weaver described a confiscated mare as "perfectly sound" and a "splendid animal." William Izzard testified to the loss of a "very fine powerful mule" and Mary Dudley described buying the "finest bed quilt." Granted, these men and women were making claims for lost property and may have exaggerated the quality of purchased goods, but the distinctions nevertheless remained important. Given the opportunity, enslaved people introduced "fine" goods into their material world through participation in the internal economy.[30]

[29] Rawick, *American Slave*, 3, pt. 4: 71; *Ibid.*, Suppl. ser. 1, 3, pt. 1: 252; Claim of Sam Osgood, Liberty County, GA, SCC; Allen Parker, *Recollections of Slavery Times* (Worcester, MA: Charles W. Burbank, 1895), 20; Olmsted, *Cotton Kingdom*, 82; Rawick, *American Slave*, 13, pt. 3: 266.

[30] Rawick, *American Slave*, 13, pt. 3: 81; Ball, *Slavery in the United States*, 167; Claim of Jacob Dryer, Liberty County, GA, SCC; Claim of Frances Brown, Liberty County, GA, SCC; Testimony of Simon Walthour in claim of Paris James, Liberty County, GA, SCC; Jordan Weaver, Orange County, NC, SCC; Testimony of William Izzard in claim of William Drayton, Beaufort District,

Clearly, like their white neighbors, slaves purchased goods that served far more than utilitarian function. Spending money allowed slaves to distinguish themselves from the provisioned masses and, through the use and display of purchased goods, to make claims about personal identity and status. An anecdote from Virginia demonstrates these processes in action. Traveling daguerreotypist John W. Bear set up shop in Winchester, Virginia, in 1843, reserving every Friday for clientele of color. Free blacks and slaves took advantage of his services at a 50-cent reduction in price. Slaves apparently paid for pictures with their own money, although their masters "gave them time" and "many of them came with them to see that they got good ones taken." Bear took special care with enslaved customers, adjusting the lighting to make them appear "as light as possible," which "took with them like hot pancakes." Even though Bear did not elaborate on the appearance of the men and women posed before him, it is likely that the slaves wore their best Sunday or holiday garments. They used their money to create an image, figuratively and literally, of not only their personal wealth but also the life and status they attempted to create for themselves through participation in the market.[31]

Even though bondpeople almost certainly derived a sense of empowerment from participation in the consumer process, it is important to remember that the men and women described here were slaves and were bound, albeit sometimes unsuccessfully, by white society's restrictions on their behavior. Cato Holmes testified to claims commissioners that the slaves on Dr. Way's lowcountry Georgia plantation were allowed to "raise anything but a 'colored man.'" Holmes was only half joking – real restrictions prohibited slaves from always spending money in the manner they chose. Although sumptuary laws were on the books in several states, by the nineteenth century, most remained unenforced. More troublesome to would-be consumers were feelings of resentment and jealousy harbored by whites toward black property ownership. Former Virginia slave James Lindsay Smith recalled purchasing a suit for $15 and wearing it to church one Sunday along with his own purchased watch and chain. Along the way, he and his master encountered a neighbor who eyed the two men with amusement, commenting, "Who is master; Lindsay or you, for he dresses better than you do? Does he own you, or do you own him?" Smith did not relay how his master responded, but the experiences of other slave consumers give some hint to his possible reaction. One slaveholder rebuked North Carolina slave Friday Jones for "dressing [his] wife finer than he was his wife." Sam Aleckson relayed a similar story – "Silla," a Charleston maid faced harsh criticism from a disapproving mistress. Clothing subject to her mistress's approval, the young slave woman regularly clad herself in the "coarsest

SC, SCC; Testimony of Mary Dudley in claim of Alexander Dudley, Marlborough District, SC, SCC.
[31] John W. Bear, *The Life and Travels of John W. Bear, "The Buckeye Blacksmith"* (Baltimore: D. Binswanger, 1873), 147–148.

material." Further, the woman was not permitted to wear a bonnet, wearing a bandanna instead when in the presence of her mistress. But this young woman, a seamstress, possessed a certain flair for dress, cared deeply about her appearance, and most importantly had the means to purchase materials needed to create a fashionable outfit. One Sunday morning she appeared in a "beautiful dress made in the latest style, a rich mantilla, and a bonnet that was not inexpensive." Upon seeing her, the plain-looking mistress handed her a match, demanded that she burn the bonnet, and ordered her never to wear the dress again. The limitations slaves faced as consumers hint at the ambivalent role of the market in bondpeople's lives. Although many slaves likely felt empowered by the consumer process, restrictions on when, where, and how they might spend their money likely dampened some of their enthusiasm.[32]

These restrictions were not limited to the physical. In purchasing, possessing, displaying, and using tangible goods, consumers project an image of themselves to the world around them. For better or worse, the objects and the process by which those objects are obtained become part of the consumer's identity. As we have seen, bondpeople engaged in this process, seeking to distinguish themselves from the image masters imposed through provisioning. In so doing, the ability to buy goods equated in many ways with an ability to buy respect. Take, for example, the childhood experience of Henry Gladney who remembered receiving a "copper two-cent piece wid a hole in it" as a young boy. Unlike other children, Gladney did not run to the store to buy candy with this bit of money. Instead, he "run a string thru dat hole and tied it 'round my neck and felt rich all de time." According to Gladney, "Little niggers always wanted to see dat money and I was proud to show it to them every time." In other words, Gladney saved and displayed his money, potentially buying the respect and attention of his young playmates.[33]

Even at a young age, Gladney understood that money conferred power and status. As he and his fellows grew older, they recognized even more fully the power of cash and property. Some slaves imagined that, in addition to a plug

---

[32] Testimony of Cato Holmes in claim of July Lecounte, Liberty County, GA, SCC; James Lindsay Smith, *Autobiography of James L. Smith, Including, Also, Reminiscences of Slave Life, Recollections of the War, Education of Freedmen, Causes of the Exodus, etc.* (Norwich, CT: Press of the Bulletin Company, 1881), 28; Friday Jones, *Days of Bondage. Autobiography of Friday Jones. Being a Brief Narrative of His Trials and Tribulations in Slavery* (Washington, DC: Commercial, 1883), 7; Aleckson, *Before the War*, 110–112. Olmsted noted a similar animus against slave women wearing bonnets in South Carolina. He described the clothing of a number of slave women outside a church, commenting on their "neatly dressed appearance" but noting that none of the women wore bonnets, presuming the choice of headwear was a matter of personal choice. He stood corrected when told that "the masters would not probably allow them to wear bonnets, if they should be disposed to, and should purchase them themselves, as it would be thought presuming." See Frederick Law Olmsted, *A Journey in the Seaboard Slave States, With Remarks on Their Economy* (London: Sampson Low, Son, 1856), 454–455. For another example of white resentment, see Jacobs, *Incidents in the Life of a Slave Girl*, 32, 100.

[33] Rawick, *American Slave*, 2, pt. 2: 130.

of tobacco, a couple of fowl, or a new pair of shoes, they could also buy the same respect, status, and privilege that wealth and property seemed to confer upon masters. The detailed records of the South Carolina Court of Magistrates and Freeholders are particularly instructive on this score, recording slaves' attempts to gain recognition of their role as propertied producers and consumers. Lazarus, for example, appeared at the home of John Bruce in Anderson District in March 1841. The enslaved man called for Augustus Bruce, son of the homeowner, accusing him of letting loose his canoe and demanding compensation for it. Hearing the quarrel, John Bruce ordered the slave off his property. Lazarus angrily replied that "he would go when he pleased, that he had money enough to pay for his conduct." But Lazarus never could have acquired enough money to legitimize such defiant and disrespectful threats – only the sting of thirty-nine lashes upon his back taught him that his chattel status blunted the power that money should have bestowed. Emboldened by belief in the power of personal wealth, Lazarus had transgressed the boundary that slavery delineated. Despite seemingly legitimate claims and possession of cash and property, his conduct toward Bruce and his son were unacceptable to the white community.[34]

The power of money as perceived by slaves manifests most strongly in incidents involving the alleged seduction of white women. In July 1846, Tom, property of Joseph Finger, was accused of behaving "rudely" to Mary E. Manus by "stopping her on the path pulling out his private member and proposing to have Intercourse with her." At no time did he physically assault her, Manus explained, although he did attempt to persuade her with the offer of a $1 payment. In August four years later, Julius appeared at the Anderson District home of Mrs. Silsey Pastain. When he showed up at her doorstep, only Pastain's daughter, Maria, was at home. According to Maria, Julius "sat down in the door and winked at her ... and took a few pieces of silver out of his Pocket and shaked it at her." Julius repeated this action three times, remaining at the Pastain house until Maria's brother Lindsey came home. As he left the property, he stopped by the window to the house; spying Maria, he winked, pointed to the woods, and shook his money at her once more. Emboldened by the silver in his hand, Julius imagined he could shed the bonds of slavery at Maria Pastain's doorstep and enter the white world as an equal – perhaps, with money to back his masculine advances, even a superior. Such was the power of money and property in his eyes. Unfortunately for Julius, the silver he jangled before Maria had little effect. As empowering as his money may have seemed, ultimately it could not protect him from the constable's whip.[35]

34 Anderson Trial Papers: *State v. Lazarus*, 4 March 1841, SCDAH.
35 Spartanburg Trial Papers: *State v. Tom*, 17 July 1846, SCDAH; Anderson Trial Papers: *State v. Julius*, 3 September 1850, SCDAH. We will never know what really transpired between Mary Manus and Tom, Maria Pastain and Julius. That the women's accusations were true is certainly a possibility – the court, after all, punished the men. As Diane Sommerville notes in her study of the "rape myth" in southern society, such convictions may have been exceptional, given the

Within the slave community, the silver in Julius's pocket may have garnered him respect from fellow bondpeople. The court cases outlined above demonstrate that buying esteem from the white community was more difficult. Enslaved men and women could secure goods and services proffered by a burgeoning market economy but could hardly purchase whiteness. But was "whiteness," practically speaking, always a desirable quality?[36] Even though white men and women – certainly the poorer members of society – faced the same judgments and moralism that enslaved consumers did, law and custom less circumscribed their market activity. Money and the power it seemed to confer was indeed desirable. But enslaved men and women, as consumable goods themselves, never forgot the ambivalent power of cash and property. After all, white avarice, many bondpeople assumed, was the very root of their enslavement. One former slave asked: "But what is de law now and what was de law then, when bright shiny money was in sight? Money make de automobile go. Money make de train go. Money make de mare go, and at dat time I 'spect money make de ships go." Were black people, as spenders of money and possessors of property, subject to the same sort of greed as their masters? Dave, a literate enslaved potter from Edgefield, South Carolina, made note of the potential danger in July 1840, inscribing on one of his pots, "Give me silver or; either gold / though they are dangerous; to our soul." Looking back on her life, ex-slave Mom Hagar Brown was more explicit still. Asked whether she had used money as a slave, she exclaimed, "Only cash the gospel! Have to get the gospel. Give you cloth! Give you ration!"[37]

Mammon's gospel, Brown understood, would judge all with equal force. Masters sought both economic profitability and confirmation of their mastery – and so it is not surprising that they would couch slave spending in

low regard in which poor white women were held in some southern communities. But historians have also documented cases in which white women caught with black men turned on their enslaved lovers, turning acts of prostitution or intimacy into false accusations of rape. In any case, the striking imagery of glittering, jangling coins serves as a stark reminder of the clash between cash-backed expectations of social leveling and the harsh reality of bondage faced by enslaved consumers. See Diane Miller Sommerville, "The Rape Myth in the Old South Reconsidered," *Journal of Southern History* 61 (1995), 481–518. See also Martha Hodes, *White Women, Black Men: Illicit Sex in the Nineteenth-Century South* (New Haven, CT: Yale University Press, 1997); Joshua D. Rothman, *Notorious in the Neighborhood: Sex and Families across the Color Line in Virginia, 1787–1861* (Chapel Hill: University of North Carolina Press, 2003); Merril D. Smith, ed., *Sex without Consent: Rape and Sexual Coercion in America* (New York: New York University Press, 2001); and Merril D. Smith, ed., *Sex and Sexuality in Early America* (New York: New York University Press, 1998).

[36] The literature on whiteness begins with the estimable work of David R. Roediger. See especially, *The Wages of Whiteness: Race and the Making of the American Working Class* (New York: Verso Books, 1991) and *Working Toward Whiteness: How America's Immigrants Became White* (New York: Basic Books, 2005).

[37] Rawick, *American Slave*, 2, pt. 1: 30; Jill Beute Koverman, ed., *"I made this jar...": The Life and Works of the Enslaved African-American Potter, Dave* (Columbia: McKissick Museum, University of South Carolina, 1998), 91; Rawick, *American Slave*, 2, pt. 1: 113.

paternalist terms. Determining the motivations of the enslaved, as we have seen, is more difficult. On some level, certainly, slaves desired the consumer trappings of freedom – to separate themselves from their group, to give comfort to their families, to make distinct their life from the provisioned masses, and to take part in the glad feast of consumption market society proffered. But to acquire such *things* was a process never entirely within their control. Legal and managerial restrictions hemmed slaves in at every turn and, more ominously, so did the spending habits of their masters. Overmatched though they were, bondpeople imposed paternalist judgment on the choices masters made. As consumer and consumed, they understood better than slaveholders the risks and rewards of market exchange.

3

Servants Served

Enslaved, for the most part, from birth until childhood, ex-slaves interviewed in the 1930s by the Works Progress Administration reveal a wide variety of experiences within the institution of Old South slavery. Tempered by both time and Jim Crow realities, the narratives vary in tone, in some cases gushing praise about "de' old times" and, in others, venting lingering frustration about the hardships of bonded life. Children, as portrayed through the narratives, experienced both of these extremes and in later years recounted those events that had affected them most with vivid detail. For South Carolina ex-slave Gus Feaster, his first visit to the trading post was one of those experiences. According to the aged South Carolinian, "Mammy said 'howdy' to all de darkies what dar and I look at dem from behind her skirts. I felt real curious-like all inside ... I seed so many things dat I never had seed befo', not in all my born days." Although colorful bolts of cloth, barrels of sundries, and shelves of tools, trinkets, and clothing likely stood before him, one particular set of goods drew Feaster's attention. He remarked with wonder, "Red sticks o' candy was a laying right dar fo' my eyes, jes' like de folks from de big house brung us at Christmas. It was not near Christmas den ... I wondered how-come dey was having candy in de store fer, now-how." Following the boy's gaze, Feaster's mother turned to the clerk, a man with a beard, and asked, "Marse, please sir, give me five cent worth peppermint candy." Having satisfied her young son, his mother turned to the errand at hand, purchasing a bonnet for "ten dollars worth o' cotton."[1]

As he grew older, Feaster's childish wonder with the store environment likely dwindled. But he, like his mother, continued to patronize local merchants. For enslaved people and whites alike the store served as creditor, repository for needed supplies of food and raiment, and tempting world of goods in which

---

[1] George P. Rawick, ed., *The American Slave: A Composite Autobiography*, 41 vols. (Westport, CT: Greenwood Press, 1972–1978), 12, pt. 2: 69–70.

they fashioned and, in some cases, fulfilled material wants and desires.[2] For bondpeople with cash in hand or goods to trade, the store offered the opportunity to vary the material life established by masters, allowing them choice and self-expression denied in other aspects of life in bondage. Masters and merchants understood the appeal of such choice and, like the enslaved, sought to harness the power economic exchange offered. This tripartite relationship was unsteady, constantly shifting, and marked by opportunity and risk for all. Profits and power, mastery and money: it was clear to all that more than goods were involved in transactions across storekeepers' counters.

Frederick Law Olmsted and Fanny Kemble, astute observers and critics of Dixie's social mores and consumption, commented on the unsophisticated nature of southern stores. According to Olmsted, in small crossroad towns and major cities alike, marketing was "quaint, provincial, and excessively slovenly." He noted that the majority of shops and stores sold "raisins, nailrods, and nigger-cloth, from the same counter with silks, and schoolbooks, and 'bitters.'" Even harsher in her criticism was Kemble, who complained about the "goods or rather 'bads,'" of southern mercantile establishments. Galled by both the selection and quality of the products offered, she also criticized "the incredible variety and ludicrous combinations of goods to be met with in one of these Southern shops." Like Olmsted, she contrasted the trinkets and accoutrements of daily life available in the average store with "one class of articles, and probably the most in demand here … cowhides and man-traps, of which a large assortment enters necessarily into the furniture of every Southern shop."[3]

Bondpeople likely noted these distinctions too, but appreciated the variety of goods community stores offered in a way that a middle-class Yankee or English traveler simply could not understand. Enslaved consumers interacted with store environments on a variety of different levels. From a young

---

[2] Literature on antebellum southern merchant establishments is scarce. Lewis E. Atherton's 1949 *The Southern Country Store* remains the defining monograph in the field. Examining the store as creditor and factor as well as the storekeeper's role in the southern social order, Atherton's account is useful but dated. His discussion of purchases is anecdotal with little attention devoted to the consumer process. Frank Byrne has completed a study on antebellum southern merchants and their families, examining their unique and sometimes ambivalent place in southern society as welcomed harbingers of market progress and scorned symbols of Yankee dishonesty. Neither study addresses the issue of slaves' purchasing ability in detail. Moreover, to date, no historian has studied these establishments as a means of gauging market change in the South on a scale akin to Christopher Clark's study of rural Massachusetts, *The Roots of Rural Capitalism*. Work on the internal economy is a small but necessary and important step in this direction. Lewis E. Atherton, *The Southern Country Store, 1800–1860* (1949; Westport, CT: Greenwood Press, 1968); Frank J. Byrne, *Becoming Bourgeois: Merchant Culture in the South, 1820–1865* (Lexington: University Press of Kentucky, 2006); Christopher Clark, *The Roots of Rural Capitalism: Western Massachusetts, 1780–1860* (Ithaca, NY: Cornell University Press, 1990).

[3] Frederick Law Olmsted, *A Journey in the Backcountry* (New York: Mason Brothers, 1860), 280; Frances Anne Kemble, *Journal of a Residence on a Georgian Plantation in 1838–1839* (New York: Harper and Brothers, 1863), 116–117.

age, slaves could identify differences between homemade items and goods purchased from a merchant. Although some bondpeople, like Georgina Gibbs of Virginia, claimed to have grown and made everything they consumed on the plantation, "store-bought" goods held special appeal to the vast majority of slaves. Ex-slave Sarah Anne Greene explained that her master assigned ten women to do all of the weaving for the plantation but that every bondwoman was allowed "one Sunday dress a year made out of store bought cloth." Melvin Smith made a similar distinction, explaining to WPA interviewers that most slaves wore coarse, heavy, plantation-made brogans. His shoes, however, were "store-bought." He and other slaves "felt moughty proud when us dressed up in dem store bought clothes." In short, "store-bought things was a treat den" and provisioned goods purchased off the plantation were highly-prized. Although slaves likely would have preferred to choose their own clothing, they eagerly anticipated their master's monthly/semi-annual/annual provisioning trips. Irving Lowery recalled "listen[ing] for the rumbling of the wagon wheels and the sound of horses' hoofs" as he and his fellows dreamed of "new suits, new shoes, new caps and new dresses." Similarly, Julia Bunch remembered anxiously waiting a week or more for the return of her master from market trips to Augusta. He and the lucky men he chose to assist him "would come back loaded down wid 'visions and clothes, and dere was allus a plenty for all de Niggers too."[4]

Accompanying the master to the store was a great privilege, an important responsibility, and an unique opportunity. Favored because she was the master's daughter, North Carolina slave Emily was permitted to accompany her mistress on shopping trips. We can only imagine the excitement as these chosen few watched and perhaps influenced their master's purchase of provisions, as they dreamed of grand purchases they might one day make on their own behalf, and perhaps as they spent money of their own. James Avirett remembered that "Uncle Suwarro," his father's trusted servant, would travel to Wilmington, North Carolina, during the week before Christmas on behalf of both master and slaves. Driving a cart "well laden with barrels of lard, turkeys, ducks, geese and other poultry, eggs, butter, roasting pigs (with shuck foot mats, baskets, horse collars and other products of the servants' private industry)," the "judicious old servant" bought desired goods for members of the quarters and the big house alike.[5]

The trust placed in Suwarro by his master was not uncommon. Slaveholders sent bondpeople to the store, usually with a handwritten order to the clerk

---

[4] Rawick, *American Slave*, 16, Virginia Narratives: 15–16; Ibid., 14, pt. 1: 342; Ibid., 13, pt. 3: 290; Ibid., 12, pt. 2: 317; Ibid., 2, pt. 1: 228; Irving E. Lowery, *Life on the Old Plantation in Ante-Bellum Days* (Columbia, SC: The State, 1911), 66–67; Rawick, *American Slave*, 12, pt. 1: 157–158. See also Rawick, *American Slave*, 13, pt. 1: 27.

[5] Rawick, *American Slave*, 15, pt. 2: 397; James Battle Avirett, *The Old Plantation: How We Lived in Great House and Cabin Before the* War (New York: F. Tennyson Neely, 1901), 174.

specifying desired goods and method of payment. As a young boy, Wesley Jones's first job was "gwine fer de papers up to de sto' at Sardis [South Carolina]." Candis Goodwin's owners gave her more explicit responsibilities. She explained, "de al'ys sen' me down tuh stow fo' tuh buy things." Even northerners accommodated themselves to this system of purchase by proxy. Frustrated with his sparsely lit accommodations in North Carolina, Olmsted ordered a slave to go to the store and buy candles for his room. The enslaved man, however, knew the store's hours and calmly explained that it was no use – "ain't no stores open, Sunday, massa." In some cases, slaves knew exactly what their shopping trip would entail, but in others they simply carried a note to the clerk. Take, for example, the experience of eight-year-old Rebecca Grant, a South Carolina slave. Sent on an errand to the store, the young girl handed the clerk a note written by her mistress. With little more than an "uh-huh" the clerk turned away and then handed her a package. Upon returning to the residence, Grant unhappily found that she had just purchased a "raw cowhide strap bout two feet long" with which her mistress whipped her. Her crime? She had neglected to call the mistress's three-year-old son, "Marse Henry."[6]

There is no discernible pattern in store account books regarding how often slaves purchased on behalf of their masters. Factors not readily apparent in extant business records – the distance from the store, the labor duties of those running the errands, or, as Rebecca Grant's story indicates, the whim of a harsh mistress – influenced decisions about who obtained needed or desired goods for the plantation. Such transactions were not rare, however. Georgia slaveholder Ulysses Lewis (or a member of his family), for example, sent his "girl" to a Hancock County shop to buy a yard and a half of black silk one Friday in August 1826. Three days later, he sent her back for more silk and some black twill. Another Georgia slaveholder, Felix James, patronized a Marietta shop; records show purchases made once or twice a week between September 1848 and April 1849. Out of sixty-five trips to the store, he sent his "servant" in his stead six times, picking up one or two items per trip, varying from soap to calico. One of James's neighbors, Mary Gibson, engaged in a similar sort of arrangement. Out of fifty-eight trips to the store, she sent her "servant" or her "girl" six times. On each occasion, the errand runner brought back sundries such as molasses, sugar, and potatoes. Gibson's sister and Gibson herself purchased sundries as well, but also sewing supplies such as calico, thread, and buttons. Whether they simply enjoyed picking out these items themselves or did not trust slaves' presumably less discerning eyes is unclear.[7]

[6] Rawick, *American Slave*, 3, pt. 3: 73; *Ibid.*, 16, Virginia Narratives: 19; Frederick Law Olmsted, *The Cotton Kingdom: A Traveller's Observations on Cotton and Slavery in the American Slave States, 1853–1861* (1953; New York: Da Capo Press, 1996), 145; Rawick, *American Slave*, 2, pt. 2: 177–178.

[7] Audas and Rogers Store Account Books, Daybook, 1826, GDAH; Noel Burton Knight Journal, September 1848 – May 1849, GDAH. For more examples of slaves purchasing goods on their master's account, see Thomas Ballance Ledger, AB.124 (1846), NCOAH; [Valleytown Store Ledger],

Trust was central to such arrangements. Historians Rosalind Williams and Elaine Abelson have described the dreamlike worlds of temptation that were late nineteenth-century department stores in France and the United States. The southern general store in no way matched these venues of consumption in size or variety of offerings, but to a slave dressed in coarse negro cloth, they likely evoked similar emotions. Sometimes the temptation was too great, and bondpeople took advantage of the responsibilities given to them. Ex-slave Julia Larken recalled that her master sent her and "Mary" to the store to purchase for themselves a pair of shoes each, the bill for which would be placed on his account. He failed to specify the type of shoes they should purchase, assuming that the young slave women would choose shoes of quality befitting their status. Larken complied with her master's unstated wishes and chose a pair of coarse, brass-toed brogans. Mary, however, "wanted a fine pair of Sunday shoes and dat's what she picked out and tuk home," changing into them as she neared the plantation. Their master, not surprisingly, was "mad as a hornet" – he could not return the shoes because they had already been worn – and threatened Mary with a beating. He never followed through, however, remarking to his wife that "dat gal Mary was a right smart Nigger."[8]

Slaveholders could, of course, use this venue of temptation to their advantage. A shop full of colorful cloth, ready-made clothing, plugs of tobacco, and items of personal adornment was incentive to industry on slaves' own time, and, as we have seen, some slaveholders hoped this productivity would translate to labor performed on the plantation. Others calculated that the opportunity to acquire goods of slaves' own choosing would allay long-term discontent. The temptation to flee, they hoped, would pale in comparison to temptation to purchase goods the country store offered. Runaway Harriet Jacobs's master made use of such allurement to entice Jacobs's children to reveal her hiding place. Threats failed to elicit a desired response; so Jacobs's owner, Dr. Flint, took a more novel, consumer-oriented approach. According to Jacobs, the doctor took young Ellen and Benny to a shop and "offered them some bright little silver pieces and gay handkerchiefs if they would tell where their mother was." As it turns out, the children had no knowledge of her whereabouts, a deliberate choice on Jacobs's part as she prepared her plot for escape and refuge.[9]

North Carolina Store, 1850–1871, NCOAH; McNeely, Young, and Company, Daybooks, vols. AB.196.1 (1858–1859), AB.196.2 (1858–1859), AB.196.3 (1859), AB.196.4 (1859), NCOAH; Richwine and Harrison Daybooks, AB.198.3 and AB.198.4 (1853–1858), NCOAH; Bagby and Gresham Account Book, 1841–1851, VHS; W. L. Cleveland Store Account Books, 1830–1831, 2 vols., GDAH; [Coweta County] Store Account Book, 1829–1831, GDAH.

[8] Rosalind H. Williams, *Dream Worlds: Mass Consumption in Late Nineteenth-Century France* (Berkeley: University of California Press, 1982). Elaine S. Abelson, *When Ladies Go A-Thieving: Middle-Class Shoplifters in the Victorian Department Store* (New York: Oxford University Press, 1989); Rawick, *American Slave*, 13, pt. 3: 44.

[9] Harriet Jacobs, *Incidents in the Life of a Slave Girl. Written by Herself*, ed. Lydia Maria Francis Child (Boston: Printed for Author, 1861), 178.

These temptations manifested varied levels of transgression against both their master and, in some cases, merchants. The issue of theft as a means of consumption will be addressed in detail in Chapter 4 but here, a brief assessment of criminal activity within store environments is in order. Familiar with stores as repositories of both cash and goods, some slaves turned to illicit means of procurement. Shopkeeper Cannon Brezeale, for example, brought a young slave boy, Charles, before the South Carolina Court of Magistrates and Freeholders in 1839, claiming to have caught him shoplifting – stealing a bunch of spun thread from his store. Clerks were surely vigilant against thefts during daylight hours but were more likely to suffer depredations once their stores were closed for the night. Despite his best efforts at theft prevention, South Carolina shopkeeper A. Kraker was the victim of several burglaries. In June 1860, he arrived at his store to find clothing and, more importantly, a watch missing from the "show case" in which he displayed it. The case was presumably made of glass – easy for customers to examine valuable goods but also an alluring temptation and a ready target for burglars. The morning after the robbery, Kraker could think of many suspects but no one in particular stood out. Other victims of store theft focused suspicion on their customers. In July 1856, for example, William, an enslaved South Carolinian, faced charges that he had stolen a lot of shoes from an Anderson District store. At the trial, clerk James Ingram claimed to have seen the defendant "at the shop twice examining the shoes." The "fine" shoes were in boxes, leading Ingram to conclude that "whoever took them must have known where the best shoes were." In light of lost property, then, shopping became prowling, the temptations of the marketplace working against merchants' profits rather than building them.[10]

Cash, too, was stolen. Although southern stores operated largely on systems of credit, all knew that clerks kept significant amounts of bills and coin in store money drawers. For example, in January 1842, witnesses testified that Mike, a Virginia slave, used an augur to break into a store to "get some money." Eight years earlier, another Virginia shopkeeper testified that Jim had stolen $55 from his store, claiming that he had seen the slave "in the store that day." Besides sturdy locks, there was little a keeper could do to protect his wares,

---

[10] Anderson Trial Papers, *State v. Charles*, 4 December 1839; *State v. Simon, Alfred*, 14 July 1860, SCDAH; Anderson Trial Papers, *State v. William*, 1 July 1856, SCDAH. In an interesting twist on the linkage between store thefts and enslaved buying behavior, Anderson District resident Joel Towns accused the slave Amos of stealing shoes from his brick storehouse at some point during the year 1851. In this case, however, Amos's conspicuous shopping may have saved the slave a whipping. In Amos's January 1852 trial, a local merchant reported that he had seen the defendant and his wife at his shop a few weeks earlier, that they might have purchased a pair of "womans shoes without heels." This testimony (combined with statements from several other witnesses) cast enough doubt on Towns's assertion that Amos's store-bought shoes were stolen that the slave was exonerated. Anderson Trial Papers, *State v. Amos*, 1 January 1852, SCDAH. For other examples of slaves accused of thefts from stores, see Anderson Trial Papers: *State v. Marshall*, 1 July 1860, *State v. Nero*, 14 July 1838, SCDAH; Spartanburg Trial Papers: *State v. Frank*, 6 October 1847, *State v. Jack*, 4 January 1838, SCDAH.

although one Virginia storekeeper made the attempt in May 1846. The proprietor of Noel and Cline's store in Albemarle, Virginia, was fed up with depredations against his establishment. He kept watch over a span of several days,
placing a weight on the cash drawer "calculated to fall and give notice if it
was disturbed." The success of his plan, in other words, was contingent on
the temptation the cash drawer possessed. Unfortunately for bondmen Watson
and Jacob, they walked into his trap, were arrested, tried, and condemned to
be hanged.[11]

In addition to theft, southern storekeepers suffered from poor reputations.
As Frank Byrne has noted in his discussion of southern merchant culture, storekeepers faced accusations of dishonesty from local communities – especially
from slaveholders concerned with maintaining surveillance over slaves' activities, economic or otherwise. In southern popular culture, the stereotypical store-
owner was a Jew, a Yankee, or a European immigrant – all seen as "cultural
interlopers – individuals lacking those virtues essential to southern character."
In both South Carolina and Virginia, Olmsted reported complaints by planters
about the "swarm of Jews ... many of them men of no character, opening cheap
clothing and trinket shops; ruining, or driving out of business, many of the old
retailers, and engaging in an unlawful trade with the simple negroes." Many of
these articles, Olmsted supposed, were secondhand castoffs from the North.[12]

This "unlawful trade" was one of slaveholders' most worrisome concerns.
Son of a prominent North Carolina planter, James Avirett condemned the "hurt-
ful influence of small stores." Poor white operators "were ready, by night, to
carry on a system of demoralizing barter" consisting primarily of goods stolen
from the plantation and overpriced trinkets and liquor. Sumter District planters John Miller and his son-in-law John Furman recognized the problem too.
Listed second under their "Rules for Government" of Cornhill Plantation was
the decree: "They [slaves] are not to be allowed to go to any Village Store, Shop
or Tavern without my express permission – nor to go to any place suspected of
trading with negroes." In 1860, residents of Fauquier County, Virginia, echoed
these anxieties, complaining of "two existing & wide-spread evils" perpetrated
by dishonest shopkeepers: trade in liquor and trade in stolen goods.[13] These
dual concerns shaped the ambivalent relationship of master and merchant and
influenced management strategies enacted to deal with threatening but needed
venues of consumption in their communities.

[11] Albemarle Commonwealth Causes, *Commonwealth v. Barnett*, 14 January 1842, LVA; Albemarle
Commonwealth Causes, *Commonwealth v. Jim*, 5 May 1834, LVA; Albemarle Commonwealth
Causes, *Commonwealth v. Watson and Jacob*, 4 May 1846, LVA.
[12] Byrne, *Becoming Bourgeois*, 41–42, 54; Frederick Law Olmsted, *Journeys and Explorations in
the Cotton Kingdom. A Traveller's Observations on Cotton and Slavery in the American Slave
States* (London: Sampson Low, Son, 1861), I: 252.
[13] Avirett, *The Old Plantation*, 118; "Rules of Government," n.d., "Cornhill" Plantation Book
of John Blount Miller and John H. Furman, 1827–1873, McDonald Furman Papers, Duke;
Legislative Petitions, Virginia, Fauquier County, 10 January 1860 (PAR# 11686007).

Like the citizens of Fauquier County, Charles Colcock Jones used the term "evil" to describe economic relationships between storekeepers and slaves, explaining that *"retailing shops,* established for the express purpose of *Negro-trading"* were *"the greatest nuisances and sources of evil tolerated in the country."* Jones's concern was liquor sold to slaves in "immense quantities" throughout the South. So great was this problem that, in 1854, Virginia citizens asked the state government to act, arguing for a law prohibiting the sale of alcohol to slaves without the consent of their masters. They noted that this illicit trade was "carried on with great art and secrecy" by "pretended groceries." Although laws on the books prohibited such trade, they were largely ineffective as "the profits of the trade [were] so favorably disproportioned to the chance of detection and of the penalties incurred." Merchants' methods, others added, were particularly devious. Although the "front door is shut," the *South-Carolina Temperance Advocate* warned, such stores often "have gates and by-ways" allowing alternate entrances. Others had nearly undetectable "hiding-holes, known only to those initiated." Worse, storekeepers had routinized this furtive business, some posting a "regular guard" to sound the alarm, usually a whistle, to alert traders of impending danger. Olmsted patronized one of these supposed storehouses. Traveling through rural Virginia, he came upon a cabin with a sign hung above the door marked "GROSERY," remarking that such terminology meant the same thing in Virginia as it did in Ireland, "a dram-shop." At one end of the small room was a set of shelves containing "two decanters, some dirty tumblers, a box of crackers, a canister, and several packages in paper." Another set of shelves held plates and kitchen utensils. At the other end stood the clerk's bed, his wife sitting on it nursing a sickly child. Olmsted assessed his environment, judged it an establishment of ill repute, and declined a dram.[14]

Concerned with maintaining control over the workforce, slaveholders worried that groceries, stores, and taverns willing to sell liquor to slaves would undermine discipline on the plantation. Just as worrisome to plantation owners was the inducement to steal that some stores provided. Escaped slave John Andrew Jackson reported that a South Carolina storekeeper encouraged slaves to steal cotton and corn from their masters at night in exchange for overpriced liquor. When that storekeeper later became a slaveowner himself, he never let his slaves go out after dark, afraid that they would steal from him, too.[15] For some bondpeople, these nighttime thefts funded consumption of store goods – profits that storekeepers were more than happy to accumulate.

[14] Charles Colcock Jones, *The Religious Instruction of the Negroes in the United States* (Savannah: Thomas Purse, 1842), 138; *Legislative Petitions,* Virginia, Kanawha County, 19 January 1854 (PAR# 11685402); "Grog Shops on Charleston Neck," *South-Carolina Temperance Advocate and Register of Agriculture and General Literature* (Columbia, SC), 19 February 1846; Olmsted, *Cotton Kingdom,* 57.

[15] John Andrew Jackson, *The Experience of a Slave in South Carolina* (London: Passmore and Alabaster, 1862), 39–40.

These profits are impossible to quantify, however. Charles Ball explained that storekeepers were "ready to rise at any time of the night" to "accommodate" slaves wishing to make purchases, but because this was illicit, nighttime activity, these business transactions were rarely recorded. Antebellum store accounts certainly note the presence of enslaved consumers, but their prominent presence in daybooks would seem to indicate that masters tacitly allowed the purchases. A group of store records from Georgia and Virginia, however, might hint at patterns of illicit consumption. As we shall see, accounting methods – especially in denoting slaves' purchases – varied widely from proprietor to proprietor. For the most part, if they are evident, slaves' accounts are not hidden within the ledgers. Stores owned by Sasnett & Smith in Hancock County, Georgia, Henry Freeman in Franklin County, Georgia, and an anonymous proprietor in Frederick County, Virginia, reveal a vastly different approach to slave accounting however. In each of these account books, the bulk of the ledgers contain fairly standardized listings and neatly-written accounts and transactions. On the last page and inside back cover of these ledgers are sets of undated disorganized scrawl – slave accounts. Are these records of illicit transactions? Two ledgers record alcohol sales. The evidence is admittedly speculative, but it possibly provides an interesting window on the way slaves and storekeepers transacted their nighttime exchanges.[16]

Publicly, storekeepers acknowledged problems of theft and alcohol but stubbornly resisted aspersions lobbed against them. Many found themselves under siege, furiously deflecting attempts to limit their trade. Sabbatarians struck with particular force, lobbying for Sunday retail closures. Virginian James Alexander remembered that shops in 1820s Charlottesville remained open on Sunday mornings, despite the vigorous protest of some local white townspeople, to accommodate those slaves who traveled to town to trade their crops for store-bought goods. Storekeepers sang paeans to the good order of society to vanquish these attacks. After all, commerce-oriented Columbians contended, it was better to keep the *"front doors open"* on Sundays than to risk illicit trade through the *"back* door." These debates were particularly fierce, historian Timothy Lockley argues, in cities like Savannah, where storekeepers faced stiff competition from Sunday African-American markets. Slave and free streamed in from the countryside to sell goods, but more importantly, to buy them. That general merchants had to shut their doors on the Sabbath, storekeepers argued, gave "one class of citizens privileges to the exclusion of others." In the end, Lockley explains, councilmen passed laws restricting all Sunday trade, to little

→ Really, this is where this is argued

[16] Charles Ball, *Slavery in the United States. A Narrative of the Life and Adventures of Charles Ball, a Black Man, Who Lived Forty Years in Maryland, South Carolina and Georgia, as a Slave Under Various Masters, and was One Year in the Navy with Commodore Barney, During the Late War* (New York: John S. Taylor, 1837), 191–192; Sasnett and Smith Store Daybook, 1824, GDAH; Henry Freeman Store Account Book, 1822-1823, GDAH; Ledger and Account Book, 1825–1828, Frederick County Court Records, Local Government Records Collection, LVA.

avail. Slaves and storekeepers, he argues, benefited as "the elite did not prevent them from trading, and the shopkeepers were willing to deny their racial ties to accommodate bondpeople for economic gain."[17]

Storekeepers fought to maintain enslaved patronage in other ways too. Just as important as retaining Sunday trade rights was keeping store hours and locations conducive to slave shopping. In 1827, for example, a group of Charleston merchants protested an ordinance prohibiting slaves from entering their stores after 8:00 p.m. in the fall and winter and 9:00 p.m. in the spring and summer. "Deprived of the right of purchase" by hours not conducive to slave work schedules, slaves spent their money elsewhere. Such restrictions, merchants argued, unfairly drained away honest men's profits. In 1846, Raleigh merchants condemned those who would "break up all retailing *in Town*," insisting that such action would result in the relocation of stores to "the suburbs," which lacked the "City watch and Constable to overlook and check them." Just as bad, increasing the fine for illicit trade simply drove business away from those who were honest, Camden, South Carolina, shopkeepers argued. They asked that the law allow slaves to purchase goods in small amounts, using cash. Peddlers, too, were a concern. In 1841, a group of Jefferson County citizens petitioned the Virginia legislature to restrict the sale of goods by itinerant merchants. Not only were these men an "injurious" influence upon the slave population, they also "injure[d] the business of the regular Merchants, without any benefit to the Citizens generally." By enacting such legislation, Virginia and South Carolina shopkeepers argued, honest merchants could share in the profits of less "scrupulous" business competitors.[18]

Reforming and reordering merchant space had little effect on the trade between slaves and merchants. Storekeepers suffered poor reputations throughout the antebellum period; illicit trade with slaves, however, still thrived. With such exchange came legal risk, but as Lockley and others have illustrated, storekeepers continued to accept slave dollars eagerly. Bondpeople, too, understood the risks of illicit trade. The lash was, after all, powerful inducement to consumptive obedience. More worrisome, covert commerce necessitated a contractual trust on which enslaved consumers could not always rely. Bondpeople railed against dishonest storekeepers who charged exorbitant prices for desired goods. As Charles Ball explained, "[t]he shop-keeper knows he can demand whatever price he pleases for his goods, without danger of being charged with

---

[17] James Alexander, *Early Charlottesville: Recollections of James Alexander, 1828–1874*, ed. Mary Rawlings (Charlottesville, VA: The Michie Company, 1942), 2–3; POPLICOLA, "Letter to the Editor," *Columbia (SC) Telescope*, 6 August 1833; Timothy James Lockley, *Lines in the Sand: Race and Class in Lowcountry Georgia, 1750–1860* (Athens: University of Georgia Press, 2001), 92–93.

[18] *Legislative Petitions*, South Carolina, Charleston District, ca. 1827 (PAR# 11382707); A Few Plain Thoughts for Both Sides," *Raleigh Register and North-Carolina Gazette*, 6 January 1846; *Legislative Petitions*, South Carolina, Kershaw District, 1818 (PAR# 11381805); *Legislative Petitions*, Virginia, Jefferson County, 11 December 1841 (PAR# 11684107).

extortion." [19] That some of the goods slaves traded were stolen surely added to the problem, leaving slaves with limited bargaining power. These risks become apparent when examining a court case involving a bondman from Virginia in 1831. James allegedly took bacon from his neighbor's storehouse, hid it in the woods, and then proceeded to have a dram at Samuel Thomas's grocery. After he had been there awhile, he sidled up to Thomas and quietly mentioned that he had eleven pieces of bacon to sell, but that he was afraid the storekeeper would cheat him. Thomas assured him that he would not, asking what he was going to do with the money and whether the slave might consider lending him some. James replied that Thomas could not borrow the money, as "he wanted to make a sum of money to purchase his freedom." Returning the next day to pick up his cash, James was arrested and turned over to authorities. [20]

We have seen the consternation with which southern slaveholders regarded the internal economy and have reviewed the myriad management techniques devised to allow masters to reap the benefits of slaves' consumer opportunities without forsaking discipline and control. But the fact remains that money allowed bondpeople to make choices that might challenge slaveholder mastery. Recall that Thomas Clay proposed solving this problem by maintaining a plantation store from which slaves could use money earned through overwork to buy desired goods. This system, he argued, would encourage industry and satisfy slaves' consumer desires, all under the watchful eye of the master. James Avirett provided readers of his memoir with an account of one such plantation store, explaining that Uncle Phillip, one of his father's slaves, held the esteemed role of store manager on the plantation. His establishment held a meager stock – "coffee, tea, sugar, cheese, cakes, peanuts, and home brewed beer (ginger and persimmon)," but suited the needs and desires of many on the plantation and lined Phillip's pocket as well. In addition to the modest markup he charged for providing the goods, he also extended credit, charging

---

[19] Charles Ball, *Fifty Years in Chains; or, the Life of an American Slave* (New York: H. Dayton, 1859), 130. It is worth noting that Fanny Kemble made similar complaints about southern stores, although she condemned all nature of their trade. Noting that most storekeepers were "thoroughbred Yankees, with the true Yankee propensity to trade, no matter on how dirty a counter, or in what manner of wares," she implied that all customers were cheated, not just black slaves. It is likely, however, that the prices slaves paid for goods were higher than even those about which Kemble complained. Kemble, *Journal of a Residence*, 83.

[20] Albemarle Commonwealth Causes, *Commonwealth v. James*, 4 July 1831, LVA. These transactions could backfire on storekeepers as well. Take, for example, a case that went to the South Carolina Court of Appeals in 1839. A storekeeper stood charged of selling spirituous liquors to a slave. How was he caught? A slaveholder gave his slave Charles 25 cents and a bottle and sent him to buy spirits from a merchant rumored to trade with "negroes." When the slave returned with his bottle full, the slaveholder and his partner confronted the storekeeper and brought charges up against him. "The State v. Thomas Stone" in *Reports of Cases at Law Argued and Determined in the Court of Appeals; Court of Errors of South Carolina, from December, 1838, to May, 1839, Both Inclusive*, ed. William Rice (Charleston: Burges and James, 1839), 147–150.

interest to white and black members of the plantation community. Avirett him-self remembered borrowing money from the trusted slave, depositing with him a "note given with a formal seal."[21]

Records of plantation stores are scarce but two account books – one from South Carolina, another from Virginia – offer a snapshot of this form of closely-monitored slave spending. From 1848 through 1854, St. James Parish planter John O. Willson annually bought "produce" or "truck" from his slaves, mostly corn and fodder. The amounts paid varied, ranging from 63 cents to just over $12. How and where slaves spent that money is more difficult to dis-cern. Accounts from 1848 and 1849 mostly note Willson's produce payments, but by 1850 it is clear he kept extensive credit accounts with his people. In the fall of 1850, eight of his slaves bought bacon with their earnings, eight others used their "cash in Charleston" or "in town." Accounts from 1851 through 1854 note similar earnings from truck or produce but also registers of pur-chases – some scratched out or noted paid, others still open – for cloth (home-spun, plaid, striped, osnaburg, muslin), staples, nails, shoes, bacon, flour, coats, coffee, molasses, lard, bed tick, soap, and tobacco. Whether Willson provided a storeroom of options or simply took requests, we cannot know. Moreover, because Willson did not itemize purchases, we cannot be certain what percent-age of money slaves allotted to foodstuffs, cloth, and other sundries respectively. Thankfully, John Segar Eggleston's Nottaway County, Virginia, slave planta-tion book reveals a more complete accounting of slave spending. Whether the Eggleston plantation possessed a physical store is unclear but Eggleston acted as storekeeper, both crediting his bondpeople for overwork and the production of fodder and corn, and debiting them for goods received. The range of items available for purchase was limited – coffee, sugar, and shoes appeared regu-larly, while some more expensive goods including coats, "fine" shoes, and china appear to have been requested by certain slaves and then ordered by the mas-ter. Of the $1,539.78 in earnings accumulated by Eggleston's slaves, $215.80 or 14 percent was spent on sugar and coffee (often listed together in transac-tions). Slaves spent $51 or 3.3 percent of their income on shoes and boots, and another $60.20 or 3.9 percent on miscellaneous goods, including knives, a coat, a hat, a cravat, flour, and some china. What of the other 78.8 percent of accumulated earnings? Slaves chose to receive cash payments from their account for work performed. Further, slaves used Eggleston's account system to pay debts to each other, whether by purchasing an item for another slave, paying cash debited from their account, or asking for a direct transfer of funds from one account to another.[22]

[21] Avirett, *The Old Plantation*, 63–64. Christopher Morris has noted that a slave named Montgomery ran a similar store in Warren County, Mississippi, coordinating trade among white and black members of the community and even transacting business with New Orleans suppliers. See Christopher Morris, *Becoming Southern: The Evolution of a Way of Life, Warren County and Vicksburg, Mississippi, 1770–1860* (New York: Oxford University Press, 1995), 112.

[22] Entries of 1848–1854, Account Book, John O. Willson Papers, SCL; John Segar Eggleston Slave Accounts, 1850–1864, encl. in Richard Eggleston Hardaway Account Book, 1835–1864, VHS.

Although Eggleston's slaves likely appreciated the ease with which they were able to transform their extra labor into material goods, that nearly 79 percent of their transactions involved some sort of cash payment indicates that they prized other venues of consumption more highly. Similarly, that Eggleston was willing to pay cash to his slaves indicates that he tacitly understood and accepted that opportunities for consumption lay elsewhere, presumably outside his realm of direct control. Although he likely monitored goods slaves brought to the plantation, Eggleston had to rely on the surveillance of others – neighbors and, importantly, the southern storekeeper – to oversee his slaves' consumer activity. What did slaves buy? Anecdotal evidence is inconclusive. Lizzie Davis fondly remembered purchasing a "decent dress to wear to church," exchanging it for a peck of corn, while Julia Bunch recalled buying candy. With the first money he earned, Aaron Ford bought candy too, as well as "cloth dat costs 12 ½ cents a yard." Former South Carolina slave Pick Gladdney characterized the shop near his master's plantation as an especially "good store." Why? "Didn't have to go to Newber'y to git no candy and 'Bacco."[23]

Planters' records reveal slaves' shopping trips too. During the "Christmas Holydays" of 1856, 1857, and 1858, George Kollock allowed small groups of slaves from his Ossabaw Island plantation to go "to town," presumably Savannah. What they did there, if and how they spent money, and how long they stayed are a mystery.[24] The memoir of Esther Davis, granddaughter of Carolina planter James Chesnut, helps fill in that picture. Memories of life on Mulberry Plantation hint at the excitement surrounding this time of raucous feasting and vital trade. Describing childhood Christmases, she noted that plantation wagons were at the "disposal of the people, for their great Christmas pleasure was to spend those days in town, 'doing their trading' and meeting all their friends and acquaintances from other plantations." Her siblings and cousins watched "wagon after wagon pass, crowded with happy men and women, clad in their best and brightest, sometimes singing their wild sweet spirituals." The thriving hamlet of Camden was their destination:

In the business part of the town those three days were given up to the negroes. They thronged the streets. The few stores that were open were intended just for this trade and did a thriving business. The foundations of some fortunes were laid in those same small stores with their stocks of hardware, crockery, beads and brass jewelry, calico and bandana handkerchiefs, candy, etc.[25]

This anecdotal evidence provides valuable insight into the details and emotional impact of the consumer process in the life of the enslaved, revealing

---

[23] Rawick, *American Slave*, 2, pt. 1: 297–298; *Ibid.*, 12, pt. 1: 158; *Ibid.*, 2, pt. 2: 76; *Ibid.*, 2, pt. 2: 127.
[24] Ossabaw Island Plantation Journal, 1856, p. 4; Ossabaw Island Plantation Journal, 1857, p. 2; Ossabaw Island Plantation Journal, 1858, p. 2, George J. Kollock Plantation Journals, SHC.
[25] Esther S. Davis, *Memories of Mulberry* (Brooklyn, NY: Eagle Press, 1913), 15.

TABLE 3.1 *Ledgers Containing Slave Accounts*

Proprietor	Location	Time Period	# of Slave Accounts
James Morris	Franklin County, GA	1820–1830	75
Isham Edwards	Person County, NC	1821–1828	23
John Black	Laurens District, SC	1824–1827	121
Morris and Freeman	Franklin County, GA	1847–1857	76
B. C. Rousseau	Fairfax County, VA	1855–1857	48
Charles, Milling & Co.	Darlington, SC	1856–1861	33

Note: The James Morris and Morris and Freeman Account Books are related, although whether these storekeepers occupied the same mercantile space in Hancock County, Georgia, is uncertain. Only one slave name, "Freeman's Stephen," appears in both account books. Because I cannot verify whether the Stephen who shopped in the James Morris store and the Stephen who shopped in the Morris and Freeman store was the same person, I consider them as distinct shoppers in my calculations.

Sources: Slave Account Book, 1824–1827, John Black Papers, SCL; Ledger, 1856-1861, Charles, Milling, and Company, Charles and Company Papers, SCL; James Morris Store Account Books, 1820-1830, GDAH; Morris and Freeman Store Account Book, 1847–1857, GDAH; Ledger, AB.5.2 (1821–1828), Isham Edwards Accounts, NCOAH, B. C. Rousseau Account Book, 1855–1857, VHS.

what types of goods slaves bought on occasion but offering no hard evidence of slaves' spending patterns. An examination of six southern account books reveals what, exactly, slaves purchased when presented with opportunities to trade in the formal market environment of the general store (Table 3.1).

These six ledgers, spanning the four states covered in this study, present a snapshot of slave consumption patterns across space and time. The data presented here represents accounts for 376 slaves, well over a thousand transactions. Broken down into broad consumption categories, the total expenditure of goods indicates an interest in the acquisition of items of personal adornment, particularly dress. Slaves devoted 64.6 percent of their purchases to cloth, ready-made clothing, handkerchiefs, and sewing supplies.[26] Foodstuffs,

[26] Even in books addressing southern merchant business and culture, historians have failed to exploit fully the vast amount of information available in southern store account books. The hesitancy to do so is understandable. Ledgers are often difficult to read and individual accounting methods can be tough to discern. Detecting slave consumers is particularly problematic, not because bondpeople are not present in these records, but because it is difficult to identify exactly which names denote slaves and which denote freemen. I have taken a conservative approach, only assigning chattel status to names clearly denoted as slaves by means of the words "slave" or "servant;" the use of the possessive, e.g. "McCulleys Stephen" or "John Paynes Isaac;" or if the accounts are listed in a ledger entitled "Slave(s) Accounts." For a useful guide to using account books as a historical source, see Robert Wilson, III, "Early American Account Books: Interpretation, Cataloguing, and Use," Technical Leaflet #140, American Association for State and Local History, *History News* 36 (1981): 21–28. Christopher Densmore, "Understanding and Using Early Nineteenth Century Account Books," *Midwestern Archivist* 5 (1980): 5–19.

TABLE 3.2 *Slaves' Purchases Recorded in Six Account Ledgers*

Total Purchases	$2654.04	
Cloth, Clothing, Sewing Supplies, Handkerchiefs	$1713.26	64.6%
Foodstuffs	$387.89	14.6%
Household	$112.18	4.2%
Tobacco Products	$69.01	2.6%
Miscellaneous	$271.57	10.2%
Tools	$13.30	0.5%
Cash Payments	$86.83	3.3%

including all food and drink, emerged as a distant second, comprising 14.6 percent of purchases. Miscellaneous goods comprised 10.2 percent of total goods with household goods, including kitchenware, tableware, and household accoutrements, comprising another 4.2 percent. Finally, cash payments – that is, cash debited from slaves' accounts and paid either directly to the account holder or to another account – comprised 3.3 percent of debited transactions (Table 3.2).[27]

Broken down by account book and, by default, categorized across space and time, data indicate that purchases were not proportionately consistent; nor was there a consistent pattern of percentage growth or shrinkage across time (Table 3.3).

There are any number of reasons for this lack of pattern or consistency. First, inventories varied from store to store. Second, as we have seen, enslaved consumers operated within a context of slaveholder provisioning and management. The types of food and raiment provided by their masters almost certainly influenced slave purchases.

This general categorization only hints at what material goods slaves valued, casting in broad strokes general patterns of consumption but failing to adequately convey the "world of goods" in which slaves engaged. From coats and cloaks to raisins and rice to pocketknives and pitchers, bondpeople purchased a wide variety of items. Table 3.4 lists goods purchased by enslaved consumers in the six reviewed account books.

Although several of the items listed here appear only once or twice in the reviewed set of store records, in toto, the list reveals the wide variety of choices available to slaves with money to spend. Of these items, shoes, alcohol, and calico were the most popular, comprising 13 percent, 8.5 percent, and 6.7 percent of total purchases respectively. (See Table 3.5) The popularity of footwear is understandable, corresponding with one of slaves' biggest complaints

---

[27] "Miscellaneous" goods denote articles listed as miscellaneous, sundry, or do not fall within the broad categorization listed above. The term also describes those goods whose prices were evident but the names of which were illegible.

TABLE 3.3 *Percentages of Goods Purchased by Slaves in Account Ledgers*

	Morris	Edwards	Black	Morris & Freeman	Rousseau	Charles, Milling, and Co.
	(1820–1830)	(1821–1828)	(1824–1827)	(1847–1857)	(1855–1857)	(1856–1861)
Cloth, Clothing, Sewing Supplies, Handkerchiefs	70.6%	76.3%	62%	82.3%	58.5%	60.9%
Foodstuffs	17.3%	10.3%	18.8%	2.2%	3.7%	15.2%
Household	3.2%	7.6%	5.8%	1.9%	1.5%	4.0%
Miscellaneous	6.5%	4.8%	7.8%	8.2%	34.7%	7.1%
Tobacco Products	0.7%	0	3.3%	4.2%	1.2%	3.1%
Tools	0.2%	0	0.8%	0.5%	0.1%	0.4%
Cash Payments	1.5%	1.1%	1.5%	0.8%	0.5%	9.4%

TABLE 3.4 *Items Purchased by Slaves in Stores*

- handkerchiefs (unspecified, cotton, gingham, linen, muslin, silk)
- indigo, copperas
- buttons (unspecified, pearl, vest)
- hooks and eyes
- lining, slipping, tucking
- needles and pins
- clothing patterns
- spools of thread (unspecified, cotton, silk)
- whale bones
- cloth (apron check, cotton stripe, calico, cambric, muslin, dotted muslin, muslin robe, chintz, crepe, domestic, flannel, print, gingham, homespun, jean, lace, linsey, long, osnaburg, plaid, twill, velvet, silk)
- hats and caps (unspecified, fine, fur, wool, leghorn, straw)
- cravats
- bonnets (unspecified, silk)
- drawers and pants (unspecified, linen)
- coats, cloaks, and jackets (unspecified, linen)
- gloves (unspecified, silk, leather)
- shoes, boots, gaiters, brogans, moccasins, slippers (coarse, fine, negro, men's, women's, boy's, girl's)
- skirts (unspecified, hoop)
- socks, hose, stockings
- belts, suspenders
- vest (unspecified, linen)
- foodstuffs (bacon, butter, cake, candy, cheese, coffee, crackers, eggs, extract, figs, flour, lemon, molasses, orange, raisins, rice, soda, spice, salt, pepper, sugar, syrup, tea, vinegar)

- alcohol (whiskey, wine, brandy)
- kitchenware (coffee mill, coffee pot, jug, oven pan, frying pan, pepper box, salt cellar, pot, sifter, teapot)
- tableware (bowl, dishes, tin cups, mugs, decanters, goblets, pitchers, tumblers)
- sets of plates, sets of cups and saucers, sets of knives and forks
- books (dictionary, primer, spelling, hymnbook)
- toiletries and hygiene (cologne, dressing comb, shaving box, soap, razor, Jim Crow cards)
- parasols and umbrellas
- medicine (unspecified, camphor, laudanum)
- pencils, pens, paper
- tobacco (unspecified, cigars, snuffboxes, pipes)
- axes and awl blades
- nails, screws, hinges, paintbrush, scissors, hammers
- cards and combs
- blacking and blacking brushes
- watch guard
- pocketknife
- pocketbook
- nonspecified, miscellaneous, and sundry goods

TABLE 3.5 *Top Itemized Percentages of Total Purchases*

Shoes	13%
Alcohol	8.5%
Calico	6.7%
Miscellaneous Cloth	5%
Homespun	4.4%
Goods (nonspecified and illegible)	3.3%
Sugar	2.9%
Sundries	2.8%
Hats	2.7%
Tobacco	2.4%

about provisions. As we have seen, if slaves had shoes at all, they wore coarse, wooden-soled brogans. Almost universally, slaves characterized this footwear as uncomfortable and cumbersome. It makes sense then, that given opportunity, slaves would purchase shoes for themselves.

The other goods listed likewise correspond with anecdotal evidence. In order to dress themselves in clothing not provisioned by the master, slaves purchased sewing implements such as needles, pins, thimbles, and thread, cloth, and ready-made clothing. Michael Zakim argues that Americans politicized

TABLE 3.6 *Percentages of Total Purchases Devoted to Homespun Cloth*

	Morris	Edwards	Black	Morris & Freeman	Rousseau	Charles, Milling, & Co.
	(1820–1830)	(1821–1828)	(1824–1827)	(1847–1857)	(1855–1857)	(1856–1861)
Homespun	3.6%	1.1%	8.2%	4.1%	0	0.9%

homespun, touting it as a symbol of American values of simplicity, industry, and frugality throughout the Revolution and early republic. With increased market expansion as the nineteenth century progressed, ready-made clothing became more accessible, not just to elites but to all social classes. Antebellum slaves likely absorbed this rhetoric, but they did not need symbolic homespun to remind them that they worked hard. The data reviewed in this study reveal fluctuations in the amount of homespun and ready-made clothing purchased across space and time (Table 3.6).[28]

Records indicate that homespun was a popular object of consumption – the fifth most-purchased item, comprising 4.4 percent of expenditures. Although the data fluctuate from account book to account book, by the end of the antebellum period, slaves seem to have bought proportionately little homespun in the face of growing market availability of manufactured cloth.[29]

Slaves bought a wide variety of manufactured cloth. Calico, as we have seen, comprised nearly 7 percent of total expenditures and nearly 26 percent of purchased cloth. Although bondpeople recalled receiving some calico as part of their provisions, the fabric did not constitute a large proportion of provisioned goods. Printed, plain, or dyed, calico cloth often served to distinguish visually slaves' Sunday clothes from work clothes. Likewise, striped, plaid, and checked cloth as well as chintz and velvet served as markers of individuality, contrasting greatly from the dull-colored but durable clothing slaveholders provided (Table 3.7).

Finer fabrics such as cambric, muslin, crepe, and silk further served to distinguish purchased from provisioned goods. As opposed to the coarse, scratchy texture of negro cloth, these fabrics were soft and light, affecting not just the way a bondperson looked, but how he or she felt, too (Table 3.8).

Ready-made clothing comprised 32.9 percent of total purchases by slaves. The data would contradict Zakim's argument regarding the increasing

---

[28] Michael Zakim, "Sartorial Ideologies: From Homespun to Ready-Made," *American Historical Review* 106 (2001): 1553–1586. See also Zakim, *Ready-Made Democracy: A History of Men's Dress in the American Republic, 1760–1860* (Chicago: University of Chicago Press, 2003).

[29] It is worth noting a caveat, however. Because homespun was most often, in fact, spun at home, slaves may have made homespun and created goods for themselves, thus obviating the need for purchase.

TABLE 3.7 *Itemized Percentages of Total Cloth Purchases*

Calico	25.8%
Unspecified/Miscellaneous	19.4%
Homespun	16.7%
Cambric	6.8%
Muslin	5.4%
Cotton Stripe	4.6%
Shirting	4.3%
Apron Check	3.5%
Silk	2.9%
Cashmere	1.8%
Flannel	1%
Chintz, Crepe, Domestic, Jean, Lace, Linsey, Long, Osnaburg, Slipping Tucking, Twill, Velvet, Cotton, Plaid	<1% each

TABLE 3.8 *Percentages of Total Purchases Devoted to Ready-Made Clothing*

	Morris	Edwards	Black	Morris & Freeman	Rousseau	Charles, Milling, and Co.
Ready-made Clothing	36.6%	55.6%	21.7%	40.3%	41.6%	40.3%

proportion of ready-made goods purchased by consumers throughout the antebellum period, although it is worth noting that he does not explicitly examine the South in his study. Again, variations from region to region and store to store likely account for these fluctuations, but there is another possibility worth considering. Because slaves were not responsible for their coarse work clothing, they may have more consistently devoted their earnings to ready-made garments – desired products that required no additional work to transform them into wearable items. Slaves, after all, worked hard to earn money after hours and on weekends, and they, sooner than their white neighbors, may have adopted the easy convenience of ready-made clothing (Table 3.9).

The breakdown of ready-made clothing in this table reveals a pattern of significance similar to that of cloth purchases. Although some of these items duplicated those provided by the master, the gloves, bonnets, cravats, belts, vests, and shawls were unique to slave purchasing. The quality of many of these garments was relatively high. In addition to simply "shoes," bondpeople bought boots, gaiters, moccasins, and slippers. Moreover, the account books indicate that slaves did not settle for generic merchandise. For example, slaves bought shoes described as "fine" or made of calf skin. Such descriptions apply

TABLE 3.9 *Itemized Percentages of*
Ready-Made Clothing Purchases

Footwear	57.4%
Caps and Hats	18.1%
Coats, Cloaks, Jackets	4.9%
Dresses	4.8%
Shawls, Mantillas	4.2%
Socks/Hose	2.8%
Pants/Drawers	1.8%
Vests	1.2%
Suspenders	1.0%
Gloves	1.0%
Bonnets	0.9%
Cravats	0.8%
Skirts	0.5%
Shirts	0.4%
Belts	0.2%

TABLE 3.10 *Itemized Percentages of Total Food*
Purchases

Alcohol	58.1%
Sugar	19.8%
Molasses	7.2%
Flour	7.1%
Coffee	2.3%
Rice	1.2%
Spices	1.1%
Butter	0.8%
Cheese	0.7%
Syrup	0.6%
Bacon, Candy, Cakes, Crackers Eggs, Extract, Figs, Lemon, Orange, Soda, Raisins, Tea, Vinegar	<0.5% each

to other items as well. Bondpeople purchased "leghorn," fur, and wool hats; fine caps; silk gloves and cravats; and lace mantillas.

The purchased food items recorded in slave accounts differ even more starkly from provisioned goods (Table 3.10).

Although slaves occasionally received molasses or coffee as part of their rations, slaveholders rarely deemed sugar, spices such as salt and pepper, butter, and cheese worthy of slave diets and palates. Under special circumstances – namely holidays, logrollings, supervised frolics, and cornshuckings, and the

like – masters granted their slaves drams of whiskey. Purchasing alcohol outside the bounds of slaveholder surveillance was a different matter altogether,
however. In their attacks on both unscrupulous dram shops and intemperate
"negro" character, slaveholders argued that, given the opportunity, black slaves
would spend most of their money on liquor. Yet according to store records,
only 8.5 percent of purchases by slaves was devoted to whiskey, wine, and
brandy. Clearly, spirits were a desired good but consumed in far smaller quantities than slaveholders feared. Several caveats are in order, however. First, alcohol was available to slaves in only three of the six stores reviewed in this study.
Where storekeepers were willing to sell liquor (John Black's, Isham Edwards's,
and James Morris's stores), alcohol purchases comprised 14.9 percent, a substantial portion of expenditures but still a smaller proportion than feared by
slaveholders. This rate of purchase may not be indicative of slave consumption of liquor across the board, however. Because so much of the liquor trade
occurred off formal record books, it is impossible to know the true rate of
alcohol consumption by slaves. Likewise, the relatively high rate of sugar and
molasses expenditure may very well have gone to either alcohol production or
trade for alcohol with enslaved or free neighbors.

In *The Refinement of America*, Richard Bushman argues that, in the eighteenth and nineteenth centuries, certain consumer goods became markers of
refinement, shaping notions of gentility and, in the increasingly market-oriented nineteenth century, "vernacular gentility" in the American republic.
Goods previously found only in the domain of the elite made their way into
rural trading posts and, significantly, into the hands of some antebellum slaves.
Although they do not constitute a large proportion of purchases, store records
indicate that slaves bought the occasional umbrella or parasol; sets of cups and
saucers or sets of knives and forks; specifically designated dishware, such as
tumblers, cream pots, decanters, and pitchers; cigars (instead of simply plugs
of tobacco); jewelry, such as rings and necklaces; and cologne. Bushman made
the useful point that laboring or middle-class men and women who purchased
these types of goods were not necessarily attempting to imitate their social betters; rather, they were taking part in the consumption of material symbols of
power. Slaves, too, recognized this process, rearranging these symbols in such a
way as to differentiate themselves from each other and from the vision of dis-
ciplined conformity established by masters.[30]

Some whites bristled at slaves who used goods of higher quality than their
status presumably granted, but slaveholders generally accommodated bondpeople's consumer activity within their system of management. Some goods
occasioned more alarm than others, however. Alcohol, of course, caused consternation, because it had the potential to threaten discipline. As worrisome
as alcohol was the possibility that slaves might acquire the ability to read

---

[30] Richard L. Bushman, *The Refinement of America: Persons, Houses, Cities* (New York: Vintage
Books, 1992), 406–407.

and write. Rules against teaching slaves to read, as well as against selling slaves print literature, were clear. In her review of literacy within the slave community, Janet Cornelius explains that, by the 1820s and 1830s, spurred by Nat Turner's rebellion, the Denmark Vesey controversy, and publication of David Walker's *Appeal to the Colored Citizens of the World*, legislatures in most southern states enacted repressive laws prohibiting teaching slaves to read and write. Prior to codification of these laws, efforts at promoting slave literacy faced tacit disapproval from white society. Runaway Thomas Jones recalled discreetly asking a sympathetic white clerk to sell him a spelling book, but the storekeeper responded, "it would not answer for me to sell you a book to learn out of." Undeterred, Jones patronized another store, explaining to the clerk that a white boy at his master's house had given him money and ordered him to buy the book. Jones left the store "feeling very rich with my long-desired treasure" and proceeded to teach himself how to read. Books were scarce in the six store accounts reviewed in this study, but a closer look at a cluster of the few sales that were recorded is revealing. John Black's Laurens District, South Carolina, store was an establishment from which slaves could buy print literature. Black's three years' worth of records indicate that slaves bought seven print items – three primers, three spelling books, and one dictionary. More compelling, Crawford's Gabe bought his dictionary on September 6, 1825. He returned eleven days later and bought a primer. During that eleven-day span, Young's Purn and Henderson's Jerret bought primers as well. Another slave from Young's plantation, Frank, had bought three spelling books earlier in the summer. Were these slaves collaborating on some sort of learning or literacy project? Did their masters know about these purchases? Was the storekeeper suspicious? Without further information, these questions will remain unanswered, but they indicate that, at least for moneyed slaves in Black's neighborhood, the ability to enhance one's mind was as accessible as the ability to improve one's diet or physical appearance (Figure 3.1).[31]

The slaves who purchased primers and spelling books at Black's store were men, not surprising since far fewer women than men patronized the general merchants reviewed in this study. Of the 376 slave accounts, 74 or 19.7 percent were held by women. They purchased $257.13 worth of goods, 9.7 percent of the total expenditures accounted. On the whole, women's purchases were similar to men's (Table 3.11).

Comparing the percentage breakdown of total purchases by men and women, six of the ten most popular items for men and women were the same. In general, men devoted more money proportionately to tobacco (2.5 percent

---

[31] Janet Duitsman Cornelius, *When I Can Read My Title Clear: Literacy, Slavery, and Religion in the Antebellum South* (Columbia: University of South Carolina Press, 1991), 32–33; Thomas H. Jones, *The Experience of Thomas H. Jones, Who was a Slave for Forty-Three Years* (Boston: Bazin and Chandler, 1862), 13–15; Slave Account Book, 1824–1827, John Black Papers, SCL.

TABLE 3.11 *Top Itemized Percentages of Total Goods Purchased By Gender*

Men		Women	
Shoes	13%	Sundries	15.9%
Alcohol	9.2%	Shoes	12.7%
Calico	6.6%	Dress	8.7%
Misc. Cloth	5%	Calico	7.9%
Homespun	4.5%	Misc. Cloth	5.3%
Goods (nonspecified and illegible)	3.1%	Goods (nonspecified and illegible)	5%
Sugar	3%	Homespun	3%
Hat	2.8%	Apron Check	2.8%
Tobacco	2.5%	Cambric	2.8%
Handkerchief	1.9%	Hat	2.2%

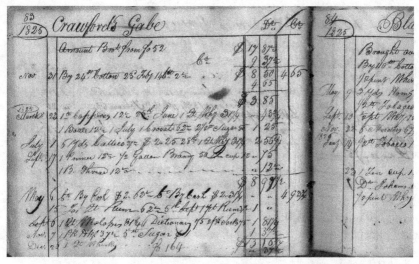

FIGURE 3.1 Slaves like Crawford's Gabe bought a wide assortment of goods – from whiskey to primers – at John Black's store in upcountry South Carolina.
Source: Slave Account Book, 1824–1827, John Black Papers, SCL, p. 83. Courtesy of the South Caroliniana Library, University of South Carolina.

of men's total spending as opposed to 1.2 percent of women's). Similarly, men devoted 9.2 percent of expenditures to the consumption of whiskey, wine, and brandy, while only 1.7 percent of women's purchases included alcohol. Options for female-specific goods were available, however. In addition to selling ready-made skirts, dresses, bonnets, and shawls, the stores in this study also sold "ladies," "womens," and "girls" shoes, although it is worth noting that both men and women purchased these items.[32]

Store records indicate that general merchants accumulated profits by meeting many of the material needs and desires of women in the community. What of the needs and desires of their enslaved customers? Merchants clearly appreciated slaves' consumer ability and made efforts to maintain their business, but did they stock goods to specifically attract black customers? Some slaveholders thought so. South Carolina planter James Gadsden lambasted the "German Jew and his family, who keep a store for the accommodation of the negroes" near his plantation, while the always alarmist *South-Carolina Temperance Advocate* condemned "odious and dangerous" shopkeepers "who look to the retail of spirits, (to slaves and others no better) for their living." Accusations of alcohol sales aside, we might consider the items merchants sold. Olmsted noted the presence of negro cloth in these establishments, but slaves rarely purchased this quality of good. (In fact, out of the $2,654.04 dollars spent by bondpeople in the six reviewed general merchant establishments, only $1.44 went to a pair of "negro" shoes.) Bondpeople desired calico and homespun, but so did white customers. The same argument can be made for any number of the goods purchased – with one exception. A number of stores stocked "Jim Crow Cards," cotton or wool cards long used by bondpeople to style their hair. Ex-slave Jane Morgan explained that "we carded our hair caze we never had no combs, but de cards dey worked better." Jacob Stroyer elaborated, explaining that the cards, dubbed "Jim-crows" were small, allowing for ease of use on the head. Although account book evidence indicates that slaves bought "fine tooth combs," by the late 1850s specifically designated "Jim Crow Cards" appeared in store accounts. Herbert, for example, purchased two Jim Crow cards from Stephen McCulley's Anderson, South Carolina, store in 1855, and Pinckney purchased one for $.13 from Charles, Milling, and Co. in Darlington District, South Carolina, in 1858. Storekeepers likely stocked goods that would satisfy both enslaved and free customers, but the presence of these items indicates that some shopkeepers may have accommodated and, indeed, targeted black tastes and needs.[33]

---

[32] Daina Ramey Berry has applied a gendered analysis of market opportunities in antebellum Georgia. In *Swing the Sickle for the Harvest is Ripe*, she observes that while, overall, enslaved Georgia women possessed fewer informal economic opportunities than men, women in coastal Glynn County reaped more benefit than women in upcountry Wilkes County. While Berry does not consider slave spending explicitly – broadly considering the fruits of slaves' informal labor in the context of family dynamics – her work substantiates the general pattern of gendered spending outlined here. Berry, *Swing the Sickle for the Harvest is Ripe: Gender and Slavery in Antebellum Georgia* (Urbana: University of Illinois Press, 2007), 104–128.

[33] "South Carolina Rice Plantation," *Charleston (SC) Mercury*, 5 July 1858; "Report of a Committee appointed for the Formation of a Temperance Society, in Columbia, So. Ca.," *South-Carolina Temperance Advocate and Register of Agriculture and General Literature* (Columbia, SC), 25 July 1839; Rawick, *American Slave*, Suppl. ser. 1, 9, pt. 4: 1576, cited in Shane White and Graham White, "Slave Hair and African American Culture in the Eighteenth

Masters, merchants, and bondpeople manipulated common market relations in complex ways. Determining the motivation of each is difficult, yet the problem itself underscores the constantly shifting nature of paternalist relations. That masters wanted to reinforce ties to their slaves, there was no doubt. Merchants could fray or strengthen those bonds. Could slaveholders risk connection with a third party – the market embodied? The commercial man was wily, slaveholders knew, concerned less with paternalism than with profit. Stereotypes aside, masters' measures of the merchants were not unfounded. For storekeepers, profits were multivalent, finding sources in both slaves and their owners. Keeping business ties to both – and themselves at the far end of the law – was the ideal. But with markets constrained by statute and custom, paternalist ties, too, had value. And so shopkeepers shifted between licit and illicit exchange – the distinction often determined by slaveholder caprice – to accommodate the master-slave relation. Slaves, as well, found themselves entangled in conflicted and conflicting ties of loyalty and interest. Double bound as always, they offered money and goods, rarely getting that which they knew other consumers purchased freely. Slaves executed material choice where they could but found that the realities of life in bondage made less liminal the potential advantages the market offered.

and Nineteenth Centuries," *Journal of Southern History* 61 (1995): 69; Jacob Stroyer, *My Life in the South* (Salem, MA: Salem Observer Book and Job Print, 1885), 14; Entry of 19 June 1855, Account Ledger, 1854–1856, Store Accounts of Stephen McCulley, SCDAH; Entry of 5 June 1858, Ledger, 1856–1861, Charles, Milling, and Company, Charles and Company Papers, SCL. Merchants throughout the South advertised "Jim Crow Cards" among their wares. See, for example, *Semi-Weekly Raleigh (NC) Register*, 10 September 1853, 28 September 1853; *South-Carolina Temperance Advocate and Register of Agriculture and General Literature* (Columbia, SC), 15 October 1846; *Daily Morning News* (Savannah, GA), 6 September 1859, 7 September 1859; *Richmond (VA) Daily Whig*, 17 March 1857. Jim Crow cards likely had other uses on the farm, though ex-slaves remembered them solely as items for personal hygiene and grooming. For more on Jim Crow cards and African-American hair practices, see Graham White and Shane White, *Stylin': African American Expressive Culture from Its Beginnings to the Zoot Suit* (Ithaca, NY: Cornell University Press, 1998), 37–62.

4

Black Markets

Richard Eppes was a meticulous man. A proponent of agricultural reform and a medical doctor, the Virginia slaveholder managed three tidewater grain plantations, overseeing a workforce that, by the beginning of the Civil War, had grown to over a hundred slaves. In addition to plantation journals and account books, Eppes kept a diary, memorializing the mundane details of daily management and expounding his own theories of profitability and social control. In particular, Eppes expressed concern for the moral character of his workforce and outlined regulations that, he thought, best promoted its welfare. In what was an annual tradition, Richard Eppes gathered slaves together for a prepared address, imparted the plantation rules, reviewed the community's accomplishments and failings, and outlined his vision for the upcoming year. Eppes explained to his slaves that he regarded them as "human beings possessing faculties similar to our own and capable of distinguishing between right and wrong" and expected them to obey the laws he decreed. The first, and presumably most important regulation addressed the problem of theft: "You shall not steal from your master, overseer, fellow servants, or neighbors." The first offense merited ten strokes of the whip; a second (occurring in the same month), twenty-five strokes; and a third, thirty-nine lashes and a shaved head.[1]

But this simple declaration of laws and expectations often failed to suffice and, in 1853, Eppes took special care to address the issue of theft among members of the gathered community. He said:

I have not spoken of stealing, for I hope we never shall hear any more of that on this plantation as you ought to know. It is to the interest of one & all of you to keep out of

[1] Clement Eaton, *The Waning of the Old South Civilization* (Athens: University of Georgia Press, 1968), 32–36; Shearer Davis Bowman, "Conditional Unionism and Slavery in Virginia, 1860–1861: The Case of Dr. Richard Eppes," *Virginia Magazine of History and Biography* 96 (1988): 31–32; "Code of Laws for Island Plantation," Section 69, Eppes Family Papers, VHS.

such scrapes but I have to ask of you if a chicken or an egg or your provision is stolen, to go and tell Mr. Rogers immediately and he will try and find out the rogue and he will surely be punished. Should we loose hogs sheep corn or other things off the plantation and the rogue cannot be detected or found out then the whole population must suffer, a day for a hog or sheep or barrel of corn, of your Christmas hollodays will be taken off until we have taken the whole when we will find out some other punishment.[2]

Evidently Eppes's address did not have the desired effect as, in 1854, he publicly chastised Toby and Archer for thefts committed earlier that fall.

Given the lashing Toby and Archer must have suffered, one wonders what sort of goods or foodstuffs might have merited such risk. Was material deprivation so great that they needed to steal bacon to supplement meager diets? Had their shoes worn thin, exposing feet to the growing chill of the fall? Did they covet their master's fine hat or a neighbor's new penknife? Did they need cash to acquire goods sold by local merchants or roving peddlers? Eppes did not elaborate on the "crimes" these two men committed, but consternation expressed in his prolific writings as well as evidence from other planters' journals, prescriptive literature, court records, and the enslaved themselves suggest that such behavior was common in the plantation South. Bondpeople acquired property through both theft and a thriving underground market for stolen goods, and in doing so they balanced the risks and rewards of illicit and contraband consumption.

The role of theft and illicit economies has been little explored in the growing historiography of consumption. Historians have tended to focus on traditional, and notably, legal means of goods and property acquisition, thus ignoring the active underground economic systems that underpinned poorer societies and the poor who lived in more affluent communities.[3] Others have made an attempt to connect a rise in criminality itself with a growing consumer culture. Timothy Breen, for example, notes that the burgeoning consumer market of the mid-eighteenth century "created its own criminal class." Quoting a pamphleteer, he asks, "For what Trifles, did this poor Wretch continually hazard his Life!" In many respects, Breen's work, and the work of others who detail the birth of the eighteenth-century consumer revolution, has been dedicated to answering this question, although he does not ultimately focus on the issue. Breen draws the reasonable conclusion that the wide variety of cloth, ribbons, silverware, teapots, and other sundries that had recently flooded the American

---

[2] "Rules and Regulations for Island Plantation," Section 69, Eppes Family Papers, VHS; Entry of 2 January 1854, Richard Eppes Diary, Section 41, Eppes Family Papers, VHS. Historian Michael Nicholls argues that the "Rules and Regulations" quoted above served as a template for Eppes's later New Year's talks. Although undated, he argues that the document can be dated between 1852 and 1854. See Michael L. Nicholls, "In the Light of Human Beings: Richard Eppes and His Island Plantation Code of Laws," *Virginia Magazine of History and Biography* 89 (1981): 67–78.

[3] Once again, historians might note interdisciplinary work on informal economies as described in note 22 in this book's introduction.

countryside "became part of a new visual landscape," tempting to those whose consumer aspirations might have surpassed their means.[4]

Elaine Abelson makes a more explicit connection between the twin themes of criminality and consumption in her discussion of shoplifting in late nineteenth-century America. Advertising agencies, mail-order catalogs, and significantly, department stores created a new consumer culture that, for many Americans, blurred the distinction between need and desire. Middle-class women, in particular, settled into the role of "shopper," eagerly perusing the tantalizing multitude of goods and making purchases based on necessity, affordability, desirability, and social conceptions of respectability. More and more often, petty theft won out as these women sought to counterbalance society's condemnations of criminal activity with an equally strong imperative to acquire goods and services deemed suitable and even necessary for the middle-class home. As shoplifting became an increasing problem for major urban department stores, a number of disconcerting questions faced management and indeed, society as a whole. How could department stores prosecute the very clientele they were trying to cultivate? And, more importantly, how could society reconcile middle-class respectability with the image of the thieving housewife? The answer lay in portraying otherwise respectable women as "victims" of kleptomania, thus allowing women to excuse their crimes as irrational indiscretions and permitting management to justify increased security and prosecution in the face of financial loss. Such diagnoses came at a cost, however; although middle-class women protected their reputation, and ultimately class status, through a discourse of consumer victimization, their willing acceptance of physiological and neurological frailties perpetuated stereotypes of female instability and irrationality.[5] Beverly Lemire has extended Abelson's analysis, arguing that theft of clothing in early modern England "fed a commercial network of second-hand trade which in turn mirrored wider social manifestations allied to popular consumerism." The depredation of elite wardrobes provided laboring classes the means to fulfill demand for "good quality, fashionable" clothing that would otherwise have been financially unattainable. For the masses, informal and illicit economic channels provided a means to challenge social hierarchies, muddling visible lines between rich and poor.[6]

Although the worlds Abelson and Lemire have painted differ substantially from the one in which antebellum slaves inhabited, the implications of their

---

[4] T. H. Breen, "The Meanings of Things: Interpreting the Consumer Economy in the Eighteenth Century," in *Consumption and the World of Goods*, eds. John Brewer and Roy Porter (New York: Routledge, 1993), 253.

[5] Elaine S. Abelson, *When Ladies Go A-Thieving: Middle-Class Shoplifters in the Victorian Department Store* (New York: Oxford University Press, 1989).

[6] Beverly Lemire, "The Theft of Clothes and Popular Consumerism in Early Modern England," *Journal of Social History* 24 (1990): 258, 261. See also Lemire, "Peddling Fashion: Salesmen, Pawnbrokers, Taylors, Thieves and the Second-hand Clothes Trade in England, c. 1700–1800," *Textile History* 22 (1991): 67–82.

studies are relevant to considerations of theft in plantation communities. Conflicting issues of morality, consumptive propriety, class, and gender loomed large in Victorian society's interpretation and judgment of white shoplifters and thieves. A study of theft as consumption in the slave community incorporates all of these issues with the added legal, social, and economic complications and implications of chattel ownership and race. Acknowledging this reality opens up a consumer realm little explored by historians, and adds another complex but significant dimension to both our understanding of the slaves' internal economy and our larger understanding of nontraditional modes of consumption across space and time.

The historiography of theft in the slave community is surprisingly limited, concerned primarily with incorporation of such activity in a dialectic of accommodation and resistance. For example, countering slaveholders' contention that bondpeople were innately disposed to theft, Herbert Aptheker cited chronic pilfering as one of the many types of "individual acts of resistance" undertaken by slaves against their masters. In *The Peculiar Institution*, Kenneth Stampp echoed Aptheker's interpretation, venturing further that theft was a sign of discontent and means of overcoming slaveholder oppression. Eugene Genovese's paternalism framework necessitated a more sophisticated interpretation, though ultimately he too argued his case using the language of resistance. Although he commended Stampp and Aptheker for looking beyond the moralizing of the slaveholding class, Genovese declared that theft "inevitably weakened [the slaves] self-respect and their ability to forge a collective discipline appropriate to the long-term demands of their national liberation."[7]

Lawrence Levine and Edward Ayers have refined Genovese's interpretation, arguing that feelings of degradation did not necessarily result from slaves' criminal activity. According to Levine, the enslaved could rationalize property crimes without significant damage to their own sense of morality because, in their interactions with whites, "the conditions permitting the application of their moral values was absent." Drawing heavily from Gresham Sykes and David Matza's concept of "neutralization theory," Levine argues that such behavior was conditional, allowing many enslaved to "create their own practical set of values and norms of behavior" without surrendering to them. Ayers, too, uses neutralization theory to explain the effect of theft on the moral fiber of the enslaved, but allows for greater variance in the motivations of those who committed these crimes. Slaves, just like their masters, possessed "no single or simple attitude about stealing" and few connected individual acts and a larger challenge to masters' hegemony.[8]

> cannot defer desire ... no discipline

---

[7] Herbert Aptheker, *American Negro Slave Revolts* (New York: Columbia University Press, 1943), 140–141; Kenneth M. Stampp, *The Peculiar Institution: Slavery in the Ante-bellum South* (New York: Vintage Books, 1956), 125–127; Eugene D. Genovese, *Roll, Jordan, Roll: The World the Slaves Made* (New York: Pantheon Books, 1974), 609.

[8] Lawrence W. Levine, *Black Culture and Black Consciousness: Afro-American Folk Thought From Slavery to Freedom* (New York: Oxford University Press, 1977), 130; Gresham M. Sykes and

Alex Lichtenstein has contributed the most significant and focused study of the linkage between theft and economy. Lichtenstein rejects "neutralization theory" outright, arguing that "the notion that the contradiction between slave behavior and slave morality was resolved in favor of stasis" was fundamentally flawed.[9] Unlike Ayers, Lichtenstein argues that property crimes challenged the hegemony of the ruling class, reminding readers that, as thieves, the enslaved were involved in "the practice of redistributing private property."[10] Drawing on the work of English labor historian E. P. Thompson, Lichtenstein instead applies the term, "moral economy" to slaves' theft of food from the plantation, arguing that slaves' conception of moral economy was "rooted ... at the most threatening level, in conflicting claims of economic rights to agricultural production." Noting that slaves often sold these goods to other (mostly non-slaveholding) whites in the community, Lichtenstein asserts that this shift from "moral economy to actual economy" threatened slaveholder hegemony, forcing masters to recognize their bondmen as economic actors and alter their management strategies accordingly.[11]

As Lichtenstein implies, theft is a form not only of criminal, but also of economic behavior. To steal foodstuffs, manufactured goods, or raw materials from one's master or neighbor was to "appropriate the goods of the marketplace" for personal use. Unlike other licit transactions, in the case of property crimes, the slave controlled the terms, essentially transforming the smokehouses, dwellings, and local shops of the antebellum South into economic forums, participation in which entailed specific risks and required particular consumer strategies not encountered in open and licit economic activity. This chapter focuses on the risks, strategies, and most importantly, choices involved in the use of theft as both direct means of consumption and indirect engagement in such illicit activity through participation in thriving black market trade. The chapter first explores the ways slaveholders relied on stereotypes about slaves' abilities and tastes as consumers to shape strategies of theft deterrence and control. After outlining these policies, it turns to detailed study of slaves' behavior as consumers of stolen goods within and in opposition to this framework of management. Hence, the chapter explores patterns of illicit consumption, the complications and risks such economic activity entailed, and the ways bondpeople altered their consumer behavior to accommodate black market realities.[12]

David Matza, "Techniques of Neutralization: A Theory of Delinquency," *American Sociological Review* 22 (1957): 664–670; Edward Ayers, *Vengeance and Justice: Crime and Punishment in the Nineteenth-Century American South* (New York: Oxford University Press, 1984), 128–130.

[9] Alex Lichtenstein, "'That disposition to theft, with which they have been branded': Moral Economy, Slave Management, and the Law," *Journal of Social History* 21 (1988): 414–415.

[10] Ian Taylor, Paul Walton, and Jock Young, *The New Criminology: For a Social Theory of Deviance* (New York: Routledge, 1973), 184–187, quoted in Alex Lichtenstein, "That disposition to theft," 415.

[11] Lichtenstein, "That disposition to theft," 415–416.

[12] According to the *Oxford English Dictionary*, the term "black market" (defined as "unauthorized

What spurred some slaves to make the shift from licit marketplace consumption to the illicit and presumably less secure acquisition of goods through theft or black market trade? Nineteenth-century commentators differed in their answers to this nagging question. South Carolina planter Nathaniel Heyward embraced what Lovalerie King has termed "the thieving negro," stereotype, explaining to a plantation visitor that the slaves of the region possessed "no morals nor principles whatever, and are all the most notorious thieves." North Carolina lawyer William Valentine was similarly cynical and was deeply troubled by the need to punish his slaves for mere *suspicion* of stealing, lamenting "all will steal and all thieves will lie and as a liar cannot be believed even when he speaks the truth, so the innocent might be punished." This was, he admitted, "bad policy," but he was at a loss as to how properly to handle a type of behavior that he had come to see as a trait common to the race.[13] Virginia planter John Walker was similarly suspicious. Although he had faced depredations from white neighbors – salvos in a prolonged fight over fencing and roaming swine – Walker blamed "evil negroes" from his neighbor's plantation for missing hogs in 1834. Antebellum reformer Charles Colcock Jones echoed this sentiment, asserting what most members of the master class believed to be true: "They [the slaves] are proverbially thieves ... They steal from each other; from their masters from any body. Cows, sheep, hogs, poultry, clothing; yea, nothing goes amiss to which they take a fancy; while corn, rice, cotton, or the staple productions, whatever they may be, are standing temptations, provided a market be at hand, and they can sell or barter them with impunity." Slaves, planters throughout the South agreed, were natural rogues.[14]

dealing in commodities that are rationed or of which the supply is otherwise restricted") first appeared in a 1931 article in the *Economist*. Despite this chapter title's obvious play on the term, the original connotation was not racial and should not be interpreted as such as it appears throughout the chapter. For the purposes of this project, "black market trade" refers to the underground and informal economic transaction of stolen or contraband goods.

[13] King argues that white southerners envisioned their region as an idyllic "paradise;" left outside of this paradise were black slaves, their inability to own property and their blackness projecting their image as natural thieves. Lovalerie King, *Race, Theft, and Ethics: Property Matters in African American Literature* (Baton Rouge: Louisiana State University Press, 2007), 29–30. See also Genovese, *Roll, Jordan, Roll*, 599. Margaret Hunter Hall, *The Aristocratic Journey; Being the Outspoken Letters of Mrs. Basil Hall Written during a Fourteen Months' Sojourn in America, 1827–1828*, ed. Una Pope-Hennessey (New York: Putnam, 1931), 223; Entry of 1 January 1851, vol. 11, William D. Valentine Diaries, SHC.

[14] Entry of 16 April 1834, John Walker Plantation Journal, SHC. Despite Walker's complaints against "abominable neighbors," white and black, his own slaves were not without fault. In addition to persistent thefts of his own stores, his bondpeople stole from neighbors too. For an extended discussion of issues of theft and internal economy in Walker's Virginia neighborhood, see Claudia L. Bushman, *In Old Virginia: Slavery, Farming, and Society in the Journal of John Walker* (Baltimore: Johns Hopkins University Press, 2002), 129–133; Charles Colcock Jones, *The Religious Instruction of the Negroes in the United States* (Savannah: Thomas Purse, 1842), 135.

As Jones implied, many whites assumed that weaknesses in "negro" character made it nearly impossible for slaves to resist the temptation of the material
world around them. Jones argued that the "government" of the slave was "*too
much physical in its nature*" and, although a master might be pious, "servants
have neither intellectual nor moral intercourse with their masters generally,
sufficient to redeem them." Faced with a lack of consistent and sound moral
guidance, the enslaved had no choice but to succumb to "temptations laid
before them against which they have little or no defense." An 1834 contributor
to the *Farmers' Register* further argued that "many a negro who would never
have committed a theft in the course of a long life, with a careful overseer or
master, has not been able to resist the temptation, when a careless overseer or
master has left keys lying about: and when once the ice is broken, and they lose
character, they soon become hardened in villainy." Many whites, northern and
southern, chalked up the prevalence of property crimes in the slave community
to assumed "negro" characteristics of improvidence, irrationality, and intemperance; in other words, in their view, slaves possessed no ability to control
their passions and could not help but take what lay before them.[15]

This temptation to steal was excited, it was thought, by the presence and
interference of calculating individuals who took advantage of morally-weak
and intemperate bondpeople. Olmsted noted that, despite an apparent animosity toward the slave population, poor whites were "said to 'corrupt' the
negroes" by encouraging them to steal. On the eve of the Civil War, a group
of citizens in Mecklenburg County, North Carolina, voiced similar concerns
and complained not of the greed of slaves themselves but of the "cupidity of
evil-disposed persons located in our midst" who induced bondpeople to steal
from their masters. The "passive nature of the negro," according to these citizens, could not resist temptations that illicit trade offered and theft was the
only means to acquire goods needed to trade for more desired items. These
items might include liquor or the means to participate in and possibly increase
their earnings through gambling. A contributor to *Farmer and Planter* noted
complaints by planters against people in the "village" who "traffick with their
negroes, thereby encouraging them to steal and giving means of buying liquor
and to engage in gambling," while Virginian Edmund Ruffin accused northern interlopers of corrupting Virginia's slaves, offering alcohol in exchange for
stolen goods. Carolina planter David Gavin perhaps summed slaveholders'
complaints best, labeling a man caught trading stolen corn with neighborhood
slaves in 1857 "unprincipled, and notorious for everything that is mean."[16]

---

[15] Jones, *Religious Instruction of the Negroes*, 119; "On the Management of Negroes," *Farmers'
Register* 1 (1834): 565.

[16] Frederick Law Olmsted, *The Cotton Kingdom: A Traveller's Observations on Cotton and
Slavery in the American Slave States, 1853–1861* (1953; New York: Da Capo Press, 1996),
66; *Legislative Petitions*, North Carolina, Mecklenburg County, 27 November 1860 (PAR#
11286001); "Trafficking with Slaves Again," *Farmer and Planter* 8 (1857): 170; Edmund Ruffin,
Agricultural, Geological, and Descriptive Sketches of Lower North Carolina, and the Similar

Even though members of the more populous poor white population faced prosecution for trade with slaves, free people of color found themselves a particular focus of slaveholder ire. In 1838, for example, Virginia planters argued for restrictions on the sale of goods by free blacks, alleging that freedpeople sold large quantities of grain on the open market – the result of association with neighboring bondpeople. Tempted by profits potentially gained from sale of purloined grain, slaves collaborated with free black neighbors, allowing them to sell grain they had stolen. White citizens throughout the South echoed such concerns. In the eyes of many whites, free blacks were "lazy," "indolent," "improvident," and overall, possessed of "bad character." They acted as "factors for the reception and disposal of the goods stolen by slaves," and their homes served as "a place of rendezvous for badly disposed slaves, where they meet to drink, gamble, & plot mischief."[17]

Virginia slaveholder Isham Keith went further, arguing that free blacks were dangerous not only because they traded illegally, but also because they set bad examples for enslaved neighbors. Petty jealousies and temptations to theft arose when slaves encountered market opportunities that their status ostensibly prohibited. A free person of color (who is married to a slave), according to Keith, "can furnish his family who are supported by their master with luxuries such as slaves cannot honestly indulge in, thus rendering the slave dissatisfied." As a result, male slaves especially, "will steal for them, from his master generally as being the one whom he thinks should support his family having the benefit of his labor." Writing in 1862, Keith found this discontent particularly troubling and in fact, argued for the removal of free black agitators.[18]

The stereotype of the "thieving negro," susceptible to both his or her own passions and corrupting influences, did not satisfy all victims of plantation crime. Some white southerners sought more nuanced rationale for thievery, if for no other reason than to find practical ways to combat declining stores and provisions. Charles Colcock Jones, a leader in this movement, sought to reform the system of slavery in such a way as to bolster the character of supposedly weak and intemperate slaves, thus making them less disposed to theft and more inclined to productive labor. Other slaveholders turned to the Lord, among

---

Adjacent Lands (Raleigh: Institution for the Deaf and Dumb and the Blind, 1861), 154; Entry of 6 February 1857, David Gavin Diary, SHC. It is worth noting that most of these concerns about the connection between trafficking and agitation occurred as sectionalist tensions were reaching their peak. For further examples of traders as promoters of theft, see "To His Honor, the Mayor," *Charleston (SC) Mercury*, 9 November 1859 and AMINADAB, "Chatham County – County Court and Turner Bynum," *Weekly Raleigh Register*, 23 June 1858.

[17] *Legislative Petitions*: Virginia, Powhatan County, 10 March 1838 (PAR# 11683833); North Carolina, Onslow County, 3 December 1848 (PAR# 11285802); Virginia, Rockingham County, 1838 (PAR# 11683808); South Carolina, Chester District, ca. 1859 (PAR# 11385908). See also *Legislative Petitions*, Virginia, Richmond, ca. 18 February 1843 (PAR# 11684305).

[18] Notes of Isham Keith, 1862, Section 14, Keith Family Papers, VHS.

them James Ladson of Charleston District, South Carolina, who explained that wayward slaves simply needed religious instruction. His slaves "have a just notion of the rights of property" and as a result, "thefts now amongst themselves are almost unknown."[19]

Ladson's belief that instruction in the value of "property rights" could serve as a deterrent to theft found support on plantations throughout the South. A contributor to the *Southern Cultivator* admonished cynics, saying, "It is a great mistake ... to assume that the negro is incapable of moral elevation – that he will lie and steal simply because he is a negro, and it is also a very great mistake to assume that the fear of the lash is the only contributing influence which can be exerted in the management of negroes." Instead, he urged fellow planters to "excit[e] his [the slave's] pride" and in doing so, "elevate the man." In other words, this reformer hoped to cultivate his "self-respect ... until it will be the most effectual preventative of crime." In his view, the malleable nature of "negro" character was such that it could be easily cultivated. Property ownership, specifically, was seen as a viable means of instilling proper values and respect for themselves, each other, and most importantly, their masters. Georgia planter Thomas Clay explained: "They have learned that without truth, there can be neither religion nor respectability. Where negroes are well-treated, the temptation to steal is less than many other temptations to which they are exposed: and we generally find a respect for property more readily cherished by them than some other of the virtues; for as soon as the negro begins to reform, he begins to accumulate some property for himself, and nothing so forcibly teaches the value of honesty, as having something to lose by dishonesty."[20]

Agricultural journals reveal similar lines of thinking on other plantations, with some modifications. A number of slaveholders actively encouraged their slaves to cultivate crops, if only to have something to take from them if their own stores were pillaged. A contributor to the *Southern Agriculturist* explained that "if one sheaf is taken from me, I take three from them; if from each other, I seize all they have; if not enough, I take the next crop." In encouraging crop cultivation, the slaveholder not only instilled pride in production, he also held out the possibility of increased consumption of articles of their own choosing. As with their master, to lose a sheaf of wheat or other produce meant a loss in

---

[19] *Proceedings of the Meeting in Charleston, S.C., May 13–15, 1845, on the Religious Instruction of the Negroes, Together with the Report of the Committee, and the Address to the Public* (Charleston: B. Jenkins, 1845), 54. This rationale is evidence of a southern reform impulse marked by an expanding temperance movement, the continued growth of evangelical Protestantism, efforts at agricultural reform, and, significantly, improvements in the material, though not necessarily social, well-being of the slave population. See, in particular, John W. Quist, *Restless Visionaries: The Social Roots of Antebellum Reform in Alabama and Michigan* (Baton Rouge: Louisiana State University Press, 1998).

[20] "Management of Negroes – Duties of Masters," *Southern Cultivator* 18 (1860): 176–177; *Proceedings of the Meeting in Charleston, S.C.,* 57–58.

potential profits (in crops sold back to their master or to neighbors) and consequently, a lost spending opportunity.[21]

But, when it came to property ownership and crop growing, slaveholders knew they were walking a fine line between the cultivation of respect and enticement. Edward Spann Hammond advocated allowing slaves to raise crops and fowl, but prohibited growing cash crops, as it was "too strong a temptation to unlimited stealing & trading." Other planters rejected the idea of crop cultivation altogether. Instead of allowing his slaves to raise stock and crops for market, a contributor to *De Bow's Review* gave each head of family $5 at Christmas in an attempt to prevent them "from acquiring habits of trading in farm produce, which inevitably leads to stealing." If caught thieving, a slave would forfeit his family's money for the year. A contributor to the *Southern Cultivator* applied a similar method, but was more exacting. Instead of a flat cash incentive, he offered each hand, "whose conduct has been such as to merit it, an equivalent in money at the end of the year." The more industrious, honest, and faithful to the plantation the hand appeared, presumably, the more money he would be given to spend. In each of these cases, slaveholders assumed that the desire to spend in a manner of their own choosing would serve as a powerful deterrent in the war against plantation thievery.[22]

For their part, the enslaved developed their own defense against white charges that they were predisposed to rascality.[23] As we have seen, Alex Lichtenstein has argued that slaves developed their own "moral economy," one that allowed them just access to the fruits of their labor and that, significantly, differentiated between "taking" from the master and "stealing" from one's neighbors. Olmsted described this calculation in detail, explaining that "the result of labour belongs of right to the labourer, and on this ground, even the religious feel justified in using 'massa's' property for their own temporal benefit. This they term 'taking,' and it is never admitted to be a reproach to a man among them that he is charged with it, though 'stealing,' or taking from another than their master, and particularly from one another, is so." Likewise, an anonymous runaway slave interviewed by the *Emancipator* explained that he "did not think it was wrong to steal enough to eat." Why? According to the runaway, "I thought I worked hard to raise it, and I had a right to it." In a very

---

[21] R[ufus] King, Jr., "On the Management of the BUTLER Estate, and the Cultivation of the Sugar Cane," *Southern Agriculturist, and Register of Rural Affairs* 1 (1828): 529.

[22] "Agriculture," [n.d.], in vol. entitled "Views on Agriculture, 1857–1858," p. 36, Edward Spann Hammond Papers, SCL; "Management of Negroes upon Southern Estates," *De Bow's Review* 10 (1851): 624; Robert Collins, "Essay on the Management of Slaves," *Southern Cultivator* 12 (1854): 206.

[23] Thomas Buchanan has explored the etymology of the term "rascality" as it applied to persons of African descent. In the view of antebellum southerners, black rascals were characterized by "lawlessness, dishonesty, and fraud" caused by too much liberty. See Thomas C. Buchanan, *Black Life on the Mississippi: Slaves, Free Blacks, and the Western Steamboat World* (Chapel Hill: University of North Carolina Press, 2004), 129.

different context, historian James Huston explains that this characteristic was a fundamental principle of revolutionary economic republicanism. Americans, wary of unequal distributions of wealth in society, sought to create a country in which every man had "the free use and sole disposal" of the products of his own industry. The individual right to one's "fruits of labor" was central to the revolutionaries' vision of an equitable and virtuous America. The slaves described here may not have ever seen or heard the political rhetoric of the revolutionary generation, but their participation in the internal economy allowed them a taste of the fruits republicans exulted. They took this republican sentiment a step further when they committed property crimes against the plantation, justifying their "crime" within the context of due compensation and just rewards.[24] Samuel G. Howe, officer of the Freedmen's Inquiry Commission, articulated this sentiment most clearly in his investigation of the condition of the ex-slave population of Canada West in 1864. His description of the population was generally positive and, although he noted the presence of crime among some newly-arrived refugees, he attributed these negative characteristics to the habits acquired from years of living under the lash, not to any sort of innate racial inclinations. Howe criticized the slaveholding class, noting that they wanted "the negro not to steal, forgetting that a man must own something

[24] Olmsted, *Cotton Kingdom*, 83; "Recollections of a Runaway Slave," *The Emancipator*, 13 September 1838; James L. Huston, "The American Revolutionaries, the Political Economy of Aristocracy, and the American Concept of the Distribution of Wealth, 1765–1900," *American Historical Review* 98 (1993): 1079–1105. James Oakes has argued that in an increasingly liberal, market-oriented antebellum South, slave culture became "the South's most powerful and enduring source of ideals long associated with republicanism." Finding little hope for the prosperity southern liberals touted, slaves heeded few of their calls and instead turned to a republican defense of their individual households, seeking to create and protect a modicum of independence for themselves and their families. Oakes's description of slaves' republican commitment to their households is valid, but the evidence presented here indicates that a refinement of his argument is in order. Slaves were emblematic of the republican legacy not because they were unresponsive to the possibilities that the market economy proffered; rather, they were standard bearers of the republican ideal in their continued, if often frustrated, contests over the fruits of their labor. James Oakes, "From Republicanism to Liberalism: Ideological Change and the Crisis of the Old South," *American Quarterly* 37 (1985): 570. Still another way of looking at this problem comes to us from microeconomic theory. In a seminal article on the "theory of innovative entrepreneurship," William Baumol argues that "payoff structure" has historically influenced entrepreneurial innovation. The concept is simple: if, for example, corruption or black market exchange or other economic activity outside the realm of state or organizational authorization offers more rewards than officially-sanctioned trade, entrepreneurs will focus their efforts in these fringe areas. The result, he argues, is that entrepreneurial innovation is not always productive for institutions, organizations, or states at large. Denied monetary payoff in the work they performed for their masters, slaves too sought shadier and perhaps riskier rewards for their efforts. In the trade of black market or contraband goods, according to Baumol's model, morality or republican entitlement mattered not, with slaves simply taking advantage of opportunities to acquire goods that the masters' provisions rarely (or scarcely) provided. See, in particular, William J. Baumol, "Entrepreneurship: Productive, Unproductive, and Destructive," *Journal of Political Economy* 98 (1990): 893–921.

in order to have any adequate conception of what theft means." Faced with the daily expropriation of the fruits of their labor, the slave violated "the less sacred right of property in stealing what he can lay his hands on." Once these men and women came to Canada, said Howe, most put their habits of theft and depredation aside, taking pride in both property ownership and an honest day's work. Again, ownership and consumerism went hand in hand; ex-slaves shrugged off their supposed thieving pasts when presented with the opportunity to produce and consume in a manner in which they chose.[25]

Justifications for property crimes were not always framed in such explicitly republican terms, however. Many slaves saw theft as simple necessity. Louisa Adams complained about the deprivation she and her family experienced during slavery, commenting that food, shoes, and clothes were "bad." Her master, she complained, "worked us hard and gave us nuthin." In her view, she and her neighbors had to "steal or parish [sic]." Travelers, particularly those with abolitionist inclinations, seized on this seemingly obvious rationale for what they otherwise would have viewed as grossly immoral behavior. One noted that "[s]lavery seldom fortifies honesty; and, besides, the slave may fancy that it is just to make reprisals on his master's property for violence done to his own person." Fellow traveler Lucius Bierce echoed these sentiments, arguing that, "by starving them [the enslaved], they acquire the habits of theft and are illy prepared for the services required."[26]

Countering abolitionist claims often concerned contributors to southern agricultural journals and many condemned thefts outright. Others, however, tempered their outrage with reasoned consideration of provisioning problems. In his "Duties of Christian Masters," minister Holland N. McTyeire classified justification of plantation thefts in moral economic terms as "sophistry," but found much to condemn in masters whose slaves "took" extra provisions to compensate for stingy allowances. Other planters were more forthright in their recognition of slaves' moral calculations and responded accordingly. A contributor to the *Southern Cultivator* urged fellow planters to "furnish them [slaves] with such things as they ought to have." What ought slaves to have? This question plagued planters, and they espoused a variety of opinions in agricultural journals. One slaveholder, for example, defined adequate provisioning in terms of quantity, noting that "too little ... will lead to pillage," while a contributor to the *Farmers' Register* commented that "the very best remedy for hog stealing is to give the rogues plenty of pork to eat." The contributor continued by explaining that merely fulfilling life necessities was not enough and that thefts could

[25] Samuel G. Howe, *Report to the Freedmen's Inquiry Commission, 1864: The Refugees from Slavery in Canada West* (1864; New York: Arno Press, 1969), 87.

[26] George P. Rawick, ed., *The American Slave: A Composite Autobiography*, 41 vols. (Westport, CT: Greenwood Press, 1972–1978), 14, pt. 1: 2–3; G.M., "South-Carolina," *The New-England Magazine* 1 (1831): 339–340; Lucius Verus Bierce, *Travels in the Southland, 1822–1823: The Journal of Lucius Verus Bierce*, ed. George W. Knepper (Columbus: Ohio State University Press, 1966), 81.

only be prevented by providing "some of the luxuries of life … all of which will save the master's fowls."[27]

Escaped slave Charles Ball would have heartily agreed with such a prescription, arguing that the slave had the right not only to appropriate basic necessities but also to "gratify his passion for luxurious enjoyment." Ball explained his reasoning:

The slave sees his master residing in a spacious mansion, riding in a fine carriage, and dressed in costly clothes, and attributes the possession of all these enjoyments to his own labor; whilst he who is the cause of so much gratification and pleasure to another, is himself deprived of even the necessary accommodations of human life. Ignorant men do not and cannot reason logically; and in tracing things from cause to effect, the slave attributes all that he sees in possession of his master to his own toil, without taking the trouble to examine how far the skill, judgment, and economy of his master may have contributed to the accumulation of the wealth by which his residence is surrounded.[28]

Ball's explanation falls well within our understanding of moral economy but he pushed the argument further, expanding the definition of what a slave "ought" to have beyond mere subsistence; that bondpeople, as sentient beings with human needs, desires, and even jealousies, deserved full access to the surrounding world of consumer goods. Property crime, quite often, was the only viable means for a slave to consume luxuries considered either financially unattainable or inappropriate for his or her race and class.

Despite the material focus of condemners, defenders, and would-be reformers, some slaveholders felt that other factors might have motivated slaves' raids on property. Rather than focusing on the end result – the presumed acquisition of a desired good – some emphasized the process of appropriation itself. In the view of one contributor to the *Southern Agriculturist*, no amount of moral instruction or provisioning would curb slaves' propensity to steal. In his mind, the bondman was not motivated by "the advantage of obtaining a desired object … but rather the excitement produced by the very act of stealing." Slavery apologist Daniel R. Hundley agreed, arguing that the most "degraded" and "thieving" slaves belonged, not to those masters who could least afford to provision them, but to those of moderate means. Overfamiliarity with and overindulgence from the master led to "saucy" and "rascally" slaves who spent nighttime hours pilfering "from hen-roosts, pig-pens and dairies." In other words, the very act of stealing, the choice one made to indulge his or her desires, the power that such an ability instilled in the thief – these were the things that drove plantation crime. Consequently, no management reform

[27] Holland N. McTyeire, "Plantation Life – Duties and Responsibilities," *De Bow's Review* 29 (1860): 359; "Management of Negroes," *Southern Cultivator* 13 (1855): 173; "The Negro," *De Bow's Review* 3 (1847): 420; "Management of Negroes," *Farmers' Register* 1 (1834): 565.

[28] Charles Ball, *Fifty Years in Chains; or, the Life of an American Slave* (New York: H. Dayton, 1859), 219.

could prevent the loss of plantation stores. Restriction and punishment, not choice and indulgence, were keys to halting criminal activity.[29]

As Edward Ayers suggests, both motivations for perpetrating property crimes and strategies for dealing with them varied among enslaved and masters. Management debates found in prescriptive literature largely substantiate Lichtenstein's assertion that slaves' actions as thieves, as a whole, challenged the hegemony of the master class, forcing slaveholders to adjust management techniques to accommodate the economic desires and actions of bondpeople. Lichtenstein's argument needs refinement, however. The behavior of both the enslaved and those who managed them clearly hinged on an understanding of slaves as consumers of goods unavailable through accepted economic channels. Masters who advocated use of provision grounds and cash rewards as deterrents to theft recognized their slaves as eager consumers who desired not only basic provisions to which they felt they were entitled, but also the ability to acquire goods of their own choosing. Even though we are unable to systematically gauge the success of these management techniques, we can develop a picture of plantation property crime as a means of evaluating the choices, risks, and strategies involved in using theft as a means of consumption.

What exactly did slaves steal? Much evidence is anecdotal. Runaway Allen Parker explained that slaves sometimes took "corn, wheat, peas, pork, mutton, or anything else they could eat, or that had a market value." Charles Ball and his cohorts stole bacon and cotton. Others tell of stealing cash, beef, eggs, and poultry.[30] These scattered accounts provide us with brief glimpses into the mechanics of plantation thievery, but it is difficult to discern any sort of pattern to presumed desires. To understand why some bondpeople chose to engage in this much more dangerous form of consumption, we have to determine exactly what it was they were interested in acquiring. The secretive nature of underground economy makes systematic analysis difficult, however. Fortunately, a set of detailed records from the South Carolina Court of Magistrates and Freeholders can provide a window to the world of illicit consumption in the South Carolina upcountry. A case study of 588 trial records from the court in Anderson and Spartanburg districts serves as a useful snapshot of what slaves

---

[29] "Moral Discipline and Treatment of Slaves," *Southern Agriculturist, and Register of Rural Affairs* 9 (1836): 74; Daniel R. Hundley, *Social Relations in our Southern States* (New York: Henry B. Price, 1860), 352–353.

[30] Allen Parker, *Recollections of Slavery Times* (Worchester, MA: Charles W. Burbank, 1895), 56; Charles Ball, *Slavery in the United States. A Narrative of the Life and Adventures of Charles Ball, a Black Man, Who Lived Forty Years in Maryland, South Carolina and Georgia, as a Slave under Various Masters, and was One Year in the Navy with Commodore Barney, During the Late War* (New York: John S. Taylor, 1837), 314–317; John Brown, *Slave Life in Georgia: A Narrative of the Life, Sufferings, and Escape of John Brown, a Fugitive Slave, Now in England*, ed. Louis Alexis Chamerovzow (London: [W. M. Watts], 1855), 22, 53, 69, 83, 192; Jacob Stroyer, *My Life in the South* (Salem, MA: Salem Observer Book and Job Print, 1885), 28; *American Slave*, vol. 14, pt. 1: 93.

may have acquired through larcenies, burglaries, and robberies. Of these cases, 40 percent (234 cases) involve some sort of property crime. An itemized list specified in court indictments is found in Table 4.1.[31]

Food and raiment were the most oft-cited items in court indictments, comprising approximately 32 and 17 percent of total items stolen respectively. On the surface, it might appear that slaves, indeed, most often appropriated goods necessary for mere subsistence. After all, clothing and staple foods, including corn, bacon, and wheat, were the items most often pilfered. In most cases, these were items already provided in some form through slaveholder provisioning, albeit in portions often considered unreasonable by the enslaved. A closer look at the indictments, however, complicates these assumptions. In the matter of clothing, stolen items included a "fine hat" and a "black velvet dress," two items among many others that were likely valued less for the basic protection clothing provides than as more ornate means of self-expression and status.

There were other items stolen as well. Thefts of looking glasses, jewelry, and a bottle of cologne suggest that enslaved thieves appropriated some items not for their value in maintaining basic subsistence but to satisfy more luxurious desires. Most surprising were the number of watches stolen, the sixth most common item mentioned in the indictments. Citing Southern Claims Commission records and WPA narratives, historian Mark Smith argues that mechanical timepieces were rare in slave communities, that in the words of one Texas ex-slave, "Dey don't have de watches dem deys fo' de nigger so dey can't tell de time."[32] Court records suggest a different pattern of ownership, one dependent on illicit activity and black market consumption. Enslaved people clearly desired timepieces, not simply as a means of telling the time, but also because they were markers of wealth and status. For most, however, a watch was clearly beyond their financial means, ranging from an average of $14 in 1805–1809 to $27 in 1839–1843. The price of a stolen watch, though costly in other respects, was financially and literally well within reach.[33]

---

[31] There are a few limitations to this study, of course. First and foremost, the court cases only document inter-plantation crime. In most cases, masters and overseers themselves tried, convicted, and punished slaves for property crimes committed on home plantations. Secondly, the study documents those trials in which slaves were indicted for, but not necessarily convicted of, crimes. Although the records for these two districts are remarkably detailed, many are incomplete, containing indictments or testimony but lacking a record of final judgments. Moreover, the capricious nature of the magistrates' system and slave trials makes some judgments (resulting in guilt *or* innocence) suspect – a survey of criminal indictments serves as one means of standardizing the range of possible action taken by some of the region's enslaved. Anderson/Pendleton and Spartanburg Districts, Magistrate and Freeholders Court, Trial Papers, SCDAH.

[32] Rawick, *American Slave*, Suppl. ser. 2, 4, pt. 3: 1082. Quoted in Mark M. Smith, *Mastered by the Clock: Time, Slavery, and Freedom in the American South* (Chapel Hill: University of North Carolina Press, 1997), 135.

[33] These prices are based on Smith's calculations from Laurens District, South Carolina. Smith, *Mastered by the Clock*, 34.

TABLE 4.1 *Items Listed in 234 Indictments for Property Crimes in the South Carolina Court of Magistrates and Freeholders, Anderson/Pendleton and Spartanburg Districts, 1819–1860*

	Anderson/Pendleton	Spartanburg	Total Items	Percentage of Total Items
Clothing	38	14	52	16.5
Cash	14	15	29	9.2
Bacon	19	4	23	7.3
Corn	11	10	21	6.6
Pocketbook	8	6	14	4.4
Watch	10	3	13	4.1
Household Goods	12	1	13	4.1
Cloth	6	5	11	3.5
Cotton	7	4	11	3.5
Bedclothes	7	3	10	3.2
Silver	6	4	10	3.2
Wheat	6	4	10	3.2
Meat	7	3	10	3.2
Hog	4	5	9	2.8
Miscellaneous	5	3	8	2.5
Leather	5	3	8	2.5
Poultry	5	2	7	2.2
Tools	1	4	5	1.6
Liquor	5	0	5	1.6
Molasses	4	1	5	1.6
Flour	5	0	5	1.6
Iron	3	1	4	1.3
Furniture	1	2	3	<1%
Horse	3	0	3	<1%
Saddle/Bridle	3	0	3	<1%
Bee Gum	1	2	3	<1%
Penknife	2	0	2	<1%
Fiddle	1	1	2	<1%
Melons	1	1	2	<1%
Jewelry	1	1	2	<1%
Potatoes	1	1	2	<1%
Gun	1	0	1	<1%
Sugar	1	0	1	<1%
Wool	1	0	1	<1%
Coffee	1	0	1	<1%
Cologne	1	0	1	<1%
Lock	1	0	1	<1%
Tobacco	1	0	1	<1%
Looking Glass	0	1	1	<1%
Silverware	0	1	1	<1%
Cornmeal	0	1	1	<1%
Plank	0	1	1	<1%

Examining witness testimony further elaborates on the connection between theft of clothing and foodstuffs and meeting basic needs. Such evidence, given by both enslaved and white witnesses, indicates that almost 31 percent of the property crimes reported involved some sort of post-theft sale. In other words, thieves and their families did not always consume goods appropriated through theft; in nearly one-third of these instances, these goods were traded or sold for cash to either neighboring whites or fellow slaves. Willingness to engage in black market trade allowed for the acquisition of more fungible cash, which in turn provided more flexible spending opportunities.

It is helpful to view the storage houses, businesses, shops, and dwellings from which all of these goods were stolen as venues of consumption that lay beyond the realm of contractual agreement and where the thief alone set the terms of purchase. In doing so, bondpeople opened up a consumer realm full of new choices and possibilities that may have otherwise been unavailable to them. But how favorable were these terms of acquisition? What ultimately was the price of consuming stolen goods? Cash and other material items were, of course, means of payment in black market trade, but what about the intangible compromises and concrete risks that illicit appropriation necessarily entailed?

Eugene Genovese argued that the cost of thieving was erosion of slaves' moral character. And while Levine, Ayers, and Lichtenstein have made valid and reasoned arguments to the contrary, the act of appropriating another's property involved some consideration by thieves of the moral consequences of their actions. Although moral economy, as outlined by Lichtenstein, might describe the motivations of many members of the slave community, such considerations were not instinctive. In fact, in describing their past conduct, many enslaved looked back with, at the very least, a need to explain their behavior, and in many cases, regret. It is also worth noting that moral economy best describes the motivations of slaves stealing from their own master and that such behavior, as Timothy Lockley explains, "is highly distinct from engaging in theft from third parties." Escaped slave Austin Steward's argument that his actions could not "be *stealing*, because 'it belongs to massa, and so do we, and we only use one part of his property to benefit another'" does not fit most property crimes in the antebellum South and certainly none of those described in the records of the Court of Magistrates and Freeholders. To appropriate the goods of a third party and/or participate in black market trade, bondpeople often engaged in moral consideration and compromise that deeply challenged their own understanding of property rights and, in some cases, their own religious beliefs.[34]

---

[34] Timothy James Lockley, *Lines in the Sand: Race and Class in Lowcountry Georgia, 1750–1860* (Athens: University of Georgia Press, 2001), 108; Austin Steward, *Twenty-Two Years a Slave, and Forty Years a Freeman; Embracing a Correspondence of Several Years, While President of Wilberforce Colony, London, Canada West* (Rochester, NY: William Alling, 1857), 29.

In some cases, this calculation was not terribly difficult. John Brown stole a bit of money from a slave trader, rationalizing that since "it had been got by selling 'niggers,' [he] had as much right to it as anybody." In retrospect, Brown felt he had to justify his actions but insisted that he made his decisions based on "the notions [he] had at the time." What is important here is not how Brown rationalized his own behavior, but rather that he engaged in the process at all. In order to appropriate the slave trader's money – to appropriate the means of consumption – Brown had to consciously evaluate his own behavior. Such justifications were even more difficult when it came to theft from fellow slaves. Such behavior rarely found approval and was universally considered "stealing" by the slave community. Fourteen cases (6 percent) of the total property crime indictments involved accusations of inter-plantation theft by slaves from slaves. Loyalties to the home plantation did not necessarily eliminate crime within the quarters, however. The presence of locks as theft deterrents merited considerable commentary from antebellum observers. Traveler William Thomson saw locks on slave cabins as necessities, "for they [the slaves] steal like rats." Charles Colcock Jones noted that "locks, bolts, and bars secure articles desirable to them, from the dwelling of the master to that of the servant, and the *keys*, must always be carried," while Olmsted remarked that lowcountry slaves "locked their outer doors, taking the keys with them" when they went out to the fields. Even though some masters may have provided such safeguards, it is worth noting that some bondpeople worried so much about depredations that they invested hard-earned money into purchasing locks of their own. Between 1829 and 1831, for example, three slave women purchased locks at 31 ¼, 25, and 25 cents a piece from their master, Thomas Ravenel. Thomas C. Law's slaves Rose and Boston invested in locks too, according to their master's 1859–1860 "Negro Book." And while slaves' suspicion might fall on white neighbors as well as black, the threat of thievery in the quarters brought potential discord to the community. Jacob Stroyer's commentary on this persistent problem is instructive here, providing readers with bondpeople's reaction to, condemnation of, and disciplinary action taken toward thieves in the neighborhood. As a community, he explained, the enslaved gathered to detect thieves among their ranks through a series of tests loosely based on principles of magic, conjure, and Christian doctrine. Clearly, some forms of illicit consumption fell beyond the bounds of acceptable behavior.[35]

---

[35] Brown, *Slave Life in Georgia*, 120; William Thomson, *A Tradesman's Travels, in the United States and Canada, in the Years 1840, 41, and 42* (Edinburgh: Oliver and Boyd, 1842), 189; Jones, *Religious Instruction of the Negroes*, 135; Frederick Law Olmsted, *Journeys and Explorations in the Cotton Kingdom. A Traveller's Observations on Cotton and Slavery in the American Slave States* (London: Sampson Low, Son, 1861), I: 237; Entries of November 1827, June 1831, and n.d. [torn ledger], unidentified account book, 1829–1833, Thomas Porcher Ravenel Papers, SCHS; Negro Book, 1859–1860, Thomas Cassells Law Papers, SCL; Stroyer, *My Life in the South*, 59–62. For more evidence of locks on the plantation, see Anderson Trial Papers: *State v. Andrew*, 4 May 1842; *State v. Sam*, 13 April 1850; *State v. Sam*, 20 January 1859, SCDAH.

Even though the moral considerations involved were significant, they were not the only challenges to consumption by theft. Charles Ball successfully rationalized his raids on others' property by arguing for slaves' appropriation of the fruits of their labor. He confessed to readers that he and fellow enslaved took peaches from their master's orchard at night and that he did not feel they had committed any wrong. He explained, however, that they did worry about the "common danger" they risked, knowing full well "the consequences that would follow detection." Just as slaveholders developed management strategies to deal with the reality of stealing, Ball and other enslaved men and women of the antebellum South altered market and consumer behavior to meet considerable and tangible risks that such activity entailed. It is worth noting that although the processes of motivation, rationalization, and justification undertaken by thieves and purchasers of pilfered items were likely very different, the risks they faced as possessors of these items and the strategies they used to avoid detection were necessarily similar. The vagaries of slave law and the capriciousness of many slaveholders meant that inconsistency marked the handling of cases in which slaves were found in possession of pilfered goods. Stealing, obviously, was frowned upon on the plantation and legislated against off the plantation. The laws were less clear, however, when it came to the prosecution of slaves who received stolen goods through purchase or trade. In July 1860, O. R. Broyles noted this oversight in an appeal to the South Carolina Court of Magistrates and Freeholders in which he argued for a stay of a sentence pronounced against his slave, Simon. The court had charged Simon with "Receiving Stolen Goods," found him guilty, and sentenced him to fifty lashes. Broyles argued that the court "had not charged him with any offence punishable by the law." After reviewing the case, the court agreed and repealed the sentence. Similarly, if a slave was found in possession of a stolen good, but during the trial was able to prove that he had indeed purchased the item, the charges would often, but not always, be dropped with no action taken against the slave.[36]

Slaves nevertheless took significant risks when they purchased stolen goods. Because states did not specifically legislate against black market purchases,

For historiographic debate over the meaning of locks on the plantation, see Genovese, *Roll, Jordan, Roll*, 606–607; Philip D. Morgan, *Slave Counterpoint: Black Culture in the Eighteenth-Century Chesapeake and Lowcountry, 1740–1790* (Chapel Hill: University of North Carolina Press, 1998), 113–114; Robert Olwell, *Masters, Slaves, and Subjects: The Culture of Power in the South Carolina Lowcountry, 1740–1790* (Ithaca, NY: Cornell University Press, 1998), 157; Lawrence T. McDonnell, "Money Knows No Master: Market Relations and the American Slave Community," in *Developing Dixie: Modernization in a Traditional Society*, eds. Winfred B. Moore, Jr., Joseph F. Tripp, and Lyon G. Tyler (Westport, CT: Greenwood Press, 1988), 37.

[36] Ball, *Slavery in the United States*, 205; Anderson Trial Papers: *State v. Simon, Alfred*, 14 July 1860. For a contemporary overview of slave law in South Carolina, see John Belton O'Neall, ed., *The Negro Law of South Carolina* (Columbia: John G. Bowman, 1848). For historical and legal analysis of the antebellum southern legal system, see Thomas Morris, *Southern Slavery and the Law, 1619–1860* (Chapel Hill: University of North Carolina Press, 1996).

punishment was meted out inconsistently. John, for example, was accused of stealing a lot of clothes from a South Carolina slaveowner in July 1860. During his interrogation, he "bitterly denied his guilt of housebreaking but acknowledged that he had worn a part of the clothes that had been taken." The freeholders, in a stunning example of the unevenness of the southern justice system, determined that "the prisoner is to some extent guilty," and sentenced him to thirty-five lashes for his transgression (although they did not identify the specific nature of that transgression). Furthermore, unless the actual thief was willing to admit that he had taken and then sold the item to the accused or, alternatively, others had witnessed the transaction, an accused slave would likely suffer stern punishment at the hands of the court.[37]

The possession and use of stolen goods clearly posed a risk to both perpetrators of thefts and those who purchased from them. Bondpeople caught with stolen property risked, at the very least, harassment or, at most, punishment by white authorities, be they slaves' masters, dreaded patrollers, or court-appointed constables. Patrollers, the bane of slaves throughout the antebellum South, possessed the right to enter slave cabins and rummage for stolen or contraband goods. In her study of slave patrols in the Carolinas and Virginia, historian Sally Hadden describes these searches in detail, explaining that patrollers could enter slave cabins at any time, overturn beds, explore beneath the floor boards, and demand the opening of boxes, trunks, and closets. Although, in practice, slaveholders resented such incursions and banned patrollers from their property, abuse of the system was rampant. Patrollers often administered beatings to slaves who possessed suspicious goods to elicit information or simply exert their authority. Petitions to southern legislatures reflected a conflicted image of the patrol. Even though they were considered vital to the security of white families and property, patrollers faced criticism from slaves and slaveholders who felt they abused their powers. Concerned with "the daring thefts and Roberies daily committed" by neighborhood slaves, residents of Nash County, North Carolina, and Buckingham County, Virginia, requested either the establishment and/or strengthening of patrol units as a means of controlling neighborhood depredations. Two Wayne County residents were more specific, asking the North Carolina legislature to extend the reach of Lenoir County surveillers, requesting that they "Patrol the Negro houses" in particular. But other slaveholders, as Hadden notes, resented patroller incursions on and against their property and, importantly, the property of their slaves. One Colleton District, South Carolina, slaveholder, for example, condemned patrollers who took his slaves' horses – property that they had acquired with their own money, but that was deemed suspicious by roving watchmen.[38]

---

[37] Anderson Trial Papers: *State v. John*, 11 September 1851, SCDAH.

[38] Sally E. Hadden, *Slave Patrols: Law and Violence in Virginia and the Carolinas* (Cambridge: Harvard University Press, 2001), 105–136; *Legislative Petitions*, North Carolina, Nash County, 21 November 1818 (PAR# 11281804); *Legislative Petitions*, Virginia, Buckingham County,

Only somewhat more restrained, court-appointed constables served warrants and conducted searches at the behest of the Court of Magistrates and
Freeholders. Aggrieved whites appealed to county magistrates who, in turn,
issued warrants for slaves that the "victim" named as suspects. As a result,
slaves were subject to search at even the slightest suspicion of impropriety. In
the case of a theft of flour and meat, for example, one deponent asked that
the "negro Houses, Kitchen, & other out Houses" of eleven separate South
Carolina plantations be searched.[39] As with the patrol system, whippings were
a routine method to compel slaves to acknowledge their guilt or to provide
information about a crime under investigation.[40]

Assumptions about both slaves' character and their tastes and capabilities
as consumers fueled the suspicions of patrollers and constables, making the
use of stolen goods risky at best. Ex-slave Robert Nelson expressed frustration
with this stereotype, one that followed him and other refugees even after they
fled to Canada. He explained that, for his white neighbors, "[i]t is very easy to
say when a thing is missed – 'O, 'tis some colored man stole it,' – although, it
has, to my knowledge, been proved, that when theft was charged on a colored
man, it turned out that a white man did it." Many a master would come "in
a-rarin' an' a-tarin'" with "his ridin' quirt" upon the slightest suspicion of a
theft, but others were more calculating. Agricultural journals urged slaveholders and overseers to hold their tempers, to calmly administer interrogations
and punishments. One slaveholder argued for patience, insisting that the best
way to ascertain a thief was to put the whole "crowd" on half allowances.
Another played on the superstitious nature of his slaves. Neal Upson remembered that his master, having lost some money, sorted out the "debbilment" by
having bondpeople line up and touch the head of a rooster contained in a coop
with his head sticking out. He claimed the rooster would crow at the touch of
the thief. An elderly couple held back from the affair; the master searched their
cabin and found the money. Such presumptions could lead to misidentifica-
tion of thieves. Caroline Seabury recounted the sad story of the brutal punishment of a young servant named Milly who was accused of stealing $20 from a
guest in a South Carolina boarding house. The northern teacher cringed as she
"heard him [the master] over & over in his rage say he would whip her till the
money was brought." As it turned out, the daughter of a neighboring planter
was eventually found with the money, but Milly's proximity to the crime scene,
along with her presumed proclivity toward theft, made her the one and only

March 1852 (PAR# 11685207); *Legislative Petitions*, North Carolina, 18 December 1830
(PAR# 11283001); *Legislative Petitions*, South Carolina, Colleton District, ca. 1824 (PAR#
11382413).
[39] Anderson Trial Papers: *State v. Lewis, Emily*, 27 January 1845, SCDAH.
[40] An example of such abuse can be seen in the trial and conviction of Sam, property of Elizabeth
Cowen, in March 1856. One of the constables appointed to the case testified that he "assisted
in *correcting* the Prisoner ... in order to make him tell if knew any thing about the money."
Anderson Trial Papers: *State v. Sam*, 28 March 1856, SCDAH.

suspect. In each of these cases, missing goods were associated with the slave population as a whole, thus making the process of acquisition and use of stolen property a perilous endeavor.[41]

Even though the process of detection often involved the population as a whole, individuals suffered most severely. Thieves not only felt the pain of the riding quirt, they acquired poor reputations as well, making consumption by illicit means even more difficult. Ella Thomas, for example, noted that Isabella, a family slave, had "an incurable habit of stealing" that prevented "one from placing any confidence in her." Asa Dupuy Dickinson expressed similar frustration with one of his family's slaves. Tired of suffering the "mortification and humiliation of having [his] neighbors continually coming to search for & find the fruits of his repeated robberies," Dickinson begged his brother to sell the slave. Even fellow slaves recognized that some individuals were more prone to theft than others. John Booth, for example, remembered a neighboring bond-woman, Charlotte, as an "incorrigible rogue." Likewise, Jacob Stroyer told the story of "Jim Swine," aptly named because of his love of purloined hogmeat. Jim's reputation made him the primary suspect in any local theft and, though he admitted his guilt on many occasions, he would occasionally face punishment when, in fact, he was innocent. Absconding following a beating sent a message to the community that, despite local perceptions of his character, his punishment was unjust. Earning an even more outrageous reputation was a slave named Rufe who was remembered as a man who "stole things he could not use, and which he had no way of turning into a gain of any kind."[42]

Stereotypes and individual reputation for theft surely added to the difficulties slaves faced as they attempted to acquire goods by illicit means. Adding to these problems were the presumptions many whites held about slaves' abilities as consumers and owners of property. Planters worried that unsupervised trade allowed slaves to possess items "under color of purchase which we know not whether they obtained honestly." They thus remained vigilant against perceived inconsistencies in the amount and quality of slave property ownership. Many whites imagined slave property, provisioned or bought, to include mundane provisions, negro cloth, and rude furniture. Slaves who possessed property considered beyond their means met immediate suspicion. Bondpeople who appropriated the goods of the marketplace, licitly or not, faced the appraisal

[41] Benjamin Drew, *A North-Side View of Slavery. The Refugee; or, The Narratives of Fugitive Slaves in Canada. Related by Themselves, with an Account of the History and Condition of the Colored Population of Upper Canada* (Boston: John P. Jewett, 1856), 371–372; Rawick, *American Slave,* 15, pt. 2: 171; "Management of Negroes," *Southern Cultivator* 13 (1855): 173; Rawick, *American Slave,* 13, pt. 4: 61; Caroline Seabury, *The Diary of Caroline Seabury, 1854–1863,* ed. Suzanne L. Bunkers (Madison: University of Wisconsin Press, 1991), 37–38.

[42] Ella Gertrude Clanton Thomas, *The Secret Eye: The Journal of Ella Gertrude Clanton Thomas, 1848–1889,* ed. Virginia Ingraham Burr (Chapel Hill: University of North Carolina Press, 1990), 157; Asa Dupuy Dickinson to William Purnell Dickinson, 21 October 1859, Asa Dupuy Dickinson Letter, VHS; Rawick, *American Slave,* 13, pt. 3: 191; Jacob Stroyer, *My Life in the South,* 52–53; Rawick, *American Slave,* Suppl. ser. 1, 11: 34–35.

of white neighbors who judged whether the acquired property fit within white conceptions of slave consumptive propriety and ability.[43]

Patrollers, in particular, were keen observers of slave property and took action if they deemed slaves' possessions inappropriate. For example, a number of slaves from South Carolina appeared before a court magistrate after patrol members found them using silver spoons to eat their evening meal.[44] Likewise, many whites became suspicious when slaves engaged in what they considered to be excessive purchasing, assuming that the slaves had acquired the cash illegally. In 1825, for example, Robert Dickeson became suspicious when Moses, one of his father's slaves, began spending a bit too freely. He explained to the Virginia legislature that although the slave Moses had been permitted to carry "on a continual traffic on his own account," Dickeson suspected that Moses had been involved in the robbery of $1000 from his former master, noting that the slave "had plenty of money ever afterwards." Similarly, South Carolina upcountry slave Madison faced questioning when he attempted to buy a gold ring for a female acquaintance. Had witnesses not testified that he "generally had money," Madison might not have escaped a guilty verdict.[45]

Our case study of upcountry South Carolina patterns of illicit consumption reveals that foodstuffs were the most frequently stolen items from plantations. Hence managers were particularly vigilant about what slaves ate. Depending on the master, this presumption of theft from plantation stores led to either intense questioning, whipping, or sometimes both. Allen Parker explained that slaves were sometimes caught as they cooked or ate contraband meals, because the master or overseer noticed that the food they were consuming was different than that allotted to them. Georgia ex-slave Levi Branham told a similar story. As a boy, he and his pals set off on a fishing expedition, fashioning dress pins into hooks and casting lines into the Conasauga River. Having little success, one of the boys spied a grapevine across the river and pulled on it. To their pleasant surprise, a fish basket full of trout emerged from the water. Excited by their find, the boys rushed home and "exhibited the fine fish to almost the whole plantation." That night, both white folks and slaves feasted on their catch. But soon after they finished eating, the owner of those baskets appeared, accusing the boys of stealing his fish. Although he was not sure how the man found them out, Branham surmised that "someone told him what fine fish they had seen a group of colored boys with."[46]

But it was not just the "fine" fish or other stolen goods that could raise suspicion; "fine living" could bring slaveholders snooping as well. Employed by his master as a fisherman, Charles Ball had taken advantage of the relative lack

---

[43] "Management of Negroes," *Southern Cultivator* 13 (1855): 173.

[44] *American Slave*, 15, pt. 2: 403; Spartanburg Trial Papers: *State v. Tim*, 15 January 1847.

[45] *Legislative Petitions*, Virginia, Russell County, 21 December 1825 (PAR# 11682510); Spartanburg Trial Papers, *State v. Madison*, 5 November 1850.

[46] Parker, *Recollections of Slavery Times*, 56–57; Levi Branham, *My Life and Travels* (Dalton, GA: A. J. Showalter, 1929), 6–7.

of oversight his job entailed and traded a passing boatman three hundred shad for one hundred pounds of bacon. Ball was cautious and had executed this plan for a number of months, but was very nearly found out. How? According to a group of neighborhood "gentlemen," Ball appeared to live too well, an almost certain indication that he had been stealing meat. Ball attempted to explain his healthy appearance to the group of men:

I was almost totally confounded at the name of meat, and felt the blood rush to my heart, but nevertheless forced a sort of smile upon my face, and replied, "My master has been very kind to all his people of late, but has not allowed us any meat for some weeks. We have plenty of good bread, and abundance of river fish, which, together with the heads and roes of the shad that we have salted at the landing, makes a very excellent living for us; though if master would please to give us a little meat now and then, we should be very thankful for it."

But his explanation failed to satisfy them and Ball's overseer insisted that he tell the truth – or at least a version of the truth that fit more squarely with their perception of slaves' well-being. The overseer insisted:

"Charles, you need not tell lies about it; you have been eating meat, I know you have, no negro could look as fat, and sleek, and black, and greasy, as you, if he had nothing to eat but corn bread and river chubs. You do not look at all as you did before you went to the fishery; and all the hands on the plantation have had as many chubs and other river fish as they could eat, as well as you, and yet they are as poor as snakes in comparison with you. Come, tell us the truth, let us know where you get the meat that you have been eating, and you shall not be whipped."

Despite his overseer's cajoling, Ball knew telling the truth would result in physical punishment and, as important, loss of his privileged position as a fisherman. He refused to give in to his inquisitors and relied on his wits to defuse the confrontation.

I begged the overseer and the other gentlemen not to ridicule or make sport of me, because I was a poor slave, and was obliged to live on bread and fresh water fish; and concluded this second harangue by expressing my thankfulness to God Almighty, for giving me such good health and strength as to enable me to do my work, and look so well as I did upon such poor fare; adding, that if I only had as much bacon as I could eat, they would soon see a man of a different appearance from that which I now exhibited. "None of your palaver," rejoined the overseer – "Why, I smell the meat in you this moment. Do I not see the grease as it runs out of your face?" I was by this time in a profuse sweat, caused by the anxiety of my feelings, and simply said, "Master sees me sweat, I suppose."

All the gentlemen present then declared, with one accord, that I must have been living on meat for a long time, as no negro, who had no meat to eat, could look as I did; and one of the company advised the overseer to whip me, and compel me to confess the truth.[47]

---

[47] Ball, *Slavery in the United States*, 314–315. Cf. Mark M. Smith, *How Race is Made: Slavery, Segregation, and the Senses* (Chapel Hill: University of North Carolina Press, 2006), 34–35.

As with Levi Branham and Allen Parker, Charles Ball had chosen to engage in illicit trade as a means of supplementing his meager provisions. Watchful whites deemed his diet, his health, his countenance, his very lifestyle, too good for the common slave. Ironically, theft as a means of consumption simultaneously elevated these bondmen's standard of living and introduced risks to their physical well-being.

By far the greatest risk a slave faced in possessing stolen goods was, paradoxically, their everyday use and display. Anthropologist Grant McCracken argues that consumers transfer meaning to acquired goods through possession rituals such as "cleaning, discussing, comparing, reflecting, showing off, and even photographing many of their new possessions." Slaves, no doubt, enacted these rituals daily as they displayed, wore, talked and bragged about, and consumed the goods that entered into the slave community. But slave consumers faced restrictions that McCracken does not envision in his theoretical study. To flagrantly consume and display the clothing, shoes, watches, jewelry, tools, and food items that entered the slave community through illicit means risked almost certain detection, loss of the goods, and often punishment.[48]

In some cases, consumers incurred punishment because they deliberately drew attention to themselves and, unwittingly, their crimes. Witnesses in a South Carolina court recalled that Lewis appeared on a neighbor's plantation with a silver watch (stolen from a shop a few weeks earlier) bragging that "he had as good a watch as any man." Others risked acquisitions through everyday use and wear. Mary Smith remembered one such incident from her childhood. One Sunday, as her family was preparing for church, her mother opened the drawer in which their clothes were held and found them missing. As the mother searched for the clothes and young Mary cried, a fellow slave returned from church and reported to Mary, her mother, and their master that "She saw Fannie dar wid all ma's clothes on." Fannie's master retrieved the stolen items, sent them back to their rightful owners, and whipped her. A similar incident occurred on John Harper's plantation one Saturday in September 1856. Dan, admiring George's shoes, offered to buy them, but was rebuffed. George awoke the next morning with his window open, the string to his shutters cut, and his shoes gone. Even though he had his suspicions, George did not make any accusations until the following week at Hopewell Church when he saw his shoes on Dan's feet. Stephen made an even more egregious mistake when it appeared he wore the shoes he was accused of stealing to his own trial for theft. Stephen's claim to have purchased the shoes a week earlier (not knowing they were stolen) fell on deaf ears and he was sentenced to twenty-five lashes with a hickory switch.[49]

---

[48] Grant McCracken, *Culture and Consumption: New Approaches to the Symbolic Character of Consumer Goods and Activities* (Bloomington: Indiana University Press, 1990), 85.

[49] Anderson Trial Papers: *State v. Lewis*, 20 July 1842, SCDAH; *American Slave*, 3, pt. 4: 112–113; Anderson Trial Papers: *State v. Dan*, 13 September 1856; *State v. Stephen*, 4 November 1845, SCDAH.

Consumers could also attach meaning to stolen goods by improving them, though such behavior sometimes attracted unwanted attention. For example, in 1838, Lewis faced a South Carolina court when he was caught with a stolen fiddle as he went to have it varnished for a friend. Bob pleaded ignorance to the same court thirteen years later when accused of stealing a watch from Baker Gentry, a neighboring white man. According to Jerry (who, luckily for Bob, confessed to the crime), Bob had purchased the watch from him a week earlier "for $15 to a pair of Shoes in part pay at $1.25, & Bob was some time that week three dollars and the balance." Apparently unaware that the watch was stolen, Bob took the watch to a local shop to have the crystal replaced, where the proprietor promptly confiscated it. In each of these cases, slaves openly used, discussed, or displayed black market goods without considering (or without knowing about) the consequences of their seemingly mundane actions. Those who successfully struck the balance between display and detection were able to reap the benefits of black market consumption; those who failed felt the sting of the constable's whip.[50]

Goods acquired through theft or black market purchase could serve as both means to increased wealth and damning evidence of unlawful behavior. Contractual agreements, even in the open marketplace, had always been risky for the enslaved; in this underground economy, risks involved in purchasing were even greater. Timothy Lockley and Jeff Forret have investigated the economic relationships between poor whites and the enslaved in Georgia and the Carolinas. According to Lockley, collaboration in property thefts and an extensive trade in stolen goods were hallmarks of relationships between poor whites and the enslaved of the Georgia lowcountry. Both nonracial class identification and racial animosity characterized these economic interactions, and illustrate the ambiguous and ambivalent nature of the relationships of the poorest members of southern society. Forret makes a similar argument regarding economic relationships in the Carolinas. According to Forret, although slaveholders perceived illicit economic interaction, and the thefts engendered by it, as a direct threat to their hegemony, such activities rarely challenged the bonds of racial solidarity, instead serving to fulfill basic material needs and wants of slaves and poor whites within their communities.[51] Clearly, interaction between slaves and poor whites hinged on trust and self-interest alike, thus making economic relationships profitable but often unstable. North Carolina slaveholder William Valentine pondered such risks when a local white man accused one of his slaves of offering him a stolen hog. Noting that oftentimes "white influence" caused slaves to steal when they otherwise would not, he

[50] Anderson Trial Papers: *State v. Phil*, 21 July 1838; *State v. Bob*, 14 August 1855, SCDAH.
[51] Timothy Lockley, *Lines in the Sand*, 108–119; Jeff Forret, "Slaves, Poor Whites, and the Underground Economy of the Rural Carolinas," *Journal of Southern History* 70 (2004): 783–824. See also Forret, *Race Relations at the Margins: Slaves and Poor Whites in the Antebellum Southern Countryside* (Baton Rouge: Louisiana State University Press, 2006).

counted himself lucky that the thief was caught. Others judged the perceived thriftlessness and lack of market savvy such illicit transactions revealed. A contributor to the *Southern Agriculturist* asked, with consternation, "what do the depredators get in exchange for this purloined property?" In his view, the half-diluted whiskey and "other trash of goods ... which they are compelled to take from fear of detection" were simply uneconomical, evidence of slaves' feckless and thoughtless character.[52]

Even though some planters seemed to believe that fellow slaves would never disclose a thief, bondpeople often tattled when faced with whipping or the possibility of personal reward. Despite portrayals of cohesive, collectively-empowered slave communities by John Blassingame, Herbert Gutman, and others, dissent and conflict could descend upon slave communities.[53] Self-interest or, at the very least, self-protection spurred some slaves to serve as informants to their masters, spoiling even the best-laid plans to avoid detection. Jacob Stroyer recounted such betrayals to readers of his narrative. In the case of "unfriendly" slave families sharing the same house, Stroyer explained, a thief would have to carry his plunder to the home of a trusted friend and carry only some of the meat to his own abode. Not surprisingly, this strategy often failed, with personal interest, envy, or simple dislike winning out over any sense of race or class solidarity. Court records from the South Carolina upcountry reveal

---

[52] Entry of 1 January 1851, vol. 11, William D. Valentine Diaries, SHC; A Practical Planter, "On the Management of Negroes," *Southern Agriculturist, and Register of Rural Affairs* 5 (1832): 182.

[53] Peter Kolchin, Lawrence McDonnell, and Clarence Walker have called on historians to re-evaluate their interpretations of the slave community. In a 1983 essay, Kolchin compared the American slave community with those in the Caribbean and serfs in Russia. Kolchin ultimately concluded that, in a comparative context, American slaves lacked a significant degree of community solidarity, thus undermining the claims of Blassingame, Morgan, Berlin, and others. In his view, many historians since the 1970s have painted unrealistic communal pictures of slave life and culture. See Peter Kolchin, "Reevaluating the Antebellum Slave Community: A Comparative Perspective," *Journal of American History* 70 (1983): 579–601. In *Deromanticizing Black History*, Walker criticized historians George Rawick, Herbert Gutman, John Blassingame, and others for their overly idyllic portrayals of slave life and culture. With regard to the slave "community," Walker argued that "the term is a romantic construct that obscures more than it reveals and posits community as an unproblematic *summum bonum* or *summum historicum*," and called on historians to elevate black history "above the romantic and celebratory." See Clarence Walker, *Deromanticizing Black History: Critical Essays and Reappraisals* (Knoxville: University of Tennessee Press, 1991), especially pp. i–xxvi. With regard to the internal economy specifically, Lawrence T. McDonnell has examined market relations on the plantation, implicitly questioning portrayals of a unified and harmonious "slave community." See Lawrence T. McDonnell, "Money Knows No Master: Market Relations and the American Slave Community," 31–44. Moreover, Dylan Penningroth has argued for acknowledgment of "internal diversity and conflict" within African-American communities as a means of evaluating the sum fabric of the black American experience. See Dylan C. Penningroth, *Claims of Kinfolk: African American Property and Community in the Nineteenth-Century South* (Chapel Hill: University of North Carolina Press, 2003), 187. See also Jeff Forret, "Conflict and the 'Slave Community': Violence among Slaves in Upcountry South Carolina," *Journal of Southern History* 74 (2008): 551–588.

similar betrayals. In September 1851, for example, Dick sent a key to Cornelius so that he could access Dick's trunk and send his clothes to him at his owner's house in Anderson. Upon opening the trunk, Cornelius found a watch, ascertained that it was the timepiece recently reported missing by a local shopowner, and promptly returned it to its rightful owner. Although the records do not reveal Dick's reaction to the indictment, a trial of another slave, four years later, serves as an example of the resentment that indicted slaves may have felt toward those who betrayed them. In November 1855, John compounded his troubles, and made his sentence harsher, when he assaulted Dan with a stick for reporting him to the authorities for stealing corn.[54]

When dealing with fenced goods, some amount of trust had to exist between purchaser and seller. Many slaves willingly purchased stolen goods and took care in using them to avoid trouble both for the thief and themselves. In their desire to make a profit, however, some slaves were less than forthright about the provenance of the goods they were selling, thus exposing unwitting purchasers to undue risk. In 1860, for example, John, a Virginia slave, sought to sell a lot of clothes, including a pair of "very nice pants" to neighboring bondpeople. Assured that the clothing had been freely given to John by his young master, Noah and Wilson bought a pair of pants and a coat respectively. Unbeknownst to them, the items had been recently stolen and, although they were not punished, the men lost both the property and the money they had spent on the contraband goods. South Carolina slave Clara was more cautious. In the winter of 1841, she rebuffed Nero's efforts to sell her a counterpane. The word in the quarter was that the bedding was stolen and that its owner, G. W. Masters, was on the lookout. In the trial for the theft, Clara explained to the court that she had overheard fellow slave Frank say that "Mr. Masters was searching for [the counterpane] but that he did not want to raise an interruption." Nero himself declared that he got the bedding from Ephraim, trading him for a coat. In the end, Nero was acquitted, but Ephraim's claim to have bought the contraband from yet another slave failed to convince the court and he suffered fifty lashes for the crime.[55]

We can observe all of the aforementioned risks – the use and display of stolen goods, the issue of trust between seller and buyer, the possibility of entrapment or overt tattling by fellow bondpeople – in an 1842 encounter in the South Carolina upcountry. A white man, Henry Lee, lost a lot of clothing and jewelry from his Spartanburg District residence. Wandering town the

[54] Jacob Stroyer, *Sketches of My Life in the South. Part I* (Salem, MA: Salem Press, 1879), 32; Anderson Trial Papers: *State v. Dick*, 4 September 1851; *State v. John*, 28 November 1855, SCDAH.

[55] Albemarle County Commonwealth Causes: *Commonwealth v. John Cox*, April 1860, LVA; Anderson Trial Papers: *State v. Nero, Frank, Ephraim*, 7 July 1842. For other examples of enslaved people attempting to use the market as an alibi, see Anderson Trial Papers: *State v. Lewis*, 14 March 1846, SCDAH; Spartanburg Trial Papers: *State v. Leslie, Martha, Isaiah*, 22 October 1853, SCDAH.

week after the break-in, he ran into Job, a slave from a neighboring plantation. As the enslaved man passed, a glint of gold caught Lee's eye – it was
one of his rings. Seeing that Lee "was noticing the ring," Job pulled his hand
back and walked away. Lee chose not to act immediately – he had lost a
good bit of property and wanted not only to punish Job but also to retrieve
his valuables. He concocted a plan, enlisting Abel, another slave, to trade
Job for whatever he had to offer. As it turned out, Job offered to sell one of
Lee's coats in return for a watch. Slyly, Abel asked whether "he should ware
it publickly," to which Job replied in the negative, that the aggrieved victim
was still about town.[56]

Even though Job fared poorly in this transaction, he and his fellow enslaved
recognized the risks of theft and black market consumption. Job and Abel's
discussion regarding wearing the jewelry "publickly" is just one example of
conversations that must have taken place between buyers and sellers of fenced
goods. Despite the lack of caution displayed by some slaves, bondpeople understood black market dangers and many articulated such sentiments in daily
affairs. Court testimony from South Carolina again provides us with a glimpse
of some of the concerns of consumers of contraband goods. One Saturday
night in May 1851, for example, Henry set out with a ticket presented to him
by Squire Croft to buy a few chickens for his evening meal. As he passed Reid
& Simpson's store, Joe approached him, "telling him to hold on a minute, that
he had some turkeys to sell him." Wary of the dangers of black market consumption, Henry asked Joe if the turkeys were his as "he did not want to get
into a scrape about the Turkeys." Joe assured him that he would buy the fowl
across the river and that "there would be no danger." In spite of his reserva-
tions, Henry consented, "giving Joe fifty Cents Cash a piece" for the fowl.
Willie and Aaron refused a similar temptation when Amos attempted to sell
them one of the twenty pairs of shoes he had stolen from a local shop. Despite
the reasonable price, they turned down his offer and urged Amos to take care,
that "he would be found out."[57]

A clearer articulation of such wariness occurred in an August 1845 trial,
when Anthony relayed a conversation he had had with a fellow slave regarding
the purchase of iron pieces. According to Anthony, "I told Charles to be cautious if he bought Iron of any black person at all the Reason why there are a
great many black persons making things and there will be the greatest fuss you
ever heard ... black people may go and git a bar of Iron and lay it away some
where and after think the fuss is all over – come and sell it to you and there will
be a fuss at last." Such were the risks of theft and black market consumption.
Anthony's statement is worth interrogating closely. First, he couched his warning in racial terms, recognizing that "black persons," whether they could justify

[56] Spartanburg Trial Papers: *State v. Job*, 5 November 1842, SCDAH.
[57] Anderson Trial Papers: *State v. Joe, Henry*, 5 May 1851, SCDAH; Anderson Trial Papers: *State
v. Amos*, 1 January 1852, SCDAH.

their actions or not, might draw suspicion. Secondly, he expressed concern that an opportunistic seller might deceive his friend. Finally, he worried that, even after time had passed, the open use, display, and discussion of the stolen iron might serve as evidence of his participation in illicit activity.[58]

Slaves like Charles and Anthony clearly had to create strategies with which they could derive benefit and meaning from black market goods, while avoiding detection and punishment by white authorities. Indeed, theft and evasion were learned skills, lamented by slaveholders and reformers. Charles Colcock Jones complained, "In multitudes of families, both by precept and example, the children are trained up in iniquity; taught by their parents to steal, to lie, to deceive; nor can the rod of correction induce a confession or revelation of their clearly ascertained transgressions." Charles Pinckney made a similar observation, condemning the "mischievous tendency of bad example in parents and elders," which teaches the slave child that "he may commit any vice he can conceal from his superiors." Thomas Clay unwittingly made a similar observation, urging planters to prohibit dog ownership by plantation slaves because the presence of packs of hungry animals provided immoral lessons to the enslaved children. He explained that the dogs "steal to escape starvation, and are then most unmercifully beaten: the children, seeing the cruelty of their parents, soon learn to imitate them, and both children and parents vent upon the poor animals, that passion which has been excited by some object beyond their power."[59]

The irony of this statement was clearly lost to Clay, but there is some truth to his description of parent-child interaction. Slave children learned the risks and rewards of black market consumption at an early age, acquiring many of the lessons of daily survival, not through textbooks and formal education, but through folklore. As Lawrence Levine and Sterling Stuckey have explained, songs and stories told by the enslaved to each other and passed to their children served a much larger purpose than that of simple entertainment. They conveyed both practical skills and meaning to the world around them. Kitty Hill, for example, remembered stories her mother told her of "patterollers ketchin' niggers an' whippin' 'em an' of how some of de men outrun de patterollers an' got away." Animal trickster tales, such as those about the cunning Br'er Rabbit, not only justified theft from whites but also posited the possibility

---

[58] Anderson Trial Papers: *State v. Anthony, Abram, Charles, and Teresa,* August 20, 1845, SCDAH.

[59] Jones, *Religious Instruction of the Negroes,* 113; Charles Cotesworth Pinckney, *An Address Delivered in Charleston, before the Agricultural Society of South-Carolina, at its Anniversary Meeting, on Tuesday, the 18th August, 1829* (Charleston: A. E. Miller, 1829), 11; Thomas S. Clay, *Detail of a Plan for the Moral Improvement of Negroes on Plantations* (n.p.: Georgia Presbytery, 1833), 17. This aptitude did not apply to religious and moral instruction, lamented James Ladson, who indicated that "the seed of divine truth sowed in childhood, makes but little growth in the period of youth," in *The Proceedings of the Meeting in Charleston, S.C., May 13–15, 1845, on the Religious Instruction of the Negroes,* 53.

that the weak could outwit the strong. Br'er Rabbit rarely failed to appropriate objects representative of status and power, and the fox or the bear was always humiliated by Rabbit's chicanery.[60]

As effectual as these animal tales were in conveying the possibilities inherent in theft and trickery, even more instructive, in practical terms, were the stories of Old John, the slave trickster. Lawrence Levine explains:

In John, slaves created a figure who epitomized the rewards, the limits, and the hazards of the trickster. He could improve his situation through careful deception, but at no time was he really in complete control; the rewards he could win were limited by the realities of the system within which he existed, and the dangers he faced were great. Time and again the more elaborate schemes of the slave trickster failed, and he saved himself only by last minute verbal facility and role playing – two qualities which these stories emphasized were crucial for all slaves to cultivate.[61]

In other words, John dealt with the challenges and risks facing the slave in his or her everyday life. And it is here that we see most clearly instruction on the risks and strategies of theft and black market consumption. Consider the oft-told slave tale of "John and the Pig."

John stole a pig from Old Marsa. He was on his way home with him and his Old Marsa seen him. After John got home he looked out and seen his Old Marsa coming down to the house. So he put this pig in a cradle they used to rock the babies in them days (some people called them cribs), and he covered him up. When his Old Marster come in John was sitting there rocking him.

Old Marster says, "What's the matter with the baby, John?" "The baby got the measles." "I want to see him." John said, "Well you can't; the doctor said if you uncover him the measles will go back in on him and kill him." So his Old Marster said, "It doesn't matter; I want to see him, John." He reached down to uncover him.

John said, "If that baby is turned to a pig now, don't blame me."[62]

In this popular folktale, the cunning slave trickster John purloined his master's property and used his wits in an effort to evade detection. On this occasion, as in many John tales, the trickster was caught red-handed. Did John escape a whipping? Was he able to keep the pig? The abruptness of the punchline cuts short the story but antebellum hearers learned a set of valuable lessons. The risks of illicit behavior, in this case, theft, were real. Enslaved persons needed to cultivate practical strategies, among them the skills of quick thinking and verbal aptitude, to deal with the difficulties and challenges associated with black market consumption.

---

[60] Levine, *Black Culture and Black Consciousness,* 81–135; Sterling Stuckey, "Through the Prism of Folklore: The Black Ethos in Slavery," *Massachusetts Review* 9 (1968): 417–437; Stuckey, *Slave Culture: Nationalist Theory and the Foundations of Black America* (New York: Oxford University Press, 1987); Rawick, *American Slave,* 14, pt. 1: 424.

[61] Levine, *Black Culture and Black Consciousness,* 127–128.

[62] Richard M. Dorson, ed., *American Negro Folktales* (Greenwich, CT: Fawcett, 1956), 137–138.

The enslaved drew on folktale lessons as a means of balancing consumption and evasion.[63] Among the available options was simply to limit the immediate public display of the stolen items, sequestering them until needed. Patience, in other words, was key to the proper use and consumption of goods procured through illicit means (a characteristic, it is worth noting, many slaveholders presumed lacking in black people's "intemperate" and "improvident" natures). In 1847, Spartanburg slave Lum explained to South Carolina officials that Frank and Wiley had given him a lot of stolen clothes "for safe keeping," and that he should not "say anything." He did not stay quiet enough, however, and was convicted along with the two others for the theft. In October 1850, two other Spartanburg slaves stashed their cache of stolen bacon in a gully, while neighboring slave Jefferson hid a stolen sack of wheat under "the fodder" in an "old house," until his potential accomplice Green could "sell it to whoever would buy it." Slaveholders were aware of such behavior and often despaired at their inability to find goods they were convinced bondpeople had stolen. Some slaves, such as Ellen from Albemarle County, Virginia, were simply too clever for local whites. Paul Goodloe, her master, warned the court, "[i]f she had any hand in stealing anything you will never find it – Her faculties for hiding are very great."[64]

Other slaves chose to keep their property close at hand in locked closets, trunks, and boxes in their own cabins. Jim, for example, stored stolen meat in a locked box in his cabin and Dick locked a stolen watch in a trunk. Harry admitted to "concealing" three pecks of wheat in a "chest or box by driving in the steeple [sic]." Patrollers and constables often ransacked slave cabins and demanded access to such containers. Slaves' continued use of lockable trunks and boxes to sequester stolen goods, however, indicates that they may have provided a needed (though sometimes unsuccessful) level of protection and security in the slave quarters.[65]

Finally, some slaves deliberately chose to sequester goods for long periods in hopes that the crime would be forgotten and the presence of the items ignored,

---

[63] The strategies outlined in this chapter are representative of those that were commonly used by slaves who participated in the black market economy. Much of the evidence for these strategies derives from the South Carolina Court of Magistrates and Freeholders. While these records serve as an invaluable window into everyday slave life and culture and provide wonderful descriptions of the strategies that slaves employed to evade detection and punishment by white authorities, a caveat is in order. Most of the specific strategies drawn from the court records necessarily failed – if the slaves had been successful in their endeavors, they would not have faced trial. They therefore serve as examples of the range of strategies forged by slaves as they sought to balance consumption and evasion.

[64] Spartanburg Trial Papers: *State v. Harriet, Judy, Tom, Bob, Liza, Perry, Jourdan, Tallon, Frank, Jack, Wiley, Jim, Lum*, 6 October 1847; *State v. Mathew, Toby*, 10 October 1850; *State v. Jefferson*, 19 January 1850, SCDAH; Albemarle County Commonwealth Causes: *Commonwealth v. Jim Shelton*, 3 February 1858, LVA.

[65] Anderson Trial Papers: *State v. Jim*, 6 May 1852; *State v. Dick*, 4 September 1851; *State v. Isaac, Harry*, 1 August 1839.

thereby allowing them to consume, use, and display them without consequence. Charles, for example, hid a $50 bill "secretly for four or five weeks" before attempting to get it changed, while a group of South Carolina slaves moved goods stolen from a local shop from house to house in hope of derailing white searches for the lost property. In each of these cases, white memories were long and efforts to evade detection failed, a perpetual risk that this strategy could not always overcome.[66]

In lieu of, or in addition to, sequestering stolen goods, slaves altered significant aspects of the consumption process, in some cases manipulating the appearance of a stolen item so that it could be used publicly without suspicion. A number of cases from the South Carolina Magistrates and Freeholders courts reveal the careful and creative means some slaves took to ensure they could safely use a stolen item. In 1855, for example, Henry bought a (stolen) gold watch from Dick for $10, two pairs of pantaloons, and a waistcoat. Upon receipt of the timepiece, Henry promptly painted the hands of the watch black with carriage paint. Even though he claimed that he darkened the formerly gold hands in order to "tell what time of night at night," the change in the watch's appearance also served to diminish the chance that the timepiece would attract attention from those looking for the purloined object. A similar event occurred in May 1856. W. Todd returned home from a camp meeting to find the latch and lock to his door broken and a number of possessions, including a single barrel shotgun, missing. Within a week, a local slaveholder found a gun in the possession of one of his slaves and presented it to the aggrieved Todd. Upon inspection, Todd indicated that the gun was indeed his, but complained to the court that it was "considerably damaged and disfigured, six or seven inches of the muzzle having been cut off." Although the deponents did not indicate whether the gun was functional, they commented on the exceptional workmanship of the thief, one witness noting that he "had to take his specks to ascertain the fact" that the muzzle had been filed off the gun.[67]

Apparently lacking the skills that Phil possessed, in March 1846, William Nevitt's Ellen hired a local seamstress to alter a dress she had stolen from the home of James Stiles. Per the bondwoman's urgent request, the seamstress "made the body larger and longer in the waist – ripped it out and made it 2 inches longer and larger." More important than adjusting the size, however, the seamstress also changed the appearance of the dress, straightening the sleeves and attaching three bands, removing the tucks, and creating a new collar. Even though Elizabeth Stiles, upon close inspection, identified the dress as

[66] Anderson Trial Papers: *State v. Charles*, 2 August 1855, SCDAH; Spartanburg Trial Papers: *State v. Armstead, Asa, Oliver, Henry, Isaac Hardy, and Ben*, 6 January 1842, SCDAH.

[67] Anderson Trial Papers: *State v. Dick*, 10 September 1851; *State v. Phillip*, 18 May 1856, SCDAH. English laborers engaged in similar alteration strategies. According to Beverly Lemire, some thieves and secondhand purchasers cut up stolen cloth into scraps, made shirtsleeves out of aprons, and made a table cloth out of a petticoat, all in order to reap the benefits of their

her own, she testified that "the dress being altered, it does not look natural." James Cochran found even more extreme changes made to a fiddle stolen from him by a bondman named Phil. Having retrieved the stolen item, Cochran found a different bridge attached to the instrument, "a piece of wood to which the strings were fastened removed, which piece of wood had the letters J. C. on has been removed, & now on it situated in its stead."[68]

The case of James Cochran's fiddle is significant not simply because of the extent of the changes made to the stolen item, but because of the quality of those alterations. McCracken has explained that one of the ways consumers invest meaning in goods that have been owned by others is through "divestment rituals" that "allow the new owner to avoid contact with the meaningful properties of the previous owner and to 'free up' the meaning properties of the possession and claim them for themselves." Divestment ritual is evident in much post-theft activity, but the fiddle is striking because Phil took extra care to remove the mark that identified the object with James Cochran. In practical terms, this action not only lessened the chance that he might lose his new acquisition to white authorities, it was also the first step in claiming this new piece of property for himself.[69]

In addition to the alteration of stolen goods, bondpeople adjusted the ways in which they prepared stolen foodstuffs. "Mad" Griffin recalled that he and his fellow slaves would attempt to steal a hog every Saturday night, dragging the carcasses off "to de gully what us'd to git him dressed and barbecued." Uncertain that their efforts would be enough to avoid detection, "Conjin Doc" put "a spell on ole Marse so dat he wuz 'blevin ev'y think dat us tole him bout Sa'day night and Sunday morning." Unfortunately for Griffin and his friends, "Marse come out from under de spell," began counting his hogs, and soon caught and punished the men. Other men and women enacted strategies reminiscent of ones described in slave folktales. For example, after having butchered and dressed a stolen sheep "by the light of the moon," an acquaintance of Charles Ball boiled the mutton in a large kettle in the plantation kitchen. Unfortunately for the hungry slave, his master arrived home well after midnight and saw the blazing fire through the chinks in the kitchen walls. Anxious to avoid detection, the slave stripped the shirt off his back and threw it into the pot, explaining to his master that he was merely doing his laundry. A leg sticking out from the boiling water spoiled his plan, however, and he faced a beating for his crime. Equally quick thinking saved a slave woman from

purchase without risking the chance of detection. Lemire, "The Theft of Clothes and Popular Consumerism," 268–269.

[68] Anderson Trial Papers: *State v. Ellen*, 27 March 1846; *State v. Phil*, 21 July 1838, SCDAH.

[69] McCracken, *Culture and Consumption*, 87. We can see this process at work in a case involving branding. Henry and Allen of Pickens District, South Carolina, changed the brands on a pig and claimed it as their own, thus transferring meaning and property rights from the previous owner to themselves. Pickens District, Magistrate and Freeholders Court, Trial Papers: *State v. Henry and Allen*, 9 February 1853, SCDAH.

certain punishment at the hands of a prying overseer. In possession of a stolen hog with the overseer headed toward her door, the old woman tossed the pork meat, "blood and all," into a tub of "persimun" beer, just in time for the overseer to search her cabin. Pleased to see no evidence of contraband, the man downed a dram, pronounced her brew to be "the very best beer I ever in my life tasted," and rewarded her skill with a shilling.[70]

Consumption of stolen food bore particular risks, as both the cooking and storage of perishable food items, particularly meat, gave off suspicious odors. Slaves had to suppress these smells in order to avoid detection. Take, for example, Charles Ball's acquisition of bacon described earlier in this chapter. Ever cautious, Ball buried the meat in a barrel underneath his cabin. He "enjoined our people never to fry any of the meat, but to boil it all," explaining that "no one can smell boiled bacon far; but fried flitch can be smelled a mile by a good nose." Thus, in order to enjoy the benefit of the purloined foodstuffs, Ball and his cohorts had to alter the taste and texture of the bacon. But even these precautions were not enough for some slaves. Bondpeople hid meat in "pit[s] dug under the hearth" and learned to bury feathers from stolen chickens rather than burn them, because "if you burned 'em de white folks would smell 'em." They cured meat with shucked corn, thereby preventing spoilage and attracting unwanted attention from suspicious whites. Others found that handling carcasses away from the plantation proved the safest and most efficient means of consuming stolen meat. Jacob Stroyer and his cohorts hid slaughtered and stolen hogs in the leaves until night when they could sneak back, retrieve the meat, and dress it back in the cabins under cover of darkness. Similarly, a runaway interviewed by the *Emancipator* explained that after killing a pig, his partners would bury the carcass and "get it as it was wanted," while others would simply secret the contraband off to another plantation to have it cooked.[71]

If the difficulties of sequestering or altering goods were too great, or if the plundered goods did not fulfill requisite needs or desires, slaves could use the market itself to convert booty into more fluid and anonymous cash. This strategy had the potential benefit of passing on risks associated with possession of stolen goods to another buyer without forfeiting monetary value. In describing his father's desire to buy liquor, Ben Horry explained that "he ain't have money but he have the rice barn key and rice been money!" Aaron and Berry likewise recognized the possibilities in black market trade as they excitedly discussed the possibility of "getting pay for" the meat they had recently stolen. Similarly, Crescia had originally planned "to make something" out of the coat stolen by

[70] Rawick, *American Slave*, 2, pt. 1: 2–3; Ball, *Fifty Years in Chains*, 80–81; Frances Fedric, *Slave Life in Virginia and Kentucky; or, Fifty Years of Slavery in the Southern States of America* (London: Wertheim, Macintosh, and Hunt, 1863), 13–14.
[71] Ball, *Slavery in the United States*, 303–304; *American Slave*, Suppl. ser. 1, 4, pt. 2: 345; Rawick, *American Slave*, 12, pt. 2: 322; *American Slave*, Suppl. ser. 1, 3, pt. 1: 70; Stroyer, *My Life in the South*, 48–49; "Recollections of a Runaway Slave," *The Emancipator*, 13 September 1838.

her mother, Julia, but instead "kept it concealed til Toby came down and took the coat and sold it to a Col'd man in Greenville." The records do not indicate what relationship Toby had with the two women, but Julia noted that "he comes regularly every two weeks" and that before he left he told the women that "he intended to get what he could for it." Even though the deponents in these two South Carolina court cases failed to reap the benefits of black market trade, Allen Parker provides us with an example of strategy successfully enacted. Parker stole a pig, dressed it, and had a "poor white" sell it for him. According to Parker, "With this money, I bought some cloth, which a white woman made into a coat and a pair of pants for me. A few days afterwards I wore my new clothes to a 'big meeting,' ... the fact that they were paid for with stolen goods did not trouble me at all."[72]

Parker's story is significant not only because he concealed his crime but also because he collaborated across racial lines. Bondpeople throughout the antebellum South could manipulate white fears and insecurities about class to their own advantage in illicit economic endeavors. In other words, slaves knew that one of the easiest ways to acquire and keep their goods, especially hogs and chickens, was to take advantage of the illicit economy's shifting alliances by acting in concert with whites themselves. As Lockley and Forret have demonstrated, slaves could increase material well-being by convincing local whites that covering for a crime or engaging in black market exchange worked to their benefit. But slaves could acquire goods as a result of masters' self-interest and duplicity as well. Some slaveholders, in fact, urged bondpeople to steal – from other planters of course – going so far as to educate and even assist their slaves in the art of theft and evasion. Both masters and slaves were well aware of their states' search and seizure laws, and took full advantage of the ability to hide plunder amidst the stores of masters. Isaac Green was told to "go out an' hunt me a hog tonight an' put it in my smokehouse – dey can search you niggers' house but dey can't search mine." A South Carolina slaveholder urged his bondpeople to act in a similar manner. Not only did he allow his slaves to hide plunder in his "apartment," he allowed his victimized neighbor to search the cabins, all the while maintaining that his "boys don't steal."[73]

Such assistance was, of course, conditional. Even though some masters would allow their slaves to hide stolen goods amidst plantation stores, responsibility for acquiring the items lay in the hands of the thieves themselves. Southern honor and neighborhood reputation trumped loyalty to their charges. Slaves faced the lash if detected, worse if they indicted their masters. Escaped slave Harriet Jacobs explained to readers that many a master would

---

[72] Rawick, *American Slave*, 2, pt. 2: 309; Anderson Trial Papers: *State v. Aaron, Berry*, 31 March 1860; *State v. Crescia, Toby*, 27 August 1851, SCDAH; Allen Parker, *Recollections of Slavery Times*, 77.

[73] Rawick, *American Slave*, 12, pt. 2: 58; Stroyer, *My Life in the South*, 28–29. For another example of masters collaborating with their slaves to steal goods – in this case, cotton – see "Letter to the Editor," *Columbia (SC) Telescope*, 21 January 1834.

indignantly defend an accused thief, feigning personal insult with the claim that his slaves simply had no reason or inducement to steal. Far from escaping punishment, however, the accused could always expect a whipping, not for the theft itself, but for "his lack of discretion" in committing the act. Poor whites, already frustrated with depredations of their stores, were equally exasperated with the hypocrisy of some members of the planter class. In 1832, sixty-seven Buckingham County residents called on the Virginia legislature to act, complaining that some slaveholders "encourage [their slaves] to steal various things, such as hogs, corn, poultry, etc." Further, "some owners live partly by their slaves stealing; and the owners themselves steal, and when arrested for it, place the burden on their slaves." The petitioners asked that, at the very least, the state refuse to compensate planters for slaves executed for commission of a felony.[74]

A pattern of continuous adjustment to the vagaries and realities of slaveholder and market law marked slaves' economic lives. Denied the fruits of the labor they undertook for their masters, they carved out new opportunities, fulfilling immediate material desires through informal economic channels. Faced with restrictions on spending, some slaves turned to theft as an additional means of acquiring goods. Whether they stole as an overt form of resistance or whether they laid hands on that which they thought rightfully belonged to them, bondpeople greatly expanded the consumer realm through participation in black market exchange. But here, too, slaves faced limits. The very use and display of their plunder risked the sting of the whip and loss of acquisitions. So slaves made adjustments once more, altering consumption strategies to meet the risks and realities of theft and illicit trade.

The process, indeed, was unending. Theft plagued masters and they devised measure after measure to deal with the problem. They locked doors, they threatened the whip, they upped provisions, they provided opportunities for trade that they thought might reduce the temptation to steal. They also criticized their slaves, cloaking laments and frustrations in a language of paternalist concern. Moral economy, as Thompson – and Lichtenstein – have conceived it, can only partially explain the tumultuous power dynamic that marked the master-slave relation. Elizabeth Fox-Genovese argued as much in a thoughtful but cutting critique of Thompson, noting that his theory of moral economy depended upon an overly romantic and unrealistically harmonious understanding of the old paternalist social order. Read this way, she contended, "the 'moral economy of the crowd' begins to look more like the prudence of the magistrates than pure, disinterested social conscience." The slaveholders of the Old South were standard bearers of this order. Certainly, slaves challenged and checked their masters' power through maddening and destructive everyday

---

[74] Brown, *Slave Life in Georgia*, 22; Harriet Jacobs, *Incidents in the Life of a Slave Girl. Written by Herself*, ed. Lydia Maria Francis Child (Boston: Printed for Author, 1861), 71–72; *Legislative Petitions*, Virginia, Buckingham County, 19 January 1832 (PAR# 11683204).

acts of theft and disobedience. Anxiety and frustration pushed slaveholders to make concessions they might never have considered otherwise. But in all of this, the slaveowner could find redemption – and validation of his mastery. Although, in practical terms, slaves' economic behavior changed the ways in which slaveholders executed their rule, these same behaviors at once justified their responsibility to do no less.[75]

---

[75] Elizabeth Fox-Genovese, "The Many Faces of Moral Economy: A Contribution to a Debate," *Past and Present* 58 (1973): 167.

5

Gilt Chains

"The gift-making seasons were times of pleasure to the children of the family," Jennie Stephenson recalled thirty years after Appomattox, "as well as to the servants." The Christmas merriment she described on her father's Virginia farm typifies depictions of year-end festivities in white southern memoirs. "Father was a firm, but a kind Master," she insisted, and no moment proved her point better than the holidays. Throughout the long year of work and worry that brought the plantation to harvest time, Charles Friend had guided his servants as a true paternalist, finding his "right to own slaves" in the Bible but feeling the "responsibility physically, morally, and spiritually" to lead them with the good government of a father. He ordered labor – and perhaps lashes too – but also bestowed blessings on marriages, provided medical services, and turned his charges toward church on Sundays. At the end of this year-long "fatiguing duty," the master's bounty knew no ebb. Slaves roused the white family early, awaiting a sumptuous morning feast. The "eager faces" of mothers and their "tots" milling around the Big House, marveling at gifts of "lace collars, coffee-mills, and rattles" formed a "bright picture" in memory. Celebration would last throughout the day, Stephenson recalled fondly, until evening's rituals began. In the "twilight ... all who took part in the harvest" gathered round the door "for money from Master." Among Stephenson's dearest memories was the sight of her father "bending over a chair filled with piles of coin, with a list of names in one hand, and with the other counting the money." While she saw evidence of generosity in this happy scene at day's end – mothers admiring their tatting, men counting their money, children "somer-sault[ing] on the grass" – more complex calculations were always at work. From the "bright picture" of gifts given in morning to the shadowed scene of payment at night, a politicized spectrum of exchange bookended the day. Embedded within this sentimental portrait of masterly beneficence, Stephenson highlighted her family's role on this occasion – and in all things – not just as gift givers, but as their slaves' "white auditors."[1]

Even in this most nostalgic of scenes, paternalist tension dynamized the master-slave relation. The "gift-making" season brought bounty to the quarters and broadcast the largesse of the master, slaves and slaveholders throughout the South could agree. Yet, as Stephenson's shuffling characterization of master as both benefactor and "auditor" superbly shows, no exchange was without cost. Every item transmitted between black and white came with strings – indeed, chains – attached, necessarily entangling both parties. Historians have only begun to divine the meaning of such ritual, focusing attention more on Christmas tradition than on the meaning of the presents that drew so much holiday focus.[2] Their descriptions hint at the confoundingly multivalent nature of gift exchange, but few have considered carefully the price men and women paid. In the liminal sphere of exchange – especially in the Old South – the boundary between gift and commodity was maddeningly fuzzy, subject to both sleight of hand and masquerade.

Scholars of gift theory[3] have sorted and sifted such distinctions, offering useful insights on antebellum southern political economy. There is, however, nothing like consensus in this group. On one side, neoclassical economists argue that gifts most often serve as payment for past favors or investment in future returns. They draw on theorists like Adam Smith and David Ricardo, who saw commodity exchange as universal, present in all transactions.[4] Some anthropologists

---

[1] Jane Minge (Friend) Stephenson, "My Father and His Household, Before, During and After the War," 1897, Section 3, Blanton Family Papers, VHS.

[2] See Shauna Bigham and Robert E. May, "The Time O' All Times? Masters, Slaves, and Christmas in the Old South," *Journal of the Early Republic* 18 (1998): 263–288. In *The Battle for Christmas*, Stephen Nissenbaum provides an exceptionally thoughtful analysis of Christmas gift-giving in plantation communities. My analysis extends and builds upon the discussion of the "gestures of paternalism" he introduces in a concluding chapter on Christmas in the Old South. Nissenbaum, *The Battle for Christmas: A Cultural History of America's Most Cherished Holiday* (New York: Vintage Books, 1996), 258–300. Kenneth S. Greenberg has situated gift-giving in the culture of southern honor, exploring the ways in which white men used gifts to strengthen local ties. Greenberg, *Honor and Slavery: Lies, Duels, Noses, Masks, Dressing as a Woman, Gifts, Strangers, Humanitarianism, Death, Slave Rebellions, the Proslavery Argument, Baseball, Hunting, and Gambling in the Old South* (Princeton: Princeton University Press, 1996), 51–86.

[3] The interdisciplinary literature on gift-giving is vast and it is impossible to explore all its permutations here. Instead, I use the definitional debate over gifts and commodities to help frame my study. For a useful discussion of the distinctions between the theory of commodities as explained by political economists like Adam Smith and David Ricardo and the theory of gifts as interpreted by anthropologists like Marcel Mauss and Claude Levi-Strauss, see Christopher A. Gregory, *Gifts and Commodities* (London: Academic Press, 1982), 10–28. For a more recent – and exceptionally cogent – elaboration, see Seth Mallios, *The Deadly Politics of Giving: Exchange and Violence at Acajan, Roanoke, and Jamestown* (Tuscaloosa: University of Alabama Press, 2006), 25–36.

[4] Margaret Jane Radin has sharply criticized neoclassical theorists for promoting a "worldview" of "universal commodification." Legal academics like Gary Becker and Richard Posner,

and sociologists, by contrast, point to the growth of social ties that gift exchange engenders. In his seminal study of exchange systems in Melanesia, Polynesia, and the American Northwest, French sociologist Marcel Mauss argued this point explicitly, explaining that each gift is imbued with the *hau*, or spirit, of the giver. By transmitting this token of personhood, gift-giving becomes a cyclical – and intensely political – process, creating obligations to give, receive, and return.[5] Far from disinterested and philanthropic, gifts demand reckoning, serving as tangible evidence and magical affirmation of political ties and, in the case of the unrequited, political subordination. Scholars have elaborated on this theory of reciprocity, categorizing gifts as "tie signs" between individuals, and studying societies in which gifts prove central to binding the community and keeping the peace.[6] It is important here to note distinction between the reciprocity engendered by gift exchange and the more fanciful notion of a "free gift" – a gift without attendant obligations. Scholars have struggled with this concept, attempting to identify circumstances under which such transactions might possibly occur, with most conceding that "the perfect gift, like most perfection, remains an ideal more than a reality in our gift giving."[7]

Much of this discussion pivots on the political and economic nature of the gift itself, its root in its intrinsic inalienability. "[C]ommodities are *alienable* objects transacted by aliens," anthropologist Christopher Gregory explains. That is, buyer and seller trade goods alone, explicitly ignoring past, present, or future ties to the object or each other. The movement of private property, then, underscores distinctions between groups and individuals. By contrast, "[g]ifts are *inalienable* objects transacted by non-aliens." The spirit of the giver can be isolated neither from the good nor the transactors themselves. In contrast to commodity trade, gift exchange creates and solidifies a near indissoluble bond between giver and recipient. Put simply, gifts bind; commodities alienate.[8]

---

for example, "assume everything people value is (or should be) ownable and salable." Gifts fall well within their definition of commodity. Margaret Jane Radin, *Contested Commodities* (Cambridge: Harvard University Press, 1996), 3, 6.

[5] Marcel Mauss, *The Gift: The Form and Reason for Exchange in Archaic Societies*, trans. W. D. Halls (New York: W. W. Norton, 1990).

[6] See, for example, Erving Goffman, *Relations in Public: Microstudies of the Public Order* (New York: Basic Books, 1971), 188–237.

[7] Russell W. Belk, "The Perfect Gift," in *Gift Giving: A Research Anthology*, eds. Cele Otnes and Richard F. Beltramini (Bowling Green, OH: Bowling Green State University Popular Press, 1996), 76. See also James G. Carrier, *Gifts and Commodities: Exchange and Western Capitalism since 1700* (London: Routledge, 1995), 157–159.

[8] Gregory, *Gifts and Commodities*, 43. Gregory's discussion of "alienability" draws both explicitly and implicitly from Karl Marx. The "corollary," Gregory argues, "of [Marx's definition of commodity exchange] is that non-commodity (gift) exchange is an exchange of inalienable things between transactors who are in a state of reciprocal dependence." Karl Marx, *Capital*, 3 vols. (Moscow: Progress Publishers, 1977), I: 91; Gregory, *Gifts and Commodities*, 12. For further discussion of "alienable" and "inalienable" exchange, see Radin, *Contested Commodities*, 16–29; Annette B. Weiner, *Inalienable Possessions: The Paradox of Keeping-While Giving* (Berkeley: University of California Press, 1992).

How can this debate help us understand life in the Old South? Abstracted from reality and posed as antagonistic poles on the spectrum of exchange, theoretical definitions of gifts and commodities obscure the complexity at the heart of the master-slave relation. After all, vicissitudes of everyday life and exchange sustained this world of constant contest. To understand the centrality of gift exchange in this time and place, we have to reintegrate the thick description so effectively deployed by anthropologists and the theoretical analysis of classical political economists. Contextualized within particular space, time, and political relations, gifts and commodities rarely hewed to idealized forms. On antebellum plantations, what was gift and what was commodity was up for grabs with parties on all sides looking to impose definitions according to their own self-interest. Under constant revision and manipulation, rituals of gift-giving on southern plantations reveal the ways in which expectation – both realized and challenged – bound masters and slaves together.

Commodity exchange via payment for overwork might serve temporarily to satisfy the material desires of their workforce, but it was the inalienable nature of gift exchange masters valued most. Unsurprisingly, slaveholders desired above all else to build bonds between master and slave. Presumably, if a slave could be convinced to merge self-interest with that of the master, he would work more efficiently and increase the production of the plantation. In more practical terms, slaves with close ties to their master would not run away, or if they did, most would soon head back home, as they did overwhelmingly, after a few days laying out. Further still, when slaves came to identify their economic well-being with the masters' flourishing interests, the planter class had momentarily won its ultimate and most appalling political victory. This achievement required careful and constant strategizing. Slaveholders worked tirelessly to render all transactions – from the disbursement of provisions to wage payment and commodity purchase to gift exchange – inalienable. In doing so, they redrew the boundaries of material exchange incessantly, both underlining distinctions, real and dubious, and erasing them to take advantage of the imagined binding qualities of the gift.

But what made a gift? Extra allowances of grain, meat, salt, or sweeteners spill out everywhere from planter journals, prescriptive literature, and narratives, particularly at Christmastime. Compared to the rest of the year, the holidays were times of "plenty." Writing to her cousin Mary in 1871, Sarah Payne contrasted hardships on her family's Campbell County, Virginia, plantation with "Old time" Christmases of years past. A "merry frolicking time for old and young, white and black," she recalled, the holiday season began with the distribution of "meat and lard flour," making sure Christmas feasts were abundant. Lowcountry planter Plowden C. J. Weston was more precise and gave his slaves "Christmas allowance[s]" of salt, molasses, rice, and meat. His bondpeople could expect such provision over the course of the year, but Weston made particular note of this special holiday ration. Fellow rice planter

John Milikin followed a similar schedule, issuing an additional quart of molasses and 12 quarts of rice during the celebrating season. Slaves, too, noted a superabundance of ordinary provisions. Ex-slaves like John Smith remembered that he "had plenty to eat, shoes etc." at Christmas. James Bolton recalled the holiday with similar fondness, explaining "Christmas we allus had plenny good sumpin' teat." Certainly not all were lucky enough to collect such bounty, but there were those also who were more exacting. Jefferson Franklin Henry explained to WPA interviewers that there was "only plenty to eat and drink," but "thar warn't nothin' extra or diffunt give" at Christmas. In account after account, it was the qualitative "extra" not the quantitative "plenty" that caught the eye of ex-slaves. Frances Willingham of Athens, Georgia, called to mind the "fresh meat, cake, syrup, puddin' and plenty of good sweet butter" her mistress "'lowanced out to her slaves at Christmas." Countless others noted similar year-end remembrances: "a little fresh meat and sweet bread," "white flour," "great big round peppermint balls."[9] Higher quality marked the clothing accessories distributed as well: colorful handkerchiefs, bright ribbons, and sturdy wool hats.[10] The more novel the gifts, the more they merited comment. Mary Colbert remembered "candy, dolls, and everything you can imagine" while Will Sheets recalled "de groundpeas" and "de good old hunk of cheese dey give us den."[11] Across the decades, elderly ex-slaves remembered these gifts as special treats, remarkable not for their absolute quality but, rather, because they stood out so distinctly from mundane provision and daily fare.

The descriptors "extra" and "plenty" defy concrete definition, as their meaning differed according to time, place, and regular ration. Between masters and slaves, too, the goods that passed from hand to hand could take on different connotations. Year-end gifts that whites imagined as enriching slaves' material lives offered bondpeople a tangible and tempting morsel of the world they had made – and lost. Every item handed over from master gave slaves a small, delectable taste of a rich feast of consumption, one that slaves understood as distinctly different than their own. Indeed, the gifts slaves received were not unfamiliar. Preparing meals for their white family, laundering linens for mistress, watching master's children frolic on the lawn, daily they saw and felt and

---

[9] Sarah P. Payne to Mary McClendin, 2 January 1871, Payne Family Papers, VHS; P[lowden] C. Weston, "Management of a Southern Plantation," *De Bow's Review* 22 (1857): 39; Entry of 26 December 1853, John B. Milikin Plantation Journal, SCHS; George P. Rawick, ed., *The American Slave: A Composite Autobiography*, 41 vols. (Westport, CT: Greenwood Press, 1972–1978), 15, pt. 2: 278; *Ibid.*, Suppl. ser. 1, 3, pt. 1: 85; *Ibid.*, 12, pt. 2: 188; *Ibid.*, 13, pt. 4: 157–158; *Ibid.*, 12, pt. 1: 311; *Ibid.*, 13, pt. 4: 223; *Ibid.*, Suppl. ser. 1, 3, pt. 1: 189.

[10] For examples, see Stephenson, "My Father and His Household, Before, During and After the War," VHS; James R. Sparkman to Benjamin Allston, 10 March 1858, in *The South Carolina Rice Plantation as Revealed in the Papers of Robert F. W. Allston*, ed. J. H. Easterby (Columbia: University of South Carolina Press, 2004), 347–348; Caroline Howard Gilman, *Recollections of a Southern Matron* (New York: Harper and Brothers, 1838), 101; Jacob Stroyer, *My Life in the South* (Salem: Salem Observer Book and Job Print, 1885), 47.

[11] Rawick, *American Slave*, 12, pt. 1: 221; *Ibid.*, 13, pt. 3: 242.

smelled these once-a-year goods in the hands or on the plates and bodies of their masters. Recall Camilla Jackson's explanation of the difference between the "shorts" used for baking in the slave quarters and the "first grade" white flour used in the masters' house, or Green Willbanks's distinction between fine flax "for the white folks" and "coarse" for the slaves. White flour, cheese, candy, soft and colorful cloth – these "diffunt" goods marked masters' world of consumption, painfully tantalizing but, for most enslaved, just out of reach. Just as variety, novelty, and quality determined whether a good was a necessity or a luxury, these characteristics also distinguished gift from provision.[12]

But it was not just goods that made the gift. As cultural analyst John Frow has argued, "Gifts are precisely not *objects* at all, but transactions and social relations." The rituals that adorned such transactions played the crucial role in gifts' definition.[13] Inalienability could be solidified, slaveholders knew, precisely at the moment of exchange; hence, they took care to cultivate rites of transmission that took full advantage of the socially-binding powers of the gift.

On southern plantations, inalienability was rooted in the master's personalization of the gift-giving process.[14] When masters bestowed goods upon slaves, white hands and black hearts were meant to touch; black hands and white inevitably came together; so, too, did black and white lives, and were thereby entangled. The political purpose of gift-giving was not to connect masters to their "people." Instead, it meant to affirm the individual relationship between slave and master, extricating the slave, in this moment of exchange, from the mass of the black community. It thereby isolated and subordinated ties to bond kin and community in favor of the tie to and tacit recognition of a manifestly benevolent master. Ex-slave Mahala Jewel noted such care, explaining that she and her kin always met their master, Hamp McWorter, at the train station. They looked forward to his trips to "Gusty" (Augusta, Georgia) for he always came home laden with treats for his people. "Marster never forgot none of us," she recalled, in what was surely an eagerly-anticipated and mindfully-planned outpouring of largesse. Jennie Stephenson's mother, too, recognized the importance of this process of individuation. She "chose gifts suited to the individual need," Stephenson explained.[15] Here too, recipients were remembered, not as part of a grasping mass but as singular beings with distinctive feelings

---

[12] Rawick, *American Slave*, 12, pt. 2: 297; *Ibid.*, 13, pt. 4: 139.

[13] John Frow, *Time and Commodity Culture: Essays in Cultural Theory in Postmodernity* (New York: Oxford University Press, 1997), 124.

[14] Gift theorists have studied the process by which goods are rendered inalienable. James G. Carrier calls the act of imbuing an object with personhood, the "work of appropriation," while Igor Kopytoff labels the process, "singularization." Carrier, *Gifts and Commodities*, 112; Igor Kopytoff, "The Cultural Biography of Things: Commoditization as a Process," in *The Social Life of Things: Commodities in Cultural Perspective*, ed. Arjun Appadurai (New York: Cambridge University Press, 1986), 73.

[15] Rawick, *American Slave*, 12, pt. 2: 317; Stephenson, "My Father and His Household," VHS.

and desires. The personal touch made a lasting impression on ex-slave Junius Quattlebaum. "I can see missus so plain now," he recalled,

on Christmas mornin', a flirtin' round de Christmas trees,[16] commandin' de little misses to put de names of each slave on a package and hang it on de tree for them. She was always pleased, smilin' and happy, 'cause she knowed dat she was doin' somethin' dat would make somebody else happy. She tried as hard to make the slaves happy as she did to make her own white friends happy, it seem lak to me. Close to de tree was a basket and in dat basket was put in a bag of candy, apples, raisins, and nuts for all de chillun. Nobody was left out. Christmas mornin', marster would call all de slaves to come to de Christmas tree. He made all de chillun set down close to de tree and de grown slaves jined hands and make a circle 'round all. Then marster and missus would give de chillun their gifts, fust, then they would take presents from de tree and call one slave at a time to step out and git deirs ... After all dis, everybody was happy, singin' and laughin' all over de place.[17]

Quattlebaum's recollection of Carolina Christmases past stands out as particularly tender, and doubtless romanticized. And while not all slaveholders were as exacting in their choices, they made sure to distinguish constituent groups in the allocation of spoils. Some slaveholders, for example, divided gifts according to age and gender. Freedman Peter Clifton described Christmas morning on Biggers Mobley's South Carolina plantation this way: "Every girl got a ribbon, every boy a Barlow knife and every man a shin plaster." So well-known was Mobley for these remembrances, Clifton tells us, that "[d]e neighbors call de place, de shin plaster, Barlow, Bandanna place." Georgia slaveowner Ben Body annually "remembered" children on his Harris County plantation with "candy, nuts, and toys" and adults with "more substantial gifts." Elsie Moreland recalled her master, Isaac Moreland, giving "women an' girls new dresses an' the men an' boys new suits" on his Georgia farm. In each of these cases, freedpeople remembered not only their gifts but others' too – deliberate distinctions made by master seared in memory. We miss the central meaning of these offerings by focusing on the materiality of a head cloth or a plug of tobacco. As important as the gift itself was, the means by which the slaveholders transmitted it – and the meaning they imagined it imparted – was far more potent. Strategizing slaveholders aimed to see their own benevolently omnipotent self-image affirmed on the most basic personal human level. For the master, it was that moment of conjured propinquity – the fleeting and thankful gaze, the particular word of gratitude – in which slavery was most splendidly affirmed.[18]

The geography of southern gift-giving was central to this process of isolation and subordination. Such exchange was almost always public performance

---

[16] Quattlebaum describes these trees as a "big holly bush wid red berries all over it."
[17] Rawick, *American Slave*, 3, pt. 3: 285–286.
[18] Rawick, *American Slave*, 2, pt. 1: 207; *Ibid.*, Suppl. ser. 1, 3, pt. 1: 72; *Ibid.*, Suppl. ser. 1, 4, pt. 2: 455.

FIGURE 5.1 Christmas celebrations brought masters and slaves into conflict and communion on the ground of gift-giving.
Source: "Winter Holydays in the Southern States, Plantation Frolic on Christmas Eve," *Frank Leslie's Illustrated Newspaper*, 26 December 1857, p. 64. Courtesy of the Library of Congress, Prints and Photographs Division, LC-USZ62–49657.

enacted upon a middle ground joining black and white spheres of experience. Porch or yard served as sites of transmission (Figure 5.1). Masters summoned and, as we shall see, slaves intruded, each giving and demanding in turn. Tarheel planter James Hervey Greenlee, for example, "called up the Black people" every Christmas for distribution of both holiday offerings and winter clothes. Slaves gathered for meals and ministrations in "marster's backyard" or, less commonly, "de big house" itself for a presentation of gifts – a ritualized task rarely delegated to an overseer. James Avirett remembered two such scenes on his father's coastal North Carolina plantation, separate performances for house servants and field hands. In an intimate ceremony, he recalled, all members of the family – house servants included – gathered in the breakfast room to exchange presents. "[N]o one is forgotten," Avirett gushed, "not even Buck, George or Cain – for, at this season especially, the old planter's home is a republic of love." In the cozy confines of the breakfast room, master could share such affections with his intimates. Recreating this feeling with field hands required further orchestration. Following breakfast, Avirett's mother and father, mistress and master, took their places on the back veranda as the assembly bell rang. Slaves filed past, "each receiving some present – a bandanna handkerchief, a

Barlow knife, a doll baby or a package of tobacco." Such rites played out on plantations throughout the South. "When the slaves came up to their master and mistress," Jacob Stroyer explained, "the latter would welcome them, the men would take off their hats and bow and the women would make a low courtesy." In return for faithful enactment of this submissive ritual, Stroyer's master, Col. Matthew Singleton, handed over a token of his approval – sweetened and diluted whiskey usually, along with "hats and tobacco for the men, handkerchiefs and little things for the women." In such performances, slaveholders showcased their power: not by hoarding and protecting bounty but by bestowing it; not by emphasizing material difference but by allowing momentary entry to the outermost fringes of their world. Each item exchanged served as tangible token of this culminating moment of connectedness, as both scar and laurel of the order and good government that the master strove to create. In gratuities given and rituals performed, slaveholders rooted reminders of their mastery in the quarters. Here we see the paternalist agenda of the master class functioning with repressive precision.[19]

Provisions could never be presents, masters knew, yet they sought to blur the boundary, imbuing gift-giving characteristics to provision distribution. When Carolina planter John Peyre Thomas doled out "usual allotment[s]" of Christmas beef, whiskey, tobacco, molasses, and hogmeat between 1828 and 1832, his plantation book conflated categories promiscuously. Described as "allowance," "supply," and "presents," the melding of categories in the book reflected the political purposes in his mind. No matter what the appellation, the intent was clear. In shrouding required rationing with ceremony most oft associated with gifting, slaveholders introduced yet another opportunity to bestow and singularize. Plantation journals, prescriptive literature, and black and white narratives described the holiday season as a time when slaves received annual or semiannual allotments of provisioned clothing. Swedish traveler, turned Palmetto-state governess, Rosalie Roos described Christmas as "the Negroes' great treat, for their winter clothing is handed out to them," while ex-slave Emma Blalock recalled getting "shoes once a year, at Christmas Eve." Samuel Gourdin Gaillard explained that wagon trips to Charleston "were always timed so that they would return in time for Christmas," when young and old alike would gather round for "useful presents" like "blankets, clothes, shoes, and handkerchiefs and other articles." Others remembered receiving annual allotments of shoes, "new dresses," or "new suits" during the holiday season, provisions, ex-slave Irving Lowery emphasized, his master "made it a point to give out … Christmas morning." Countless plantation books and memoirs confirm their accounts, bondpeople's names

[19] Entry of 25 December 1847, James Hervey Greenlee Diary, SHC; Rawick, American Slave, Suppl. ser. 1, 3, pt. 1: 25; Ibid., 15, pt. 2: 145; James Battle Avirett, The Old Plantation: How We Lived in Great House and Cabin Before the War (New York: F. Tennyson Neely, 1901), 178–180; Stroyer, My Life in the South, 47.

listed individually and, occasionally, in family groups, correlated with allocated shoes and clothes. Amidst the bounty of holiday celebration, even this
mundane provisioning – the very least a master could provide – took on a
festive air. "'Now Cuffee,' 'Now Nebuchadnezzar,' 'Now Jeremiah,' 'Philis,'
'Chloe,' 'Clarissa,'" planter's daughter Celestine Lowndes remembered, each
slave advancing "promptly in response to their names" to receive Christmas
allotments of "many hued garments for themselves and their households."
This allocation of "winter clothing" and "brogans" – each pair containing
"the stick sizes with the names of the owners upon them which had been sent
on to town for measurement in advance" – inspired "ecstasies of delight" and
"summersets" in the yard.[20]

That provisioning was but prelude to the "gifts ... to be distributed" at
Lowndes's Kelvin Grove plantation only served to heighten enthusiasm. As
ex-slave Irving Lowery explained, the buildup to distribution day at his master's Sumter District, South Carolina, plantation was "indescribable," tinged
with feelings of "anxiety ... longing and solicitude for the dawn of Christmas
morning." Excitement began to build a month prior when each slave had his
foot measured for new shoes – an annual tradition on Jack Frierson's South
Carolina plantation. On Christmas morning, slaves "repair[ed] to 'the house'"
to find the front piazza lined with piles of clothes, each containing "shoes, a
suit, or dress, and a cap." Master did not disperse these goods indiscriminately.
Rather, "on each pile there [was] a tag with the name of the person written
on it for whom it is designed"; master's people waited with "exquisite joy" to
hear "his or her name called." Lowery's recollection might seem overly romantic, but we can imagine that, from the perspective of provisioned people, the
crisp and clean newness of their clothing ration, however scratchy and stiff,
combined with the relative rarity of its distribution, inspired happy expectation. That Lowery's master separated rations into separate allotments, that he
tagged each pile, that he called each slave by his or her name: such rituals
were played out across the South. Was this simply a convenient and efficient
way of distributing like goods? Hardly. Such rituals acted to singularize and

---

[20] Entries of 25 December 1828, 25 December 1829, 25 December 1830, 25 December 1831,
25 December 1832, John Peyre Thomas Diaries, Thomas Family Papers, SCL; Rosalie Roos,
Travels in America, 1851–1855, trans. and ed. Carl L. Anderson (Carbondale: Southern Illinois
University Press, 1982), 102; *American Slave*, 14, pt. 1: 105; Samuel Gourdin Gaillard, Memoir,
1934, p. 6, SCL; *American Slave*, Suppl. ser. 1, 4, pt. 2: 455; Irving E. Lowery, *Life on the
Old Plantation in Ante-bellum Days* (Columbia, SC: The State, 1911), 66; Celestine Lowndes,
"Kelvin Grove, or, An Old Time Christmas on a Southern Plantation and Other Stories," 1895,
pp. 36–38, Celestine Lowndes Writings, SCHS. For another example of holiday provision distribution, see Record Book of Comingtee Plantation, 24 December 1850, Keating Simons Ball
Plantation Journal, Duke. It is worth noting that the holiday season described by slaves and
slaveholders alike lasted through January 1st. Distributing provisions at the start of the new
year made logical business sense, of course. Correlating this annual or semiannual event with
the "gift-making season" lent added festivity and meaning to distribution.

individualize the provision process, transforming basic raiment and ration into occasion for celebration and, more importantly, thanks.[21]

Rites of inalienability need not take place only on Christmas Day. Masters might ritualize more mundane provisioning, too. Carolinian Louisa McCord Smythe fondly remembered the "giving of 'lowance' when the long line of women and children with baskets and buckets would come over from the quarter to get the provisions for the week." More meaningful was the semiannual distribution of clothing. Men and women appeared, "dressed in their best," before their mistress who was standing in front of the "barred store room." One at a time, representatives made their way "up the piazza steps" where "the men dropping their hats on the bottom steps, and 'pulling their wool and scraping their foot' as they took what was given to them." Women, too, "made a little bob curtsey" as they got their "share." It was, as Smythe described it, "a sort of Fair day for them." For Smythe, too. Weekly and semiannual provisioning served as one of the "occasions and people so vividly impressed" upon her mind many decades after slavery's end. Rituals on Smythe's father's plantation matched those on Charles Manigault's estate, but the rosy nostalgia that tinged her memoir was markedly absent from his own. In a post-bellum justification of his family's slaveholding past, Manigault railed against the treachery of both those who would criticize the peculiar institution and the "Lazy, Improvident" African-American population that so eagerly embraced emancipation. As evidence of the attention with which he and his family cared for their slaves, he pointed to provision distribution. "We assembled them, old & young, around US," he explained, "to give them punctually their Clothes, Blankets, calling each by name, & handing it to them." Far from nameless drones, Manigault emphasized, slaves on his plantation received more than raiment; rites of recognition and belonging marked provisioning too.[22]

Even though ritual remembrances – counted, measured, and individualized tokens of recognition – shine as beacons of beneficent largesse in plantation memoirs, giving was far from apolitical. Indeed, on the master's plantation, gifts explicitly came with strings attached. On James Ritchie Sparkman's rice plantation, this accounting took place on Christmas Day itself when "all plantation tools [were] inspected and a memorandum taken of each, as a check and guide for the overseer and the master." "[A]ll who are not defaulters" and those "who [had] not been found guilty of any greivous [sic] offense during the year" earned "an extra Ration of Rice, Peas, Molasses, and Meat," and tobacco to boot.[23] But what of those who did commit "greivous" offenses?

[21] Lowndes, "Kelvin Grove or An Old Time Christmas on a Southern Plantation," 37; Lowery, Life on the Old Plantation, 67.
[22] Louisa McCord Smythe, Recollections of Louisa Rebecca Hayne McCord, [ca. 1928], SCL; Charles Manigault, "Respecting Slavery," Writings, n.d., Manigault Papers, SCHS.
[23] James R. Sparkman to Benjamin Allston, 10 March 1858, in The South Carolina Rice Plantation as Revealed in the Papers of Robert F. W. Allston, ed. J. H. Easterby (Columbia: University of South Carolina Press, 2004), 347–348. Sparkman's Direlton Plantation Journal confirms this

Some planters preferred sticks to carrots, threatening to deduct from anticipated future presents. One Savannah River planter kept superior "small Rice"
for his slaves "unless on one or two occasions when they have done anything
wrong, when I have sold the whole of it." Similarly, Robert Allston normally
gave out "a ¼ proportion of Small Rice" to "those who lost not a day of work"
over the course of the year. In 1859, however, his slaves were "shared out of
Xmas" until they ratted out a hog thief from the quarters.[24] Slaves on Davison
McDowell's two South Carolina plantations understood this accounting all
too well. Christmas was indeed a time of reciprocity and McDowell used the
holiday to reinforce expectations of obedience and subservience. Yearly tallies
of "crimes and misdemeanors" indicate that Christmas offerings were disciplinary tools used to reward or punish at will. The following entries drawn
from McDowell's diaries illustrate the Janus-faced nature of Christmas ritual
on Asylum and Lucklow plantations.

7 August 1827	Since I have been from house Terry & Jackson has Killed a Beef. The runaway Marlboro was concern'd in it also but not so deeply. *Give them no Christmas nor Summer Cloths.*
21 November 1828	Small came home last night after being gone 18 days – No Christmas
31 October 1829	Give the Negroes to day. The Negroes Stole corn & *Dick* is one of the thieves. *No Christmas for him.*
27 March 1830	The Fences in the neighborhood of the Negro Houses are continually destroyed & burnt up – remember to make the Negroes during the Christmas Holydays split rails – carry them in & repair the fences.
16 September 1830	Sibby Miscarried, believed She did so on purpose. Stop her Christmas and lock her up.
25 December 1830	Balanced the acct in the Distribution of Beef & Whiskey. Stopped Sibby's & give small pieces according to the days the Negroes lay'd up. Promised next Xmas to stop days for burning fences.

But withholding Christmas gifts or mandating extra work was the least
troubling of McDowell's holiday plans. "Nobody took the Cow hide of the
Steers Kill for Xmas," his first entry under "1830 Crimes and Misdemeanors"
announced. The beeves killed every Christmas yielded more than meat to sate
the weary, all understood; hides made whips, too. Even though McDowell's

policy. On 25 December 1854, for example, Sparkman's journal lists an "Inventory of Plantation
Tools." Entry of 25 December 1854, Dirleton Plantation Journal, 1853–1859, James Ritchie
Sparkman Papers, SCL.

[24] Charles Manigault to Jesse T. Cooper, 10 January 1848, in *Life and Labor on Argyle Island:
Letters and Documents of a Savannah River Rice Plantation, 1833–1867*, ed. James M. Clifton
(Savannah, GA: Beehive Press, 1978), 62; Entry of 14 January 1859, Robert F. W. Allston Diary,
in *The South Carolina Rice Plantation*, 454.

sadistic sneer showed that his slaves were spared the crueler side of his Christmas offering, both sides knew that his whip hand remained raised over their heads throughout that year and for years to come. Escaped slave Jacob Stroyer distilled the essence of such transactions, owners' gift policies made clear. "Some of the masters would buy presents for the slaves," he explained, "these things were given after they had been pleased with them." In Stroyer's analysis, we see just how deeply the paternalist agenda might penetrate. Slaves were bound by both moralizing judgment and apparently beneficent gift. Even among slaves who were not gulled by paternalism's promises, the desire to acquire such goods must have had a powerful effect on their everyday behavior, leading others to conform and influence in return.[25]

Masters and slaves understood gifts as those that exceeded typical rations in quantity and quality. Yet, through ritualized exchange, provisions might be transformed into gifts as well. The practice of giving small amounts of money as Christmas presents muddied categories of exchange even further, making unclear the distinction between gift and commodity transactions. Recall Jennie Stephenson's father, piles of coin at his side, distributing money to all who participated in the harvest. Other sources reveal similar images. In addition to monthly allotments of meat, sugar, and coffee, Robert Allston's slaves Phillip and Sary received "some gratification in money at Xmas," while Georgia planter Thomas Hawkins sent a barrel of spirits and $20 to be "distribute[d] among the negros" on his Woodville plantation during the Christmas season. Ex-slave Philip Evans cherished the "small coins" his master gave, while Benjamin Johnson recalled that he sometimes received a "dollar at Christmas." At Kelvin Grove, Celestine Lowndes bragged, "it rained a shower of small coin, pennies, fourpences, and sevenpences," the "uproar" from her father's slaves "tremendous." Ex-slave Richard Jones remembered that "master allus carried a roll of money as big as my arm." When the mood struck him, he would "get up on a stump" before his slaves and "throw money to 'em. De chilluns git dimes, nickels, quarters, half-dollars, and dollars. At Christmas he would throw ten dollar bills. De parents would take de five and ten dollar bills in charge, but Marse made de let de chilluns keep de small change." Did Jones and Lowndes exaggerate slaveholders' generosity? We cannot say, but the image of mastery and subordination here is clear and could not have been lost on those who scrambled for the material opportunity glittering coin might offer.[26]

More than distributing outright gifts of cash, disguising payment as selfless generosity was a political tactic planters employed wherever possible.

[25] Entries of 7 August 1827, 21 November 1828, 31 October 1829, "1830 Crimes and Misdemeanors," Asylum Plantation Diary, Davison McDowell Papers, SCL; Stroyer, *My Life in the South*, 47.

[26] Entry of 1 February 1860, Robert F. W. Allston Diary, in *South Carolina Rice Plantation*, 456; Entry of 4 December 1856, Gilbert Isaac Germond [Overseer] Plantation Journal, 1855–1867, GHS; Rawick, *American Slave*, 2, pt. 2: 36; *Ibid.*, 12, pt. 2: 325; Lowndes, "Kelvin Grove," 37; Rawick, *American Slave*, 3, pt. 1: 66.

Anecdotes across a wide array of sources reveal small transactions or "tips" given to bondpeople for bits of attentiveness or good work. Isaac Williams, for example, always rushed to open the gate for cotton speculator John Braxton. Why? The brash young suitor who would eventually become his master "was always free with his money, and generally threw me a quarter." Such displays were common – and expected – Letitia Burwell remembered, "the neglect of this rite being regarded as a breach of politeness." Levi Branham put up visi-tors' horses for "nickels and dimes," while Pierce Cody recalled picking nits from the heads of the "young white men" who visited his quarters. Surely an unpleasant task, Cody and his fellows were offered "a gift of some sort" in return.[27]

Slaveholders more stridently strove to blur the line between gift and com-modity exchange especially at Christmastime, overlaying the sometimes grim atmosphere of year-end financial reckoning and payment of accounts with gift ritual. Slaves might garner year-end compensation for the production of staves, crops, and other goods, paid in cash or credit, providing them with the power to consume in exchange for supposedly independent labor throughout the year. On Christmas Day 1856, for example, Burke County, North Carolina, planter James Hervey Greenlee "[p]aid the black people part of the money" for their corn before handing over gifts of "flour sugar & coffee." Virginia planter Richard Eppes paid Tom and Bob for sawyering completed over the course of the year 1852, and Stewart "$5 for woodslabs 50¢ a hundred." A more striking example from Georgia makes this connection to gift transaction clear. According to the *Southern Cultivator*, a planter paid "so much per load (*cash*) for all the *manure* [his bondpeople] can make or save." Not only were his slaves' quarters clear of "decomposed vegetation, old bones, 'night soil,' soap-suds, or slops," but the transaction "'puts money in his [the slave's] purse,' and gives him annually, at the good old Christmas times (when the yearly manure account is paid up) the means of supplying himself with necessaries and lux-uries to him otherwise unattainable."[28] This scatological bargain was clearly and measurably rooted in commodity trade yet was explicitly tied to the gift season, explained as a way for bondpeople to obtain luxurious items that were not part of routine provisions. Commodity transaction, then, served as surro-gate for gift itself.

Such transactions became even more convoluted when this annual reckoning was tied, not to independent production, but to behavior and labor efficiency.

---

[27] Isaac D. Williams and William Ferguson Goldie, *Sunshine and Shadow of Slave Life. Reminiscences as told by Isaac D. Williams to "Tege"* (East Saginaw, MI: Evening News Binding and Printing House, 1885), 7; Letitia M. Burwell, *A Girl's Life in Virginia Before the War* (New York: Frederick A. Stokes, 1895), 4–5; Levi Branham, *My Life and Travels* (Dalton, GA: A. J. Showalter Co., 1929), 9; Rawick, *American Slave*, 12, pt. 1: 198.

[28] Entry of 25 December 1856, James Hervey Greenlee Diary, SHC; Entry of 25 December 1852, Richard Eppes Diary, Section 41, Eppes Family Papers, VHS; "Management of Negroes – Bathing Feet, Remark," *Southern Cultivator*, 11 (1853): 302.

On Henry Middleton's Weehaw plantation, for example, slaves received extra Christmas rations of rice, molasses, fresh meat, and sugar. Additionally, drivers and watchmen as well as the trunkminder, children's cook, cattleminder, head carpenter, and head cooper received $5 each. "Each sewer," he noted, received 50 cents "if clothes are well made," and nurses were granted 75 cents for "infants that lived." But even more than gifts of goods, cash payouts proved easily slashed if slaves failed to measure up to masters' demands. One contributor to the *Farmers' Register* gave each laboring hand an annual gift of "a barrel of corn, or its equivalent in money" at the annual "time of settlement," Christmas. This gift came with conditions, however – if anyone on the plantation committed a theft in the preceding year, his "negroes [were] responsible for it," with "double its value deducted ... from the Christmas present." A contributor to *De Bow's Review* had a similar policy, giving $5 to "each head of a family and to every single Negro on Christmas day." If they broke plantation rules, however, they lost the gifted money.[29] Each of these tactics is laid out in a typically-detailed exposition from Richard Eppes's diary. On December 25, 1853, he wrote:

The following servants from plantations came over to receive their annual Christmas present for good conduct, it being a part of my management to reward all who conduct themselves properly during the year who I myself am not compelled to have punished. To each I allow one dollar apiece at Christmas except my foremen hogfeeders who receive five dollars, provided the former conduct themselves well and the latter have no hogs stolen. My ploughmen receive two dollars each for every field ploughed provided their ploughing is done well, no mules gauled for each gaul something is taken off from the amount.[30]

Eppes's diary after that date indicates that he hewed to this policy. Henry, for example, received a dollar beyond his master's usual presents for "not drinking Whiskey," while Patty, Elizabeth, and "their mutual paramour Henry" gave up potential profits after Eppes charged them with "Adultery." That the depredations, "crimes," and bad behavior Eppes sought to reform continued year after year suggests that cash contracts were not always effective, but they did serve as means by which his charges could be measured. Slaveholders stood in judgment of all forms of slave behavior – from spending to stealing to personal mores. The promise of cash – the lure of the market – amplified the importance of his appraisals.[31]

Witnesses to rituals of accounting such as these might have difficulty determining just what sort of transactions masters and slaves were engaged in. The

[29] "Plantation Expenses," Weehaw Plantation Journal, 1855–1861, p. 75, Henry A. Middleton, Jr. Papers, Cheves and Middleton Collection, SCHS; "The Farm and Farming of the Rev. J. H. Turner – No. 1," *Farmers' Register* 10 (1842): 129; "Management of Negroes upon Southern Estates," *De Bow's Review* 10 (1851): 624.

[30] Entry of 25 December 1853, Richard Eppes Diary, Section 41, Eppes Family Papers, VHS.

[31] Entries of 25 December 1852 and 25 December 1853, Richard Eppes Diary, Section 41, Eppes Family Papers, VHS.

exchange of cash indicated payment, but the timing and mechanics of its distribution suggested paternal largesse. The very appearance of these transactions – "bright scenes" such as those described by Jennie Stephenson – could cause further confusion. Sociologist Vivian Zelizer has considered such calculated ambiguities, arguing that the seemingly impersonal medium of cash money can easily be converted into covenants more personal. Through a process of earmarking – the use of special currencies or simple gift wrapping – money can be transformed, she contends, into gift. We can observe aspects of these techniques in monetary transactions on the plantation. James Avirett's father, for example, would call his foreman before the gathered plantation and give him an "envelope with a crisp bank note in it," the carefully wrapped bill untainted by lesser and impersonal market motives. Recall, too, Georgia planter James Towns's policy regarding end-of-the-year settlements with his slaves. "I always pay them in silver," he emphasized to readers of the *Southern Cultivator*, imagining such a distinction would do far more than bolster their purchasing ability. Still another planter combined the novelty of shimmering coin with public performance, "plac[ing] silver coins on a rock and hav[ing] the men run and pick them up" as part of Christmas Eve festivities. On plantation after plantation, slaveholders ritualized payments through public ceremonies and personal recognition, molding them into exchanges that suited their needs best.[32]

Were these masters paying slaves for proper behavior and efficient labor? Were these commodity exchanges? The questions recall the vigorous debate surrounding Robert Fogel and Stanley Engerman's *Time on the Cross*. Fogel and Engerman argued that "rewards and incentives" encouraged more efficient slave labor. Critics responded that the gifts and market opportunities Fogel and Engerman described were part of a larger system of custom and negotiation between master and slave.[33] Slaveholders never made such stark distinctions. They deliberately blurred the boundary between gift and commodity because they never imagined delimiting the master's domain within the boundaries of a cost-benefit analysis. Undeniably, they sought to create a world on the backs of black labor, but it was the souls of black folk they ultimately hoped to ensnare. These transactions touched the "purses" of slaves and masters alike, the *Southern Cultivator* noted, but slaveholders' efforts to gift wrap these payments were purest politics. By ritualizing commodity exchange, masters sought to replace

[32] Vivian A. Zelizer, *The Social Meaning of Money: Pin Money, Paychecks, Poor Relief, and Other Currencies* (New York: Basic Books, 1994), 71–118; Avirett, *The Old Plantation*, 180; James M. Towns, "Management of Negroes," *Southern Cultivator* 9 (1851): 86; Rosalie Roos, *Travels in America*, 103.

[33] Robert William Fogel and Stanley L. Engerman, *Time on the Cross: The Economics of American Negro Slavery* (Boston: Little, Brown, 1974), 41, 144–157, 241–242. Herbert G. Gutman and Richard Sutch, "Sambo Makes Good, or Were Slaves Imbued with the Protestant Work Ethic?" in *Reckoning with Slavery: A Critical Study in the Quantitative History of American Negro Slavery*, ed. Paul A. David, *et al.* (New York: Oxford University Press, 1976), 73. See also Gutman, *Slavery and the Numbers Game: A Critique of Time on the Cross* (Urbana: University of Illinois Press, 1975).

the inherently alienating characteristics of market exchange with soothing fantasies of paternalism. For slaves, this was a double bind in the truest sense.[34]

For masters, too. Their attempt to frame an important component of internal economy within the paternalist ethos was bound to tie everyone, everything in knots. The narrow advantages to slaveholders seemed clear: by melding gift and commodity exchange, they would reap the material benefits of commodity transactions while strengthening social ties. But at what cost? Traveling minister Bishop Henry Whipple's description of holiday celebrations in Georgia provides telling clues. Merry scenes animate his December 1843 account. The "music of the negroes" awoke his slumber on Christmas morning. He emerged from his quarters to find the "servants ... all waiting with laughing faces to wish us a Merry Christmas." Their shining countenances expressed more than happy desire to extend holiday greetings, however. As Whipple explained, they were "expecting to receive a bit or so as a contribution." Such holiday gratuities were tradition in that part of Georgia – indeed, in many parts of the South – as Whipple would soon come to understand. Two days later, he found himself at Duncan Clinch's lowcountry plantation. Never before had he "seen any class of people who appeared to enjoy more than do these negroes," he noted. With satisfied pleasure, he described the dancing, supping, and "joyous mirth" he witnessed on "the last day of the feast and with them [the slaves] the 'great day.'" Whipple gauged the scene: "their ebony faces shin[ing] with joy and happiness," Clinch's men paraded, "a corps of staff officers with red sashes, mock epaulettes & goose quill feathers" leading the way. The crowd took full advantage of this rare opportunity for ostentatious and raucous levity, but wise to holiday tradition, they had more ambitious designs as well. "They levied contributions on all the whites they see," Whipple remarked, "& thus find themselves in pocket money."[35]

Scenes such as these potentially brought paternalism and the bottom line into conflict. The "happy effect" such gifts had on the slave population was gratifying indeed, but at what point did the "kind feeling that seemed to exist between master and slave" prove too much to bear? "To moralize and induce the slave to assimilate with the master and his interest," one slaveholder explained, "has been and is the great desideratum aimed at," and yet all knew the achievement of the goal could not possibly come without great cost. Despite carefully crafted rituals of paternalism and submission, slaveholders found themselves caught by the very schemes they had worked so hard to impose on the enslaved. Bondpeople appreciated ritual too and did their best to draw masters into their own web of reciprocity. Bondpeople often described being "called" to master's domain, but others – slave and white recollecters alike – paint a different scene altogether. Celestine Lowndes recalled peering out her bedroom window, looking out to an "expectant crowd ... grinning gleefully" on Christmas morning.

[34] Towns, "Management of Negroes," 86.
[35] Lester B. Shippee, ed., *Bishop Whipple's Southern Diary, 1843–1844* (New York: Da Capo Press, 1968), 48–52.

Unbidden, it seems, James Bolton remembered that he and his kin "runned up to the big 'ouse early Christmas morning." What awaited masters upon awakening was a world seemingly turned upside down. Even as staunch a romanticist as James Avirett described a scene of uproarious tumult. "Bang! Bang! Bang! 'Hurrah for Christmas!' No more sleep." Young slave boys had kept all the hog bladders from butchering season, inflating and hanging them round their cabins. They woke their masters Christmas morning by unleashing a veritable "fusilade" of noise by "put[ting] them down on the hard beaten paths around the great house and jump[ing] on them with both feet." Slaves amplified the clamor of these "Christmas guns" with "serenades" to the master's family, complete with "banjoes, and old tin pans and whatever you wanted to make a noise." And while the songs sung and pans beaten may have varied from place to place, the constant refrain heard by masters across the South was the same. When Bolton and his fellows burst into master's yard, they barely got out a "mornin'" before shouting a more meaningful salute, "Christmas Gif'!" This is the phrase white southerners remembered most often hearing as they roused from bed each December 25th. Most white accounts recall the tradition with fondness, but the salutation only barely masked demands and expectations more political and, indeed, more costly than cheerful countenances implied. The rituals of the day involved not just gift-giving but calculated "surprise" and subversion too. Indeed, masters did not just give gifts, they were symbolically ensnared by their "people." Explained ex-slave Louisa Davis: "Every slave ketch white folks wid a holler, 'Christmas Gift, Marster!'" Daniel Hundley was more specific, noting that "[slaves] lie in wait behind every door and corner, and the moment the end of your nose appears, they pounce upon you with a whoop, shouting furiously, 'Chrismus Giff, Mas'r ah! I cotch you dis time!'" No white man or woman found peace until he or she "conformed to [this] universal custom."[36]

And if they were caught? In some form, slaveholders had to pay. Esther Davis remembered failed attempts to "catch" her grandfather's Carolina plantation slaves on Christmas morning. "[T]hey were before us," she explained, "and their 'Christmas Gift' greeted us before we could call out 'Merry Christmas,'

---

[36] Shippee, ed., *Bishop Whipple's Southern Diary*, 51; B. McBride, "Directions for Cultivating the various Crops Grown at Hickory Hill," *Southern Agriculturist, and Register of Rural Affairs* 3 (1830): 238; Lowndes, "Kelvin Grove," 36; Rawick, *American Slave*, 12, pt. 1: 100; Avirett, *The Old Plantation*, 176–178; Rawick, *American Slave*, 12, pt. 2: 120; Rawick, *American Slave*, 2, pt. 1: 301; Daniel R. Hundley, *Social Relations in our Southern States* (New York: Henry B. Price, 1860), 360–361. For a variant of this game in which slaves were rewarded for finding a hidden master, see Rawick, *American Slave*, 15, pt. 2: 18–19. Louisa McCord Smythe claimed games such as these took place every Sunday on her father's plantation when their slaves would come over from the quarters "dressed up" and serenade the white family. "Part of the performance," she explained, "was always to 'choose' as they called it, that is to say to go over us and our belongings and claim us or them, as their special property. This was a great compliment and we were always much pleased though a little embarrassed by the claiming of our dresses or shoes, or anything else down to our toes and fingers." Smythe, "Recollections," SCL.

and this meant they claimed a present from each." Samuel Gourdin Gaillard recalled similar demands, slaves on his father's Eutawville farm holding "Master and Missus" accountable with yearly requests for goods "out of your pocket into mine" on Christmas morning. Georgia ex-slave Charlie Hudson tramped "f'um house to house lookin' for locust and persimmon beer"; children, he remembered, "went to all de houses huntin' gingerbread."[37] Other bondpeople required more than sweet treats to sate Christmas desires. Slaves who celebrated John Kuner (also known as John Canoe or John Kunering) were most forthright in their demands. This festival of subversion took place in coastal North Carolina, always around the Christmas holidays. Scholars debate its origins, some pointing to similar celebrations in the Caribbean and Africa and others noting similarities to English traditions of mumming and wassailing. Historian Stephen Nissenbaum convincingly argues for a creolized blending of both, that "John Canoers understood that convergence and exploited it." Origins aside, southerners in this region – enslaved and free – understood its implications. According to North Carolina doctor Edward Warren, a request for donations was but one part of an elaborate performance involving a "rag man" dressed in a costume of rags, cow bells, and a variety of hanging animal skins and horns. The costume obscured the bondman's identity and caused a racket to boot. A second participant, dressed in his "Sunday-go-to-meeting suit," carried a small tin cup. Other slaves gathered behind them, "arrayed fantastically in ribbons, rags, and feathers," each carrying a musical instrument called a "gumba box." Finally, the rest of the population, dressed in their "ordinary working clothes" stood guard. This "motley crowd" came to the front of the big house. The musicians played and the main actors danced with the man in his Sunday best singing a "song of a strange, monotonous cadence":

My massa am a white man, juba!
Old missus am a lady, juba!
De children am de hone-pods, juba! juba!
Krismas come but once a year, juba!
Juba! juba! O, ye juba!

De darkeys lubs de hoe-cake, juba!
Take de "quarter" for to buy it, juba!
Fetch him long, you white folks, juba! juba!
Krismas come but once a year, juba!
Juba! juba! O, ye juba![38]

37 Esther S. Davis, *Memories of Mulberry* (Brooklyn, NY: Eagle Press, 1913), 12–13; Gaillard, Memoir, 7; Rawick, *American Slave*, 12, pt. 2: 228.
38 Nissenbaum, *The Battle for Christmas*, 289; Edward Warren, *A Doctor's Experience in Three Continents* (Baltimore: Cushings and Bailey, 1885), 200–202. Runaway Harriet Jacobs quantified the Christmas tradition. Revelers left "[n]ot a door … unvisited where there [was] the least chance of obtaining a penny or a glass of rum." The penny offerings added up, she noted: "These Christmas donations frequently amount[ed] to twenty or thirty dollars." Harriet A.

The meaning of their incantation was clear. Tin cup in one hand and hat in the other, the finely-dressed slave appeared before his owner's door. Master knew what was expected of him and responded accordingly, the slave sauntering away jingling the coin in his cup. That act of paternalist compliance, that silver wrung from master's hand, was often satisfying to both, memoirs reveal. But the ring of contentment such masters thought they heard disappearing down the pathway to the quarters must have sounded differently to the ears of the slave who was so visibly and audibly shaking things up. Slaveholders gave over the stage and passed over the cash, smugly relishing their benevolence. Yet in that moment, there was anxiety too. The ties that bound slave and master were all too tenuous and needed constant tending, even when end-of-the-year accounts suggested stingier spending might be wiser. Slaveholders could not help but worry about the future, wondering how much loyalty and subservience might ultimately cost. In a letter to her father just prior to that most worrisome Christmas of 1860, South Carolina mistress Sally Baxter Hampton expressed her dread at "the Negroes peculiar festival," ruefully noting that "I am to go down on Monday & give out Sugar – Coffee – Rice & Flour to all that want." In the face of "gloomy" times, her husband's poor crop, and political crisis, responsibilities weighed heavy upon her, yet she knew obligations had to be met. In addition to the usual presents, slaves had to be paid for independent production at Christmas, "whether money is tight or easy."[39]

Hampton's letter drips with self-pity, but her concern was real. Even in flush times, it seems, there were risks associated with pursuing a strategy of open-handedness. The political economy of gift-giving tied slaveholders within a strangling web of expectation. There were worrisome consequences to be faced if gifts did not adequately measure up year after year. Sea island cotton planter Thomas Chaplin felt these concerns acutely as he fell further and further into debt in the 1840s and 1850s. "Killed 2 beefs for the Negroes," he noted on an otherwise "Dull. Dull. Dull" Christmas Day in 1845. In years following, the self-described "sufferer" would pine for such humdrum malaise. From 1846 to 1849, he did not mention Christmas gifts, more often lamenting the ills, slights, and transgressions of stolen turkeys and hogs. We cannot know whether he simply failed to note offerings or had nothing to give. By 1850, however, it was clear that failing fortunes disrupted expected rites of reciprocity. "I had nothing to give them but a few turnips," he sighed, assuring himself that "they [his slaves] are satisfied." Years later, mastery shattered, Chaplin doubted his own words, adding "pretend to be" to his description of Christmas satiety.[40]

Jacobs, *Incidents in the Life of a Slave Girl. Written by Herself*, ed. Lydia Maria Francis Child (Boston: Printed for Author, 1861), 179–180.

[39] Sally Baxter Hampton to George Baxter, 22 December 1860, in *A Divided Heart: Letters of Sally Baxter Hampton, 1853–1862*, ed. Ann Fripp Hampton (Spartanburg, SC: The Reprint Company, 1980), 79.

[40] Theodore Rosengarten, ed., *Tombee: Portrait of a Cotton Planter* (New York: William Morrow, 1986), 27, 385, 426, 448, 480, 516.

Whether wishful thinking, utter miscomprehension, or calculated delusion guided Chaplin's assessment in 1850 is difficult to say. Signs of displeasure were either absent or Chaplin chose to ignore them, lest they further weaken his already precarious image as man and master. But for other slaveholders, bondpeople's expectations – and displeasure when reckonings were not met – were all too clear. Harriet Jacobs explained that, at Christmas, slaves were permitted to "go round ... begging for contributions." Their efforts often succeeded far too well for the planters' taste, Jacobs explained, for, if master refused to hand over a "trifle," he was serenaded with mournful derision:

> Poor massa, so dey say;
> Down in de heel, so dey say;
> Got no money, so dey say;
> Not one shillin, so dey say;
> God A'mighty bress you, so dey say.[41]

To those who failed to respond to John Kuner's call, the response could be even more damning, more caustic:

> Run, Jinnie, run! I'm gwine away,
> Gwine away, to come no mo'
> Dis am de po' hous,
> Glory habbilulum![42]

This is charivari in its purest form.[43] Work slowdowns, theft, runaways – the forms of political struggle working people have always employed on the heels of such mockery as prelude to even more troubling forms of rough justice – such were the behaviors planters tried to eliminate through the allocation of material goods. When masters found themselves mastered by the expectations of their slaves, more than productivity suffered. Social ties were broken, political fault lines opened up, slaveholders' inadequacies became public. In a diary entry from December 1864, plantation mistress Dolly Lunt Burge summed up the humiliation she felt as a result of her failure – the failure of the master class – to provide. Located near Covington, Georgia, her husband's plantation lay in the path of Sherman's relentless march to the sea. By Christmas, the army had passed, the surrounding countryside in ruins. On December 25th, she awoke to an all-too-familiar refrain. Her bondpeople roused the plantation, as usual, with calls of "Christmas gift mistress Christmas gift mistress," but wartime deprivation had struck hard. There would be no white offerings. The mistress "pulled the covers over [her] face & was soon mingling [her] tears"

---

41 Jacobs, *Incidents in the Life of a Slave Girl*, 180.
42 Dougald MacMillan, "John Kuners," *Journal of American Folklore* 39 (1926): 55. Quoted in Levine, *Black Culture, Black Consciousness*, 13 and Nissenbaum, *Battle for Christmas*, 289.
43 E. P. Thompson, *Customs in Common: Studies in Traditional Popular Culture* (New York: New Press, 1993), 467–531; Edward Muir, *Ritual in Early Modern Europe* (New York: Cambridge University Press, 1997), 85–116.

with her daughter's. Such tiny episodes, mingling joy and pain, expectation and dread, point up abundantly to the irreparable and perhaps inevitable fissures at paternalism's core that had so long threatened to rupture. With no whip to threaten and no goods to guile, bonds so carefully tended could not but fail.[44]

Political and economic implications of melding of gift and commodity exchange resonated far beyond transactions themselves. By providing slaves with "trifles" or "luxuries," practical patriarchs aimed to dampen discontent, cultivate compliance, and boost production. In gift wrapping provision and commodity exchange, political paternalists revealed more ambitious designs. Through carefully-crafted rituals of subordination, individualization, and isolation, slaveowners strove to strengthen the bond between master and slave. Yet such ties bound them in ways less reassuring than vexing. Strategizing slaves compelled masters to make meaningful that bond and held owners accountable to the bargains they proffered. Gift exchange exposed an unending cycle of ties frayed, mended, and frayed once again. Momentary victories – material and political, validating and subversive – marked this process, revealing the strangling web of reciprocity at the heart of the peculiar institution.

War time example not really a good example.

[44] Dolly Lunt Burge, *The Diary of Dolly Lunt Burge, 1848–1879*, ed. Christine Jacobson Carter (Athens: University of Georgia Press, 1997), 166.

6

The Choice

My husband was a slave – he hired himself and worked hard and saved his money and bought himself – he then married me and afterwards bought me of my master about 30 years ago. My daughter Bettie was then two years old and my husband and I bought her – that is the way we became free – we then all worked hard and saved our wages until we could buy the place where I now live.[1]

Commenting on eighteenth-century probate inventories, Ann Smart Martin has characterized the furniture, silverware, candlesticks, bedding, and other material goods represented therein, not as a snapshot of spending and acquisition, but rather as a representation of a lifetime of consumption. Although she does not provide a clear timeline of purchase, through her 1873 petition, Annie Smith relayed a similar story to members of the Southern Claims Commission in Stafford, Virginia. The purchase of herself, her husband, and her daughter surely involved careful planning and, likely, material sacrifice.[2]

What were some of these sacrifices? Smith did not elaborate, but the foregoing chapters indicate that a vast array of material goods were available to slaves looking to spend their money on more immediate needs and desires, essentially creating a material image of themselves and their surroundings, however temporary, that was markedly different from the ones prescribed by their masters. Harriet Jacobs, a woman who eventually would appropriate her body through theft rather than purchase, commented on the drab clothing provisioned by her master. Regarding the "linsey-woolsey dress" supplied to her and her fellow bondwomen every winter, she exclaimed, "How I hated it! It was one of the badges of slavery." As we have seen, through engagement in the

---

[1] Claim of Annie Smith, Stafford County, VA, SCC.
[2] Ann Smart Martin, "Buying into the World of Goods: Eighteenth-Century Consumerism and the Retail Trade from London to the Virginia Frontier" (Ph.D. diss., College of William and Mary, 1993), 39. See also Ann Smart Martin, *Buying into the World of Goods: Early Consumers in Backcountry Virginia* (Baltimore: Johns Hopkins University Press, 2008), 121–127.

internal economy, enslaved men and women could replace material "badges of slavery" with, presumably, markers of freedom – a gold watch, a silk vest, a dram of liquor drunk in a tavern with local white and black men. They may have dreamed of one day purchasing themselves or their families, but the risks, limitations, or simple impracticalities of the marketplace for slave bodies often made more immediate material spending more gratifying.[3]

This chapter explores the process by which slaves engaged in the ultimate act of consumption – the procurement of themselves and their families. Enslaved people's experience in the internal economy provided some with means to make self-acquisition a reality and, equally importantly, prepared them for the risks and rewards of doing so. The skills, strategies, and justifications employed by bondpeople as consumers of material goods and property translated to acquisition of their bodies through purchase, theft, or gift. Even though the risks and rewards were greater, the choices, skills, and perils of such exchange were necessarily similar. Admittedly, the slaves and masters described here represent but a small portion of the antebellum southern population. But in highlighting the "choice" made by bondpeople and masters alike, we see slavery in its most twisted and tragic form. In the exchange of human bodies, risk was amplified – for master, slave, and the peculiar institution itself.

Slaves involved in self-purchase generally characterized their transactions in one of two ways. First, they explained the consumer process in the form of the tangible. "I was formerly a slave. I bought myself in 1850 of my master" or "I bought myself and finished paying for myself about 20 years ago." Others referred to the intangible concept of freedom. "I was born and lived a slave till 1853 at that time I bought my freedom" or "I bought my freedom about a year before the war." Most, it seems, showed little preference, using the terms interchangeably. According to freedwoman Charlotte Baker, "She [her mistress] allowed me a chance to buy my freedom. I worked and paid for myself."[4] Even though southerners, black and white, might have cared little about such terminology, thinking about the terms "freedom," "self," and notably, "time" allows us to think more critically about the mechanics and, as a conclusion to this chapter and this project, the meaning of the consumer process.

Dylan Penningroth has aptly described slaves' market activity as an "economy of time," with bondpeople accumulating the time to earn money

---

[3] Harriet Jacobs, *Incidents in the Life of a Slave Girl. Written by Herself*, ed. Lydia Maria Francis Child (Boston: Printed for Author, 1861), 20.

[4] Claim of James Simpson, Warren County, Virginia, SCC; Claim of Lewis Dunn, Cumberland County, North Carolina, SCC; Testimony of John Wilson in claim of Charlotte Thompson, Chatham County, Georgia, SCC; Testimony of Charles Bromfield in claim of William Anderson, Chatham County, Georgia, SCC; Testimony of Charlotte Baker in claim of Sarah Ann Black, Chatham County, GA. For an enlightening investigation of strategies enacted by families seeking manumission, see T. Stephen Whitman, *The Price of Freedom: Slavery and Manumission in Baltimore and Early National Maryland* (Lexington: University Press of Kentucky, 1997), esp. ch. 5.

claims commissions

and amassing property by completing tasks early (if laboring under the task system), performing overwork for their master (if laboring under the gang system), and/or significantly, hiring out. Under the hiring-out system, slaveholders essentially rented their slaves' time and labor to other white men or women. The hiring-out system has been described in detail, and the historiography does not bear repeating here, but as it relates to bondpeople's rental of their own bodies or time, a brief overview is in order. In most cases, the lessor and the lessee arranged these contracts and transactions. Some slaves, however, arranged their own contracts, agreeing to pay their master a certain amount of money, month to month or less commonly, year to year. Any money earned over the stipulated monthly or yearly payment went to self-provisioning and, if anything was left, personal profit. Jacob Allman of Marlborough District, South Carolina, for example, explained to claims commissioners that he would "hire my time from my owner and would then make little profits." Thomas David, also of Marlborough District, made more explicit the circumstances of his hire, explaining "When ever I could get a good job I hired my time at $26-per month." Charles Verene of Georgia hired himself at $12 per month, Pompey Bacon at $15 per month, and Alonzo Jackson at $140 per year. More interesting was Abraham Johnson of Chatham County, Georgia, who, after paying for himself, proceeded to hire his wife for $7 per month as well as both of his children for $6 per month each.[5]

Those slaves who hired their own time lived with a relative lack of oversight and, with the money left over from the rental fee they paid their masters, could provision themselves. It was not an easy life by any means, but self-hired bondpeople valued the opportunities to spend or save the excess fruits of their labor without the constant monitoring of a prying master. This relative autonomy, it is worth noting, spurred complaints by whites who not only feared unnecessary competition with black laborers, but also worried that these men and women had too much unsupervised time to themselves during which they could move freely and in secrecy, easily devising plans for insurrection.[6] Fears of insurrection, as we know, largely proved unfounded, but the relative autonomy of choice allowed by the hiring-out system equated to quasi-freedom for some bondpeople. In some cases, this line was difficult to determine. A deposition

[5] Dylan C. Penningroth, *Claims of Kinfolk: African American Property and Community in the Nineteenth-Century South* (Chapel Hill: University of North Carolina Press, 2003), 49; Claim of Jacob Allman, Marlborough District, South Carolina, SCC; Claim of Thomas David, Marlborough District, South Carolina, SCC; Claim of Charles Verene, Chatham County, Georgia, SCC; Claim of Pompey Bacon, Liberty County, Georgia, SCC; Claim of Alonzo Jackson, Georgetown District, South Carolina, SCC; Claim of Abraham Johnson, Chatham County, Georgia, SCC. For a thorough overview of slave-hiring practices, see Jonathan D. Martin, *Divided Mastery: Slave Hiring in the American South* (Cambridge, MA: Harvard University Press, 2004).

[6] See, for example, *Legislative Petitions*, South Carolina, Richland District, ca. 1822 (PAR# 11382222).

contained within the records of the Southern Claims Commission reveals this fine line. Interrogating a claimant, Ray Johnson, a commissioner asked:

Q: You were a slave?
A: Yes Sir, once.
Q: When did you get your freedom?
A: I rented of him.
Q: You mean you bought yourself?
A: Yes Sir, during the war, but I rented a farm in the first part of the war.[7]

There was obvious miscommunication on the part of the two men, but this confusion only serves to highlight the complexity of the freedom process. Johnson, at some point, hired himself out to his master, giving him not wages but two-fifths of everything he raised. With the rest of his crop and his profits, he provisioned himself and bought a couple of horses (among other items not listed specifically in his claim). In other words, prior to the war, Johnson, like some other bondpeople, had been able to acquire some trappings of freedom, whether material goods or simply the ability to buy them, and then through this process had accumulated enough money to purchase himself.

In any case, renting oneself or renting one's time goes to the heart of the contradictions inherent in slavery, and required a good bit of mental gymnastics by both defenders and critics of the institution. Abolitionist critiques of slavery as a labor system, as Amy Dru Stanley has argued, rested fundamentally on principles of classical liberalism, specifically the notion of freedom of contract. Many abolitionists, among them William Lloyd Garrison, celebrated the freedom that wage labor allowed, using it as a foil to the coerced nature of bonded labor. According to Stanley, "the autonomy expressed in wage labor was but an offshoot of the underlying right of property in the self that constituted the taproot of contract freedom."[8] Self-proprietorship was key to this equation. Northern proponents of labor reform, of course, disagreed. In true republican fashion, they argued instead that the wage system itself was a form of slavery, equating wages with the loss of productive property. To Garrison and his followers, the purchase of the body was enough. To those concerned with the growing loss of independence by free wage labor, freedom was something entirely different. Under the lash, antebellum slaves could conceive of their enslavement in both ways. The fruits of the labor they reaped for their master denied, they could identify with northern laborers who struggled to preserve their independence as workers. But, based on their experience with the internal economy, they harbored classically liberal desires to transact their economic affairs freely.

[7] Claim of Ray Johnson, Warren County, Virginia, SCC.
[8] Amy Dru Stanley, *From Bondage to Contract: Wage Labor, Marriage, and the Market in the Age of Slave Emancipation* (New York: Cambridge University Press, 1998), 21.

Just as enslaved men and women were aware of the monetary value of common goods and services, many were acutely aware of, if not their current market value, then at least their price at the time of original purchase. Take, for example, an experience relayed by a northern traveler in the 1830s. As she stopped and chatted with a group of slave children, Barbara Bodichon recoiled in horror as a young girl seized one of her playmates and shouted, "I'll sell you this child for two dollars." In practical terms, the child likely would have earned much more on the auction block, but the lesson was clear to Bodichon. At a young age, these children knew they were a commodity to be bought and sold. As they grew older and became better versed in commodity culture, they came to comprehend their value and that of their fellow slaves in more realistic monetary terms. Escaped North Carolina slave John Quincy Adams recalled members of his master's family wandering the plantation, putting "their hand on one of the little negroes, and say[ing], 'here is $1,000, or $1,500 or $2,000,'" while Sarah Debro recalled her mistress threatening to put her grandfather "in her pocket," in other words, "sell him den put de money in her pocket." Likewise, traveler John Ingraham observed a conversation between two enslaved men about not only their market value, but what it meant in terms of personal reputation. According to Ingraham, one slave mocked the other, exclaiming, "You sell for only seben hun'red dollars! ... my massa give eight hundred and fifty silver dollars for me. Gom! I tink dat you was more 'spectable nigger nor dat."[9]

Naturally, enslaved people, well aware of their market value and well-versed in the mechanics of the internal economy, could at least dream of the possibility of purchasing themselves. But as in the internal economy, enslaved people ran up against limits to their spending. As Liberty County slave July Leconte recalled, slaves on one lowcountry plantation "were allowed to raise anything but a <u>colored man</u>." More specifically, state legislatures regulated manumissions, imposing more limits and restrictions as the antebellum period progressed. In South Carolina, until the beginning of the nineteenth century, manumission, whether by will or by purchase, was a contract between master and slave requiring no state approval. The Act of 1800, however, required the blessing of the Court of Magistrates and Freeholders. Designed to ensure that slaves were not too old, ill, or depraved to handle the responsibilities

---

[9] Barbara Leigh Smith Bodichon, *An American Diary, 1857–1858*, ed. Joseph W. Reed, Jr. (London: Routledge and Kegan Paul, 1972), 77; John Quincy Adams, *Narrative of the Life of John Quincy Adams, When in Slavery, and Now as a Freeman* (Harrisburg, PA: Sieg, 1872), 9; George P. Rawick, ed., *The American Slave: A Composite Autobiography*, 41 vols. (Westport, CT: Greenwood Press, 1972–1978), 14, pt. 1: 248; [John Holt Ingraham], *The South-West, By a Yankee* (New York: Harper and Brothers, 1835), 2: 30–31. Walter Johnson has described this process of commodification as the "chattel principle," arguing that "children were taught to experience their bodies twice at once, to move through the world as both child and slave, person and property." Walter Johnson, *Soul by Soul: Life Inside the Antebellum Slave Market* (Cambridge, MA: Harvard University Press, 1999), 22.

of freedom, the act did little to limit manumissions. By 1820, however, the state had become wary of the growing influence of the free black population, declaring that only the state legislature could grant acts of manumission and prohibiting free blacks from freely entering or leaving the state. By 1841, the state prohibited manumission altogether, voiding private wills and contracts. Georgia's and North Carolina's legislation was more strict much earlier. In 1741, the North Carolina legislature limited manumission to those men and women who had performed "meritorious service" as determined by a county court. Ostensibly seeking to remove the possibility of a freed slave becoming a "burden" to the state, North Carolina in 1812 began to require bonds for all freed slaves. Despite these limitations, the legislature itself continued to grant manumissions freely, with little discussion of "meritorious service." But by 1830, North Carolina too had become wary of unchecked increases in the free black population. An 1830 legislative act required that manumitters file a petition and pay a bond in the sum of $1,000. In Georgia, the laws were more forthright. In 1801, a law decreed that a slave could only be manumitted by a special act of legislature; in 1859, the law decreed manumission mandates in wills could be ignored. In both of these states from 1830 to 1861, the laws were enforced intermittently and capriciously with little overall effect on the growth of the free black population. In Virginia, manumission laws were less prohibitive, as white Virginians were loathe to submit to the state's interpretation of what they could do with their own property. In 1782, the legislature removed restrictions on manumission, though requiring masters to ensure subsistence for their former slaves. While free blacks faced growing restrictions on their movement and livelihood as the antebellum period progressed, masters retained the right to manumit slaves as they pleased.[10]

These laws were not inflexible but were capricious, setting uncertain standards for manumission from state to state and often from court to court. Slaves sought to elide them, either by finagling contracts that allowed bondpeople to live lives of quasi-freedom or, in the case of runaways, engaging in a more advanced form of moral economic behavior – stealing their own bodies. In each of these cases – manumission by purchase, emancipation through theft, or

[10] Testimony of Cato Holmes in claim of July Leconte, Liberty County, GA, SCC; Marina Wikramanayake, *A World in Shadow: The Free Black in Antebellum South Carolina* (Columbia: University of South Carolina Press, 1973), 31–46; John Hope Franklin, *The Free Negro in North Carolina, 1790–1860* (1943; Chapel Hill: University of North Carolina Press, 1995), 20–29; Benjamin Joseph Klebaner, "American Manumission Laws and the Responsibility for Supporting Slaves," *Virginia Magazine of History and Biography* 63 (1955): 443–453; Tommy L. Bogger, *Free Blacks in Norfolk, Virginia, 1790–1860: The Darker Side of Freedom* (Charlottesville: University Press of Virginia, 1997), 8; John Henderson Russell, *The Free Negro in Virginia, 1619–1865* (1913; New York: Negro Universities Press, 1969), 42–87. For concise overviews of all of this legislation, see Ira Berlin, *Slaves without Masters: The Free Negro in the Antebellum South* (New York: Oxford University Press, 1974), 138–157 and Andrew Fede, *Roadblocks to Freedom: Slavery and Manumission in the United States South* (New Orleans: Quid Pro Books, 2011), 87–138.

freedom through gift – enslaved southerners in their capacity as consumer and consumable drew on their understanding of the market to formulate skills and strategies to deal with the perils of the purchase of black bodies.

Slaves who saved their money, thereby confounding stereotypes of imprudence and intemperance assigned to them by white southerners, might establish freedom as the goal of their patient efforts. From a young age, children could make the connection between the money they earned from small chores and gifts and the possibility of one day buying themselves. Traveler Charles Grandison Parsons related a conversation between a young slave boy and a "Yankee" boarder in Georgia. The boy ran up to the man and said, "Mr. L., I want you to give me a dollar." Asked what he was going to do with the money, the boy proudly announced, "I am going to keep all the money I can get, so when I get enough, I can buy my FREEDOM!!" Lunsford Lane recalled similar childhood aspirations, relaying to his readers the moment he began saving for freedom. As a young boy, his father had given him a small basket of peaches that he sold for 30 cents, the first money he had ever earned. Shortly after, he won some marbles, again selling them for a pittance. Later he received $1 from a guest of his master for his attentiveness as a house servant. According to Lane, "These sums, though small, appeared large in my estimation; and hope again revived in my bosom that at some future time, by perseverance and economy, I might purchase my freedom. Henceforth I longed for money, and plans for money-making took principal possession of my thoughts." North Carolina slave Tom Jones would carry this sense of delayed gratification with him to adulthood. With the goal of family purchase, he and his wife "made a box, and, through a hole in the top, we put in every piece of money, from five cents up to a dollar, that we could save from our hard earnings." A source of both security and anxiety, Jones and his wife constantly feared that thieves or patrollers would steal their savings, with Jones starting in alarm every time he "dropped a piece of money into my box, and heard its loud ring upon the coin below" for fear that a "prowling enemy" should hear it.[11]

Core values of temperance, industry, prudence, and patience clearly underlay strategies for pursuing freedom. "By honest industry," for example, North Carolinian Roger "acquired money sufficient to purchase his freedom" in 1838. Cato, a Virginia slave, engaged in a "steady course of industry and frugality" until he too saved enough to purchase himself. Henry Beadles of Fulton County, Georgia was more specific, explaining that he worked for himself "until midnight every night to make all I could for myself." His goal? "My wife

[11] Charles Grandison Parsons, *Inside View of Slavery: or a Tour Among the Planters* (Boston: John P. Jewett, 1855), 41–42; William G. Hawkins, *Lunsford Lane; or Another Helper from North Carolina* (Boston: Crosby and Nichols, 1863), 21; Thomas H. Jones, *Experience and Personal Narrative of Uncle Tom Jones; Who Was for Forty Years a Slave. Also the Surprising Adventures of Wild Tom, of the Island Retreat, a Fugitive from South Carolina* (Boston: H. B. Skinner, n.d.), 26.

and I were trying to make money to buy me." Even casual observers understood the importance of these values. Commenting on the weekly peck of corn
and occasional bit of rice and yams given slaves, a traveler to South Carolina
noted, "This is not sumptuous living; but the slaves have their own private
fields, poultry, and swine, and can often purchase delicacies; and I believe that
one, very prudent, might, in twelve years, collect enough to purchase his freedom." Such prudence, of course, required sacrificing immediate material luxuries. Frank Freeman of North Carolina recalled, "I had decided many years
before to save all my nickles [sic]. I kept them in a bag. I did not drink, chew,
smoke or use tobacco in any way during this time." When freedom came, he
was prepared, having saved $47.75 to help start his new life.[12]

But saving money was not easy, and it often took the collaboration of bondpeople, free blacks, and white acquaintances to make purchase possible. Claims
commissioners reacted with surprise when they found that Nancy Brewer had
purchased her husband, noting on her claim, "He was formerly a slave, but she
had bought him & he belonged to her!" More astonishing, Elijah Thomas, a
Virginia freedman, bought his first wife (while married to, presumably, his second). Elvira Jones purchased her son and daughter in 1823, and Isaac Motes
bought his seventeen-year-old nephew in 1830. In some cases, having patiently
saved and emancipated themselves, freedmen set freedom of another family
member or acquaintance as their next spending goal. Phil Sewell, for example,
bought himself for $650 and then bought his daughter and son-in-law, while
James Dunn purchased himself, his mother, wife, and son over the course of
his lifetime. Petitions to southern legislatures are filled with stories of such
sacrifice.[13]

Formal and informal contracts for payment were often complex, involving
collaboration with white men, payment by installment, and extensions of debt
and credit. Billy Brown borrowed money from a Virginia "gentleman," later
paying off his purchase price. Likewise, Moses, a Virginia slave, hired his time
to a local white man who in turn offered to purchase him, allowing him "at
reasonable and stipulated wages to serve him a time sufficient to reimburse
the purchase money as a ransom of his subsequent liberty." Similarly, William
Williams purchased a slave couple and their child following their masters' death,
allowing them to pay their purchase price in return for manumission. David,
in 1848, advanced a white man, Alexander McNight, $1,000 so that he might

[12] *Legislative Petitions*, North Carolina, Davie County, 25 December 1838 (PAR# 11283805);
Legislative Petitions, Virginia, Amherst County, 16 December 1822 (PAR# 11682201); Claim
of Henry Beadles, Fulton County, Georgia, SCC; G. M., "South-Carolina," *The New England
Magazine* 1 (1831): 339; Rawick, *American Slave*, 14, pt. 1: 320.

[13] Claim of Nancy Brewer, Orange County, North Carolina, SCC; Claim of Jane Thomas, Roanoake
County, Virginia, SCC; *Legislative Petitions*, Virginia, Richmond, 5 December 1823 (PAR#
11682304); Claim of Joseph Sneed, Chatham County, Georgia, SCC; Claim of Phil Sewell,
Dinwiddie County, Virginia, SCC; *Legislative Petitions*, North Carolina, Richmond County, 2
November 1854 (PAR# 11285401).

purchase him from his current master, with the understanding that McNight would then emancipate the slave. At age thirty, Georgia slave Charlottte Baker arranged for a white man, John Sewell, to act as her guardian, convincing him to buy her for $800 and paying him the purchase price in return.[14]

Just as with any market transaction, the purchase of oneself or family involved extraordinary risks. The capriciousness of the law and its enforcers and the uncertainty of nineteenth-century southern life meant that considerable complications could accompany purchases of slave bodies. Dishonest sellers or creditors proved most worrisome for bondpeople looking to purchase freedom. David West, a refugee to Canada, recalled being cheated by a slaveholder over the sale and purchase of corn, commenting, "He was worth ten thousand dollars, and I was not worth ten cents." In chattel terms, West, of course, was worth far more. Had it been his body up for purchase, West would have had a more difficult time assigning monetary worth in the transaction. In any case, West's comment reveals a mindful wariness of the susceptibility of black slaves to white fraudulence in the marketplace. Silvia Baker applied this wariness to the market for freedom, explaining to claims commissioners that "many slaves made enough in that way to buy their freedom but they often got cheated out of there [sic] freedom but few would risk it." Those who did choose to take such a risk sometimes faced frustrating consequences. Toby Adams, for example, had to buy himself twice, paying $650 the first time, getting "cheated out of that," and then paying another $750. Such deception could come in a variety of forms. Overt bribery derailed Henry's aspirations toward self-purchase. A witness to his former mistress's will refused to validate the agreement for him to buy his freedom following her death unless he, the witness, received half of the testator's property. Another Virginia slave, James, agreed to pay one hundred pounds for his freedom, but once the sum was paid, his master demanded more money. A similar fate befell Catherine, a South Carolina slave who agreed to pay $300 for her freedom. Catherine paid for herself in full but, in the meantime, her master had died and his family refused to honor the contract. How heartbreaking was this chicanery? William Robinson revealed his family's bitterness at his father being cheated out of both freedom and the cash he put up to buy it. Having begun to "pay for himself on the installment plan," Robinson's father had given $800 to his master and then hired himself out to a surveying company in California. A short time later, his family received word that he was "returning in chains," his master content to "rob him of what he had paid."[15]

---

[14] *Legislative Petitions*: Virginia, Prince Edward County, 14 December 1825 (PAR# 11682506); Virginia, Goochland County, 18 December 1822 (PAR# 11682205); North Carolina, Martin County, 28 November 1811 (PAR# 11281101); North Carolina, Franklin County, October 1848 (PAR# 11284801); Testimony of Charlotte Baker in claim of Sarah Ann Black, Chatham County, Georgia, SCC.

[15] Benjamin Drew, *A North-Side View of Slavery. The Refugee; or, The Narratives of Fugitive Slaves in Canada Related by Themselves, with an Account of the History and Condition of*

Some would-be freedpeople suffered less as a result of deception than of simple ignorance of the law. Georgia ex-slave James Deneson, for example, bought his freedom in 1850 but failed to get his papers and was sold back into slavery. Likewise, Willis fulfilled a contract with his master and received a "Certificate of Emancipation" from a North Carolina court. Unfortunately the certificate did not give him "a name or title" by which he could purchase or sell property, sue, or "otherwise enjoy many of the rights and privileges of a free person of color." Others succumbed to the will of the legislatures, their contracts for freedom falling through as legal statutes regarding free blacks became harsher. In South Carolina, Simon had contracted with his mistress for his freedom, and by 1821 had paid her $400. Unfortunately, South Carolina outlawed manumissions in 1820, thereby negating their private contract. Another South Carolina slave faced an even worse fate as a result of the 1820 law. Faced with the prospect of being sold, he arranged to have a white acquaintance purchase and manumit him. The slave, John, had saved a sum of money and had convinced the prospective buyer to contribute some funds of his own with the understanding that John would pay him back in full. Again, the shift in state law nullified the contract.[16]

Even if a man or woman purchased freedom without incident, special considerations complicated the consumer process. By the 1850s, only Arkansas, Delaware, and Missouri allowed manumitted blacks to remain in the state in which they had been enslaved.[17] North Carolina judge and slaveholder William Valentine commented on the plight of the newly-emancipated, explaining, "they cannot acquire [a residence] here and are not allowed to stay where they once could." Frustrated, just as freedpeople must have been, Valentine exclaimed, "What can be done for them!" Petitions to southern legislatures reveal the conflicted choices that accompanied many bondpeople's purchase of freedom. Jacob, for example, had agreed to pay fifty-six pounds, five shillings to his master's creditor; he had paid twenty-five pounds when in 1806, the Virginia legislature mandated that emancipated slaves had to leave the state. An elderly Virginia slave, James Butler, patiently saved his money and paid his master for his freedom in 1812. His joy at his release from bondage was short-lived, however, as he faced the prospect of having to emigrate from Virginia.

---

the *Colored Population of Upper Canada* (Boston: John P. Jewett, 1856), 90; Claim of Silvia Baker, Liberty County, Georgia, SCC; Claim of Toby Adams, Chatham County, Georgia, SCC; *Legislative Petitions*, Virginia, Richmond, 11 November 1814 (PAR# 11681412); *Legislative Petitions*, Virginia, Hampshire County, 1813 (PAR# 11681302); *Legislative Petitions*, South Carolina, Charleston District, ca. 1822 (PAR# 11382227); William H. Robinson, *From Log Cabin to the Pulpit, or, Fifteen Years in Slavery* (Eau Claire, WI: James H. Tifft, 1913), 16–17.

[16] Claim of James Deneson, Sr., Chatham County, Georgia, SCC; *Legislative Petitions*: North Carolina, Bertie County, 20 November 1816 (PAR# 11281608); South Carolina, Charleston District, December 1821 (PAR# 11382104); South Carolina, Charleston District, 16 November 1821 (PAR# 11382105).

[17] Berlin, *Slaves without Masters*, 138.

Ben Johnston faced a similar problem. Having contracted with his master for his freedom in 1807, Johnston broke his leg and was unable to immediately pay off his debt. Five years later, though still disabled, Johnston was able to pay the price in full, only to be told that he would have to leave the place of his birth. Another Virginia slave, Stephen Bias, was so distraught that he took drastic measures regarding his newly purchased freedom. He had bought himself and, in compliance with Virginia law, immigrated to Ohio. Having endured the "difficulty, danger, and expense attendant on his trip," he found that he could not live among the people there "with the least happiness or content-ment." So desperate was he to return to Virginia, that he "would prefer being sold into slavery in Virginia to being again compelled to emigrate to & reside in the state of Ohio."[18]

But it was not simply attachment to the homeplace that tempered the satisfaction of self-purchase, it was the certain separation from family that affected many slaves' choices with regard to freedom.[19] Among the worst horrors of the slave system was the constant worry that, as property, they could be bought or sold at a moment's notice, thereby rending asunder ties between sisters and brothers, parents and children, and husbands and wives. Frances Fedric, among many other slaves, lamented this sad fact, explaining, "A slave possessing nothing, and rarely hoping to possess anything, except a wife and children, has all his affections concentrated upon them; hence often, when torn from them, he pines away and dies." Fedric, of course, overlooked the material goods that he and his fellow enslaved were able to acquire, but the sentiment he conveys is significant. Family was important and, for those slaves who had the good fortune to have their family members close-by, the decision to purchase one's freedom and face the prospect of leaving them behind was heartbreaking and almost impossibly difficult. Lunsford Lane's narrative about his life as a North Carolina slave relayed, in detail, the moment he paid off his master and obtained freedom. This account was tem-pered, however, by the realities of slave life. Describing Lane, his biographer

---

[18] Entry of 26 November 1852, vol. 12, William D. Valentine Diaries, SHC; *Legislative Petitions*: Virginia, Fairfax County, 29 October 1814 (PAR# 11681411); Petersburg, 6 December 1810 (PAR# 11681002); Virginia, Stafford County, 3 December 1812 (PAR# 11681207); Virginia, Albemarle County, 14 February 1839 (PAR# 11683913). Careful readers will note that the Virginia petitions cited above were submitted prior to 1815 and might be considered outside the purview of this project. In state after state, flurries of petitions were submitted to legislatures in the five to ten years after the passage of these residency laws. In the case of Virginia, the act ordering free people of color to leave the state after manumission was passed in 1806. Because these petitions so vividly illustrate the excruciating choices newly-freed people faced, I have decided to include them in this study. For a chronology of the so-called "removal act," see Berlin, *Slaves without Masters*, 139.

[19] Recent work by historian Emily West provides a thorough and thoughtful assessment of the heartbreaking choices faced by African Americans in the wake of manumissions. See West, *Family or Freedom: People of Color in the Antebellum South* (Lexington: University Press of Kentucky, 2012), esp. 53–74.

wrote, "his cup of enjoyment is mingled with sorrow still; for his wife and children are all slaves, and may be separated in a moment when he dreams not of it."[20]

Lane's sadness stemmed from the continued worry that his family's master might sell them from their current home. But what of those who willingly left their families behind? Amid all of the choices an enslaved man or woman had to make as a consumer, this was likely the most difficult. James Langford purchased himself in 1852, but his wife and children remained slaves. In a petition to the North Carolina legislature, residents of Northampton County explained that his devotion as a father and husband was so great that he refused to leave them and that, in turn, he desired to remain in the state. As with many legislative petitions, the outcome of Langford's request is unknown. Virginia slave Jacob Spenglar was more specific. He had bought his freedom in 1825 but was tortured that, in the area, he had "numerous family connection, all of them slaves, and none of whom, could he possibly take with him for want of means to purchase their freedom." Burke submitted a similarly impassioned plea to the Virginia legislature in 1815, explaining that "although he is a person of Colour, he has attachments and affections, perhaps as strong as if it had pleased heaven to give him a whiter skin." He begged the legislature not to compel him "to adopt an alternative So distressing to his feeling they will not insist on maintaining a policy Verry questionable in its character and So Subversive of humanity."[21]

Especially when multiple family members were involved, timing was crucial in the process of self-purchase. Having diligently and patiently saved the money to buy freedom, bondpeople carefully calculated the time and money it would take to purchase family members. Uncertainties plagued this process. What were the relative profits of remaining provisioned as a slave and earning money during evenings and weekends versus working as a free laborer and provisioning oneself? How long would it take to earn enough money to purchase the freedom of another family member under each of these circumstances? Those less willing to take risks saved enough money under slavery to buy their entire family at the same time. Others calculated that as free persons they could earn enough before being forced out of the state. Edmund Keen,

---

[20] Frances Fedric, *Slave Life in Virginia and Kentucky; or, Fifty Years of Slavery in the Southern States of America* (London: Wertheim, Macintosh, and Hunt, 1863), 25; William Hawkins, *Lunsford Lane*, 15.

[21] *Legislative Petitions*: North Carolina, Northampton County, ca. 1852 (PAR# 11285203); Virginia, Rockingham County, 8 December 1825 (PAR# 11682503); Virginia, Washington County, 9 December 1815 (PAR# 11681506). In an interesting twist on a common problem for the newly-emancipated, a Virginia slave, Will, saved money to purchase, not himself, but his wife, who lived thirty miles away. "He was," according to the petition, "willing to devote all his little Savings during a Life of honest Industry to her Emancipation, that she might be at Liberty to choose a Residence near him." *Legislative Petitions*, Virginia, Campbell County, December 1815 (PAR# 11681518).

for example, purchased his freedom in 1849, but had failed to raise sufficient funds for the purchase of his wife and children. He petitioned the legislature to allow him to remain in the state until he could earn this money.[22] Frederick Williams also miscalculated the amount of time it would take to free his family. He explained his dilemma in detail to the legislature:

The petitioner, by long and patient industry was enabled to lay up a considerable sum of money, with part of which, during the last fall he purchased his freedom from his master at the price of $450. Your petitioner believed at that time that with the residue of money then in his possession and such additional sum as he could raise in twelve months he would be enabled to purchase his wife and children ... Your petitioner has found himself disappointed in this expectation – being unable at this time to pay a reasonable price for his family.[23]

An untold number of newly-freed men and women, particularly in Virginia where manumission remained legal, faced this same heart-wrenching calculation. Judith Hope summed their frustrations in a desperate plea to the Virginia legislature. Faced with the choice of "securing the blessings of liberty" or giving up "every friend and natural connexion upon earth," freedom appeared but a "cruel mockery."[24] Emancipation, Virginia freedpeople would come to understand, meant something entirely different than "the free use and disposal" of their own bodies – more often and more pernicious, freedom brought the breakup of families so often feared during their life in chains.

The stories relayed above present dismal portraits of the difficulties of a portion of the manumitted population. Certainly, other black men and women made the transition from slavery to freedom with less difficulty and fewer regrets. As we have seen, bondpeople naturally felt a sense of satisfaction, though perhaps only temporarily so, at having purchased a new hat or a fine pair of "store-bought shoes." Relatively speaking, the pleasure of having completed a successful transaction for purchase of oneself must have been exponentially greater and was one that some slaves went to extraordinary lengths to enact. Elizabeth Keckley was one of these bondpeople. Keckley approached her master and asked if he would allow her to purchase herself. If so, she queried, what price would he charge her? Irritated with the question, her master explained that, if she really wanted to be free, then she should just leave. Keckley was taken aback, assuring her master, "I do not wish to be free in such a manner. If such had been my wish, I should never have troubled you about obtaining your consent to purchasing myself ... By the laws of the land I am your slave – and you are my master, and I will only be free by such means as the laws of the country provide." Pleased by her answer, her master agreed to take $1,200 for herself and her son.

---

[22] *Legislative Petitions*, Virginia, Frederick County, 6 December 1849 (PAR# 11684904).
[23] *Legislative Petitions*, Virginia, Lynchburg, December 1834 (PAR# 11683410).
[24] *Legislative Petitions*, Virginia, Richmond, 11 December 1820 (PAR# 11682002).

Similarly, Booker T. Washington relayed the story of a slave who contracted with his master for freedom, agreeing to pay him in installments. In 1863, when the Emancipation Proclamation was passed, the slave still owed his former master $300. Explaining that "his word he had never broken," the man fulfilled his financial obligation. In most cases, it would seem, bond-people paid money for their freedom out of practical necessity. Although never a secure transaction, it was the safest way to procure their bodies. Slaveholders might have argued otherwise, but it is unlikely most bondpeople who bought freedom sought to legitimize masters' claims to their bodies. Keckley and Washington's fellow, however, actively sought the satisfaction of self-purchase, whether to fulfill a promise to their owner or to feel the sense of accomplishment of having earned what had once belonged to their masters. Washington, in fact, relayed this example as a means of exhibiting the essential honesty of African-American people, thereby countering claims of innate racial "rascality" so often assumed by white southerners.[25]

Slaves who ran away calculated the satisfaction of the consumer process quite differently. Working within a moral economic framework similar to that which justified theft of material goods from masters, runaways took something they believed to be their own – their time and their bodies. John Quincy Adams most clearly expressed this sentiment, remarking, "Well I do not know that I ever stole anything very valuable but one thing, and I think that every just man will say that I done right. In 1862 I stole John Q. Adams from Mr. George F. Calomese, of Winchester, Va. They valued me at $2,000. At that rate I stole $2,000." Likewise, Harriet Jacobs's brother William provides a stark contrast to Elizabeth Keckley and the slave Washington described. Following the death of their father, William and Harriet discussed hope for "brighter days" ahead. Harriet dreamed of hiring herself out and earning enough money to purchase her freedom. William scoffed at this notion and declared that "this was much easier to say than to do; moreover, he did not intend to *buy* his freedom." As it turned out, William and, eventually, Harriet refused to purchase themselves, both running North. Harriet, it is worth noting, eventually was purchased by a compassionate white New Yorker who wished to see her live without fear of recapture. To this transaction, Jacobs reacted with ambivalence, happy to finally live openly as a free woman but frustrated that it took a bill of sale to make such status a reality. Gone were childhood dreams of self-purchase. According to Jacobs, "The more my mind had become enlightened, the more difficult it was for me to consider myself an article of property; and to pay money to those who had so grievously oppressed me seemed like taking from my sufferings the glory of triumph." And, as much as she valued freedom, she

[25] Elizabeth Keckley, *Behind the Scenes, or, Thirty Years a Slave, and Four Years in the White House* (New York: G. W. Carleton, 1868), 48–49; Booker T. Washington, *Up From Slavery: An Autobiography* (Garden City, NY: Doubleday, 1900), 15.

"despise[d] the miscreant who demanded payment for what never rightfully belonged to him or his."[26]

Compared with the process of self-purchase, the act of stealing oneself entailed risks and rewards much more stark than those experienced with the appropriation of material goods. The rewards were obvious and similar to those resulting from self-purchase. The risks and associated punishments could be far worse. As Ira Berlin has astutely noted, "it took a special kind of person to leave the familiarity of a relatively small, if harsh, world and risk the almost certain punishment that would follow failure." Even slaveholding whites described the perils of running away. Recalling the experience of Essex, his father's favorite slave, J. G. Clinkscales explained: "The position of the runaway was unique. His freedom was purchased at a terrible price. With the silent stars his only sentinels, his house a hollow log or a hole in the ground, he had to be as sly as a fox and as alert as an Indian. Hunted by day and night, sometimes hungry and often cold, and with a constant dread of being betrayed by one of his own race, his life must have been a very hell." In Clinkscales's romantic description of the Old South, the sacrifice was not worth the risk. The responsibilities of freedom were too much to bear, he argued, as evidenced by the voluntary return of a weary and contrite Essex three years after his absconding.[27]

The risk of punishment or sale to a harsher master, the certain difficulties of the journey, and ties to home and family surely prevented many from embarking northward to freedom. Hence slaves only occasionally absconded on a whim, usually plotting their escape, waiting for the right moment, and earning money for food and bribes along the way. An acquaintance of Charles Ball, for example, decided to run "as soon as the corn was so far ripe, as fit to be roasted," allowing him plenty of time to prepare for his journey. Likewise, Virginia slave Isaac Williams sold fish as a means of "making money to come away." John Holmes was more rash. Unwilling to accept a promised one hundred lashes from his increasingly cruel master, he decided to appropriate himself and acted on it within the span of twenty-four hours. Although he had "some good clothes" purchased from money working nights, he had little money. He ventured sixty miles from his home "and got work, and stayed until I got some clothes and a little money." With these funds, he proceeded on his journey.[28]

With money in hand, bondpeople could use the market to facilitate their run to freedom. But as goods themselves, slaves had to take special care to conduct

[26] Adams, *Narrative of the Life of John Quincy Adams*, 47; Jacobs, *Incidents in the Life of a Slave Girl*, 19, 299–301.

[27] Berlin, *Slaves without Masters*, 45; J. G. Clinkscales, *On the Old Plantation: Reminiscences of His Childhood* (Spartanburg, SC: Band and White, 1916), 18–19.

[28] Charles Ball, *Slavery in the United States. A Narrative of the Life and Adventures of Charles Ball, a Black Man, Who Lived Forty Years in Maryland, South Carolina and Georgia, as a Slave under Various Masters, and was One Year in the Navy with Commodore Barney, During the Late War* (New York: John S. Taylor, 1837), 130–131; Drew, *North-Side View of Slavery*, 58, 172.

themselves as contraband – in other words, limiting the display of their bodies and altering appearance and behavior to adjust to realities of illicit or underground self-possession. For black southerners, self-ownership was anything but presumed. Almost inevitably, enslavement was inferred, and black men and women required constant positive proof of freed status in the form of documents or testimony of a white guardian. Even though they had taken possession of themselves, they could not use their own bodies publicly and freely. James Smith was lucky. In the fall of 1847 he "made arrangements and walked away." No one questioned him except for a man who knew him and proved to be a friend. Charles Lucas and two fellow runaways took more significant risks, but were similarly fortunate. Having lost their way, they stumbled upon a sleeping white man tending a lime kiln. They woke him, explaining they were looking for hire and asking directions northward. The man called their bluff, but proved friendly and advised them to "[k]eep away from the big road, walk near it, but not on it, – walk in the daytime, but keep in the woods."[29]

But fugitives could not always count on luck and, as Charles Lucas did, enacted strategies for self-appropriation via theft that were markedly similar to the illicit appropriation of material goods. Among the techniques for avoiding detection by slave catchers was simply to go into hiding, sequestering oneself until a move north could be made. In Spartanburg District, South Carolina, for example, members of a slave patrol found a runaway "boy" on a neighbor's plantation hiding in his friend Tom's locked cabin. Likewise, in Anderson District, a South Carolina court indicted Maryann for harboring runaway Simon, "by carrying to him victuals, and spirits & by sleeping with him ... in a camp in the woods." Sold away from his mother and siblings, John Little escaped a slave trader in Norfolk, Virginia. He ran, not to the North, but back south to North Carolina, where his mother and siblings lived. For two years, he "dodg[ed] here and there in the woods" until he was betrayed by a free black neighbor. James Sumler sequestered himself for less time, "remain[ing] concealed nine months," several times "run[ning] back to [his] hiding-place" when he felt the risks of heading north were too great. Harriet Jacobs spent six years in the garret of her grandmother's shed, not three miles from her owner's house. Her children remain enslaved, and she spent many days and nights clandestinely listening to their voices when they visited the house as she awaited safe passage to the free states.[30]

Just as enslaved people could alter stolen goods as a means of using them publicly, so too could they attempt to manipulate their appearance, wearing disguises to mask their identities. But these alterations could only go so far. Loren Schweninger and John Hope Franklin have argued that, although most

[29] Drew, *North-Side View of Slavery*, 352–353, 107–109.
[30] Spartanburg Trial Papers: *State v. Tom*, 28 July 1860; Anderson Trial Papers: *State v. Maryann*, 5 May 1843; Drew, *North-Side View of Slavery*, 205, 98; Jacobs, *Incidents in the Life of a Slave Girl*, 173.

slaves fled wearing the clothing provisioned by their masters, runaway advertisements reveal that they took with them an astonishing variety of clothing
and accoutrements. Slaveholders took special care to note a runaway's proclivity for "fine" clothing, with a few exhorting newspaper readers to watch for
black men and women wearing "Casimere breeches," "black silk or a white
Muslin gown," or "a double-breasted, grey broadcloth coat," possessions that
had served to distinguish men and women from their enslaved brethren, raiment that slaveholders hoped would facilitate recapture.[31]

But even if a master did not advertise the specifics of a runaway's raiment,
casting off the drab, coarse clothing of servitude would have helped little, as
the incongruity of fanciful clothing on dark skin served less to camouflage
than to draw attention to absconding slaves. Ultimately, the dark-skinned slave
could do little to alter his appearance in such a way as to make his body appear
to be his own. Light-skinned men and women, however, could and did use the
currency of whiteness to facilitate efforts at gaining freedom. Light-skinned
William Grimes, for example, recalled donning a "decent suit of clothes" and
walking the streets of Savannah, taking delight in eliciting respect from the
passing slave guard. Grimes would later use this whiteness to make his escape
northward, stowing away on a merchant vessel but freely passing through
southern ports of call with a fellow black sailor acting as his servant. William
and Ellen Craft traveled to the North more openly. The light-skinned Ellen disguised herself as an invalid gentleman, the darker-skinned William acting as her
manservant. Knowing that "many persons will sell a slave any article that he
can get the money to buy," William "went to different parts of the town, at odd
times, and purchased things piece by piece" to complete the couple's disguises,
including a pair of spectacles and a set of fine men's clothing. This combination
of light skin and the possession of fine clothes and a black slave allowed Ellen
to purchase food and passage by rail and steamboat. They encountered few
problems, although William found that he had been somewhat overzealous in
the purchase of his own accoutrements. In his anxiousness to alter his appearance, he purchased a "very good second-hand white beaver," an item of luxury
he had never "indulged" in before. Not surprisingly, the hat drew attention and
scorn, a white traveler exclaiming to Ellen, "I reckon, stranger, you are 'spiling'
that ere nigger of yourn, by letting him wear such a devilish fine hat. Just look
at the quality on it; the President couldn't wear a better" (Figure 6.1).[32]

[31] John Hope Franklin and Loren Schweninger, *Runaway Slaves: Rebels on the Plantation* (New
York: Oxford University Press, 1999), 219–220.

[32] William Grimes, *Life of William Grimes, the Runaway Slave. Written by Himself* (New York:
s.n., 1825), 41, 51–52; William Craft, *Running a Thousand Miles for Freedom; or, the Escape of
William and Ellen Craft from Slavery* (London: William Tweedie, 1860), 30, 67. It is worth noting that the Crafts were able to use such stereotypes to their advantage as well. As they traveled,
William held all of their money, correctly figuring that thieves would not bother to pick the pocket of a lowly slave. Craft, *Running a Thousand Miles*, 76. For other examples of fugitives passing into freedom, including a Tennessee mulatto with "straight hair and fashionable attire," see

FIGURE 6.1 Light skin and purchased goods enabled Ellen Craft's escape from slavery. *Source*: William Craft, *Running a Thousand Miles for Freedom; or, the Escape of William and Ellen Craft from Slavery*. London: William Tweedie, 1860. Courtesy of Documenting the American South, The University of North Carolina at Chapel Hill Libraries.

Despite a few stumbles and miscues, the Crafts made it to Philadelphia and then Boston. But, even there, they could not buy security. Charles Ball identified with their situation, explaining to his readers, "By the laws of the United

Franklin and Schweninger, *Runaway Slaves*, 214–215. For a discussion of slaveholders' fears that light-skinned slaves would run away, see Johnson, *Soul by Soul*, 151. For connections between passing and auditory markers of free status, see Mark M. Smith, *How Race is Made: Slavery, Segregation, and the Senses* (Chapel Hill: University of North Carolina Press, 2006), 34.

States I am still a slave; and though I am now growing old, I might even yet be deemed of sufficient value to be worth pursuing as far as my present residence, if those to whom the law gives the right of dominion over my person and life, knew where to find me." The Constitution provided for the return of escaped slaves but the law, as written, lacked any real power of enforcement. The more stringent Fugitive Slave Law of 1793 outlawed assistance to runaways and, in effect, validated slaveholders' contention that fugitives, as absconded personal property, rightly belonged to original owners despite living in free territory. The Fugitive Slave Law, passed as part of the Compromise of 1850, destabilized escaped slaves' already uncertain status as northern freedpeople even further. It required northern officials to aid in returning runaways, established policies of enforcement and extradition, and made it more difficult for black northerners to prove free status. William and Ellen Craft would feel the impact of the law in the form of two agents sent by their former master to retrieve them shortly after the 1850 statute was passed. Only the actions of the Vigilance Committee of Boston allowed them escape to Canada.[33]

Freedom for the Crafts, Harriet Jacobs, and Charles Ball was tenuous at best and, until 1865, there was little certainty that each one's most precious possession – his or her own body – was secure. But given their desire to slip slavery's chains, what other options did they have? Accumulating money for self-purchase was possible, but material temptations and the very cost of the goods in question made such pursuit speculative at best – for both these and the many others with similar aspirations. The possibilities and pain of life in bondage were instructive, once again. "You know what 'Daily Gift'?" Jane Hollins asked a WPA interviewer. "I was Daily Gift – Mausa give me to Miss Margaret, his daughter, when she was married to Mr. Gaillard – I give to Miss Margaret – I never was sold." This biblical allusion to manna – daily sustenance given by God to his people – symbolized sanctified means to tie further slaveholders' kin. For slaves it meant more, serving as yet another means through – and potentially out of – southern networks of exchange.[34]

Indeed, what better, more lasting, present than "the gift of freedom"? The ultimate bequest of benevolence, slaveholders imagined, manumission was a selfless act. From an economic perspective, the net loss was measurable in year-end accounting, labor, and capital lost. But bondpeople knew better. There was

---

[33] Ball, *Slavery in the United States*, 136. For discussion of fugitive slave laws, see Stanley W. Campbell, *Slave Catchers: Enforcement of the Fugitive Slave Law, 1850–1860* (Chapel Hill: University of North Carolina Press, 1968); Don E. Fehrenbacher and Ward M. McAfee, *The Slaveholding Republic: An Account of the United States Government's Relations to Slavery* (New York: Oxford University Press, 2001); James Oliver Horton and Lois E. Horton, "A Federal Assault: African-Americans and the Impact of the Fugitive Slave Law of 1850," in *Slavery and the Law*, ed. Paul Finkelman (Madison, WI: Madison House, 1997), 143–160; Craft, *Running a Thousand Miles*, 88–93.

[34] Rawick, *American Slave*, 2, pt. 2: 291–292. See also *Ibid.*, 2, pt. 2: 91; *Ibid.*, 3, pt. 3: 251; *Ibid.*, 3, pt. 4: 83.

always a cost. The strings attached to master's annual gifts told them as much. So, what merited the bestowal of freedom – master's gift of one's own body? *What made a gift?* As with material goods, distinctiveness and individuation were key markers of gifts given and, in the twisted logic of the slave system, those who received them, too. Slaves deemed worthy of claim to their own bodies were, in a word, special. They distinguished themselves from kin and community by means of uncommon action and attitude. Citizens of Accomack County, Virginia, for example, asserted that recently emancipated Peter Snead, was a "man of unexceptionable character, an industrious honest and worthy Citizen." Dolly, too, merited emancipation. According to a petition submitted to the Virginia legislature in 1834, she was "unexceptionable in her conduct," exhibiting "an affection and tenderness rarely if ever surpassed in the more exalted walks of life." Likewise, Isaac found favor with his mistress, Mary Thompson, for providing "more than Ordinary Care of the plantation & the affairs belonging to it" and "Considerably better[ing] the Circumstances of the Memorialist."[35] Indeed, manumitters throughout the South argued that those they chose to free were similar to the late Samuel Hyman's slave, Ned, a "very uncommon and extraordinary Negro."[36] Petitions to southern legislatures echo with a pattern of telling adjectives, saluting slaves who were "quiet," "obedient," "trusty," "humble," "moral," "upright," "orderly," "respectful," "sober," "honest," "submissive," "frugal," and "well behaved."[37] More important than any of these characteristics, however, were qualities of "faithfulness" and "fidelity."[38]

[35] *Legislative Petitions*: Virginia, Kanawha County, 24 January 1844 (PAR# 11684405); Virginia, Accomack County, 6 January 1845 (PAR# 11684505); Virginia, Henrico County, 9 January 1834 (PAR# 11683403); North Carolina, 1 December 1827 (PAR#11282707). See also *Legislative Petitions*: South Carolina, Edgefield District, 17 November 1823 (PAR# 11382310); South Carolina, Clarendon District, November 1836 (PAR# 11383601).

[36] *Legislative Petitions*, North Carolina, Martin County, 10 October 1833 (PAR# 11283306).

[37] See, in particular, *Legislative Petitions*: North Carolina, Wake County, ca. 1838 (PAR# 11283804); North Carolina, Randolph County, 21 December 1840 (PAR# 11284007); North Carolina, Montgomery County, November 1850 (PAR# 11285002); North Carolina, Northampton County, 9 December 1850 (PAR# 11285004); North Carolina, Cumberland County, 12 December 1850 (PAR# 11285008); North Carolina, Rockingham County, ca. 1850 (PAR# 11285104); North Carolina, Cumberland County, 20 November 1854 (PAR# 11285405); South Carolina, Union District, ca. 1820 (PAR# 11382020); South Carolina, Charleston District, 27 November 1821 (PAR# 11382110); South Carolina, Dorchester District, ca. 1821 (PAR# 11382122); South Carolina, Union District, ca. 1822 (PAR# 11382228); South Carolina, Pendleton District, 22 October 1824 (PAR# 11382401); Virginia, Amherst County, 27 December 1833 (PAR# 11683313); Virginia, Charlotte County, 10 December 1834 (PAR# 11683409); Virginia, Rockingham County, 2 December 1834 (PAR# 11683412); Virginia, Nicholas County, 9 December 1836 (PAR# 11683622); Virginia, Goochland County, 18 February 1840 (PAR# 11684006); Virginia, Halifax County, 15 December 1841 (PAR# 11684108); Virginia, Hampshire County, 20 December 1849 (PAR# 11684908); Virginia, Monroe County, 5 January 1850 (PAR# 11685004).

[38] See, in particular, *Legislative Petitions*: North Carolina, Cumberland County, 23 November 1833 (PAR# 11283304); North Carolina, Martin County, 23 November 1833 (PAR# 11283305); North Carolina, Randolph County, 22 November 1834 (PAR# 11283402); North

Barbara, for example, served her Virginia master Stephen Osborne with such "fidelity and zeal, that by the said will he emancipated her and her said children" in 1836. Thomas Hooper's will summed the terms of exchange perfectly, lauding the "wonderful fidelity, honesty, kindness, obliging & humane disposition, and trustworthiness" of his slave Matilda. The forty-five-year-old woman both distinguished herself from her fellow species of property and proved her devotion.[39]

Were slaves aware of what it took to gain freedom? A petition to the 1815 Virginia legislature indicates some did: George and Patsey understood that laws restricting manumission were needed in order to prevent the "evils consequent upon indiscriminate emancipation." Thankfully, they explained, they did not fall into *that* category themselves, "uniformly good & meritorious" as they were, and worthy of their master's gift of freedom.

Increasingly strict interpretations of manumission laws in North Carolina, Georgia, Virginia, and South Carolina meant that long tenures of diligent, devoted, and faithful service did not necessarily merit emancipation – nor would such service allow freedpeople to remain legal residents once manumitted. James Dunlop argued that although his slave had not performed a single act of "extraordinary merit," he had served faithfully "when the infirmities of your petitioner rendered such services at once doubly valuable and more than twice as difficult to be commended; and during the whole period, with a steady attention, an uniform fidelity, and an active devotion, which deserve more than mere commendation." In 1821, his petition found a hearing and a bill was drawn. As the antebellum period progressed, however, legislators were more fearful and less lenient; more and more was required to guarantee a freedperson's home

Carolina, Randolph County, 25 November 1835 (PAR# 11283502); North Carolina, Buncombe County, 26 November 1836 (PAR# 11283606); North Carolina, Cumberland County, 24 December 1840 (PAR# 11284008); North Carolina, Iredell County, 25 November 1842 (PAR# 11284203); North Carolina, Chowan County, 24 December 1842 (PAR# 11284205); North Carolina, Cumberland County, 17 December 1844 (PAR# 11284402); North Carolina, Montgomery County, November 1850 (PAR# 11285002); North Carolina, Cumberland County, 12 December 1850 (PAR# 11285008); North Carolina, 25 November 1856 (PAR# 11285601); South Carolina, Charleston District, ca. 1820 (PAR# 11382011); South Carolina, Charleston District, December 1821 (PAR# 11382104); South Carolina, Charleston District, 22 November 1821 (PAR# 11382107); South Carolina, Beaufort District, 23 October 1821 (PAR# 11382114); South Carolina, Pendleton District, 21 November 1831 (PAR# 11383105); South Carolina, Chester District, 23 January 1835 (PAR# 11383506); South Carolina, Charleston District, ca. 1836 (PAR# 11383603); Virginia, Nottoway County, 14 December 1824 (PAR# 11682402); Virginia, Pittsylvania County, 5 December 1827 (PAR# 11682714); Virginia, Franklin County, 8 December 1830 (PAR# 11683001); Virginia, Pendleton County, 7 December 1833 (PAR# 11683308); Virginia, Albemarle County, 31 January 1835 (PAR# 11683507); Virginia, Brunswick County, 9 December 1836 (PAR# 11683615); Virginia, Accomack County, 2 January 1838 (PAR# 11683809); Virginia, Prince Edward County, 13 January 1843 (PAR# 11684303); Virginia, Monroe County, 12 January 1850 (PAR# 11685003).

[39] *Legislative Petitions*: Virginia, Scott County, 17 December 1836 (PAR# 11683624); North Carolina, Cumberland County, 26 November 1834 (PAR# 11283404).

and emancipation at all. Still, petitioners plied legislatures with requests and, although fewer and fewer found satisfaction, we see the range of behaviors that rated comment and commendation. Petitioners might point to the extraordinary care given masters and mistresses in their most frail and debilitated moments. Amelia, for example, received her freedom and "sundry goods & chattels" for the "kind & unwearied care & attention" to her master "during a distressing & protracted illness which terminated in his death." The sons of Mary Campbell asked to free Sall, who cared for their mother who was "for many years blind and very helpless," while Alick earned this precious gift on account of the "zeal and fidelity" with which he cared for his ailing master. In a particularly gruesome example of such devotion, Stephen, in a 1835 petition to remain in Virginia, claimed to have been freed ten years prior on account of care given during his master's long illness. His master's "privates" had gone to stinking and rotting decay and the slave used his "rude skill to heal" the sickness. All to no avail, Stephen's master died, but expressed his gratitude through posthumous manumission.[40]

Those who risked their bodies to protect masters found favor as well. Vigilant bondmen stood watch over masters' manors and families and, on occasion, rose in their defense. Untold numbers of southerners lost life and property to raging fires. For that reason, petitioners found cause to reward those who prevented loss through courageous intervention. A group of North Carolina slaveholders noted, for example, Peter's "voluntary, prompt, and efficient aid in the suppression of fires." Sam provided a similar service in 1822, when "at the risque and peril of his life" he saved his mistress's home from fire. Twenty-six years later, his devotion remembered, his mistress's son sought manumission.[41] So, too, with more direct and perilous threats. Lewis and Jack dove into the Mud River "at the peril of their own lives" and rescued their drowning master. They were remembered in his will with the bequest of freedom. Last, not only was Adam "faithful," but "he preserved the life of his master, when unarmed and with no means of defence, threw himself between his master and a mad man who armed with a Knife had violently assaulted & wounded him." He, too, found freedom upon his master's death.[42]

[40] *Legislative Petitions*: Virginia, Richmond, 13 December 1815 (PAR# 11681510); Virginia, Petersburg, 5 December 1821 (PAR# 11682101); South Carolina, 21 November 1827 (PAR# 11382702); South Carolina, Chester District, 23 January 1835 (PAR# 11383506); Virginia, Nottoway County, 14 December 1824 (PAR# 11682402); Virginia, Washington County, 4 February 1835 (PAR# 11683504).

[41] *Legislative Petitions*: North Carolina, Cumberland County, 5 December 1848 (PAR# 11284802); North Carolina, New Hanover County, 1 December 1848 (PAR# 11284804). For more commendations for fire suppression, see *Legislative Petitions*: North Carolina, Cumberland County, November 1854 (PAR# 11285404); South Carolina, Charleston District, ca. 1823 (PAR# 11382314).

[42] *Legislative Petitions*: Virginia, Cabell County, 28 December 1836 (PAR# 11683628); Virginia, Brunswick County, 9 December 1836 (PAR# 11683615).

Were these extraordinary acts calculated investments of social capital? The question bears consideration, even if slave testimony and action provide few clues to its answer. Bondpeople understood there were advantages to be gained through cultivation of a master's good graces. Adhering to his dictates – or at least giving the impression of doing so – resulted in increased opportunities for independent production, improvement in material circumstances, and in these rare cases, freedom. Tending ties could very well pay off, it seems. But given the relative rarity and increasing difficulty of legal manumission, it seems unlikely that most bondpeople would act with such a goal in sight.

We might more profitably ask what slaveholders got by dangling promise – or simply prospect – of freedom? Bondpeople, slaveholders might calculate, would serve with devotion if they knew such a gift was forthcoming. But was there something else? Aside from questions of economy, why release that which they had striven so hard to keep close? An 1817 petition gives some insight. Aging Virginia slaveholder Peter Mock aimed to hearten his "drooping spirit" by freeing his slave Weiney and her daughter, Jean. We know little of the cause of his sadness, nor why he thought freeing his slaves would cheer him. At the end of his life, perhaps he sought lasting affirmation of the work he did on earth. After all, a woman so devoted as Weiney was proof of his good judgment, his benevolence. Or, given the decency and humane goodness Weiney modeled, perhaps guilt, not pride, had welled within him? We cannot know. What is clear is that masters freed those men and women whose devotion was unquestioned, whose fidelity was "unexceptionable." Paternalist ties strong, mastery seemingly secure, slaveholders could release slaves from their shackles. The gift of freedom, they imagined, would further cement the bonds between them. In securing those ties, they affirmed mastery. That much slaveholders desired, in life and in death.[43]

But what happened when that carefully-crafted paternalist connection was broken, not by manumission, but by those who interfered with it? Indeed, as with contracts in the market sphere, the gift of freedom ran headlong into countervailing interests. Outside the master-slave relation, unattached southerners had cause to disrupt collaborators' careful plans. In some cases, community assessments of a slave's character differed from the one imagined by the master. A group of forty petitioners in Edgecombe County, North Carolina, opposed Ely's manumission, for example, explaining that he was "what may be termed a bad Negro." Josiah Turner made a similar complaint in 1823, arguing that James, Duncan, and Stephen had "not the merits nor the moral qualities that would fit them for emancipation." Turner's character judgments warrant further examination, however. His purpose in petitioning the North Carolina legislature was to contest the will of his late wife's deceased first husband, claiming title to the slaves her first husband had wished freed. We do not know what happened to these three bondmen – Turner's petition was rejected, but

⁴³ *Legislative Petitions*, North Carolina, Iredell County, 2 December 1817 (PAR# 1128704).

we see no record of emancipation either. We do know, however, that Turner and his wife's brothers fought over the slaves for a full four years – the fate of James, Stephen and Douglas hanging in the balance.[44] Slaveholders understood their families better than others, anticipating such disputes and making plans accordingly. Set on emancipating her late-husband's slaves, Nancy Donnell worried that "distant relations, whose covetous & nigardly disposition suffer them, to oppose the object & wish of your petitioner" would contest his wishes; she asked that the legislature ensure enforcement of his will. Others forestalled potential problems with inheritors by providing stipulations in their bequests. For example, Christian Eaker wished to see his slaves manumitted upon his death. According to his will, his heirs would forfeit his estate if they failed to carry out his wishes.[45]

It was dismissals like these that highlight the compacts – realized and broken – that marked the exchange of slave bodies. As with material gifts and commodities, the boundaries between these modes of exchange were blurry, at best. The language of payment and present both echo in slaveholders' manumission petitions. South Carolinian Claude Rame, for example, sought to "recompense" Aurora, his slave, for her "faithful services, and meritorious character," thereby seeking emancipation of her and her four children. A group of North Carolina citizens made a similar request, asking that Dave and Alphonso be manumitted in compliance with their late mistress's wishes. The long sickly Mary Grover, they explained, had "confer[red] upon them the only boon in her power then to give," granting them freedom "as some compensation for the unremitting industry and devotion with which they rendered their service." North Carolina slaveholder Robert Walker made a more exacting calculation in deciding to seek manumission for his slave. In addition to being "honest & faithful," James had "amply paid him in labour for the sum he give when he purchased said James." The legislature denied his petition.[46]

Even as they spoke of compensation or payment, slaveholders knew freedom was theirs to give. Slaves knew it too and, whether through purchase or

---

[44] *Legislative Petitions*: North Carolina, Edgecombe County, 20 December 1838 (PAR# 11282306); North Carolina, Orange County, 16 December 1823 (PAR# 11282306); North Carolina, Orange County, 4 September 1819 (PAR# 21281904).

[45] *Legislative Petitions*: North Carolina, ca. 1827 (PAR# 11282721); North Carolina, Lincoln County, 12 December 1832 (PAR# 11283201). For petitions alluding to similar emancipation stipulations, see *Legislative Petitions*: South Carolina, Charleston District, ca. 1822 (PAR# 11382227); Virginia, Alexandria, 13 March 1850 (PAR# 11685012). For an extended discussion of the ways in which family relationships complicated slaveholders' manumission efforts and a wider discussion of obstacles to manumission broadly, see Ellen Eslinger, "Liberation in a Rural Context: The Valley of Virginia, 1800–1860," in *Paths to Freedom: Manumission in the Atlantic World*, eds. Rosemary Brana-Shute and Randy J. Sparks (Columbia: University of South Carolina Press, 2009), 363–380. See also Fede, *Roadblocks to Freedom*, 207–215.

[46] *Legislative Petitions*: South Carolina, Charleston District, n.d. (PAR# 11300002); North Carolina, Craven County, ca. 1844 (PAR# 11284405); North Carolina, Randolph County, 25 November 1835 (PAR# 11283502).

bequest, uneasily awaited that day of final exchange. North Carolina slave Daniel Macay expressed his "anxious wish and desire to become a Free man" in an 1834 petition. Having "been able to acquire enough money (without at all neglecting his duty to his master,) to pay for himself," he asked the legislature to legally manumit him. So, too, Sophia, who "anxiously expect[ed]" her emancipation as her master, Auguste Genty, put off his promise to free her "day to day, and from year to year." Her master, as it turned out, waited too long, his 1821 petition to the South Carolina legislature too late, her emancipation impossible. For Sophia and, as we have seen, many other men and women in chains, promises and contracts fell hard in the face of inequities that even cash and good intentions could not overcome. As crushing as such rejections must have been for slaves, the burden of expectation clearly weighed on masters too as more and more often their promises fell short in the face of state restrictions. Mary Warham explained to the South Carolina legislature that she had "covenanted and agreed with" her slave Simon, promising him freedom in return for $400. Having "paid the sum so contracted," she was ready to manumit him in 1821. Given South Carolina's recent law, the legislature refused to honor the contract. John Warren reported a similar problem, begging the legislature to "enable him to fulfill the trust reposed in him" by his slave John. John had approached Warren only a year earlier with "the savings of his industry," asking that Warren buy him and then allow John to buy himself. Warren agreed but South Carolina's 1820 law negated the contract. Palmetto State mistress Rebecca Drayton petitioned the legislature in 1820, asking that body to allow her to keep a promise to the relative who had bequeathed to her the slave Abba. The bondwoman had "always lived under the expectation of being one day free." The legislature cared not for her mistress's wishes – nor Abba's – and denied the request.[47]

In each of these cases, slaves' expectations of freedom were dashed. In that moment of denial, slaves found themselves victims of a distinctly unlevel market once again. The realization must have been devastating to those who had invested so much, but deep down, they could not have been surprised. The lessons learned here were not so different from the moral of bondage itself – for their owners too. With a shrug, slaveholders might simply have shouldered the mantle of mastery once again, but that task was now, surely, more difficult. Having promised the gift of freedom to those most devoted, they now reneged. Legal chains bound master and slave more closely than ever, but never before had they been so distant.

For those few men and women who sought freedom by purchasing themselves, stealing their bodies northward, or receiving a bequested release from

---

[47] *Legislative Petitions*: North Carolina, Rowan County, 20 November 1834 (PAR# 11283407); South Carolina, Charleston District, ca. 1821 (PAR# 11382120); South Carolina, Charleston District, December 1821 (PAR# 11382104); South Carolina, Charleston District, 16 November 1821 (PAR# 11382105); South Carolina, Charleston District, ca. 1820 (PAR# 11382011).

bondage, the hard lessons of exchange were instructive. Acutely aware of their dual role as consumer and consumable, they took special caution in acts of both material procurement and self-procurement. Indeed, few transactions were ever easy and nagging questions plagued all those who participated in southern exchange.

At its heart, what was the nature of freedom? What sacrifices were bond-people willing to make to acquire it? Frederick Law Olmsted pondered this complex issue. Noting that a number of slaves he had met as he rode through the Georgia lowcountry owned horses, he asked,

Will it be said, 'therefore, Slavery is neither necessarily degrading nor inhumane'? On the other hand so far as it is not, there is no apology for it. It is possible, though not probable, that this fine fellow, if he had been born a free man, would be no better employed than he is here; but, in that case, where is the advantage? Certainly not in the economy of the arrangement. And if he were self-dependent, if, especially, he had to provide for the present and future of those he loved, and was able to do so, would he not necessarily live a happier, stronger, better, and more respectable man?[48]

A thoughtful observer and inquirer of southern affairs, particularly aspects of "the retail traffic of life," Olmsted posed these rhetorical questions to his read-ers – queries he did not attempt to answer definitively. The well-traveled north-erner had seen enough of the South to recognize not only the inconsistencies in slaveholders' justifications of the peculiar institution, but also the fallacies of some abolitionist characterizations of universal material deprivation among the enslaved.

Certainly in a better position to judge than Olmsted, slaves hoped for the best. After all, having money and spending it as they chose allowed them occa-sional tastes of an unbound existence – bits of cultural power they hoped would translate to a life of legally-proscribed freedom, even if it meant giving up some of the provisioned security of slavery. This sentiment emerged most clearly in the testimony of those who gave up purchased property to the sol-diers who had come to liberate them during the Civil War. Even though they desired compensation for this lost property, petitioners to the Southern Claims Commission made clear their priorities. According to Peter Miller, "When they [the Union soldiers] first came if I had 3 times as much property I would have enjoyed them taking it if I could have got my freedom. I will be in favor of the Union until I die. Slavery is death." Charles Warner made a similar distinction between his hard-earned property and a life free from chains, proclaiming to commissioners, "My freedom was worth more to me than what little property I had." Still, some slaves admitted, it was difficult to watch their material goods carted away. William Gilmore explained that he had been angry at Union troops

---

[48] Frederick Law Olmsted, *The Cotton Kingdom: A Traveller's Observations on Cotton and Slavery in the American Slave States, 1853–1861* (1953; New York: Da Capo Press, 1996), 188–189.

for appropriating his property and leaving him and his fellow slaves "in very bad condition," but that he had been willing to make the sacrifice. Looking back on the experience, he explained, "I was willing to give all for my freedom I would not go back into slavery for twice the amount or any amount I value freedom too much to sell it for anything or any price." Similarly, William Lecounte, almost apologetically assured commissioners that he would "rather have [his] freedom than the property now," but he had patiently saved his time and money under the task system to acquire the horse listed in his claim. Others were "putting in for pay" and he thought he might as well too.[49]

In the uncertain years of war and emancipation, Edmund Bacon of Liberty County, Georgia, explained why he welcomed the arrival of Union troops, that he was "tired of working and not being at liberty – not being his own man."[50] Eighty years later, in the midst of the Great Depression, ex-slave Sylvia Cannon was less certain, her memories of slavery tinged with nostalgia: "Peoples would have found us colored people rich wid de money we made on de extra crop, if de slaves hadn' never been set free." Spurred by the presence of her white interviewer and current troubles, Cannon likely engaged in a good bit of hyperbole. The sentiment behind the statement, however, was sincere. Jane Johnson of Columbia, South Carolina, was more explicit and perhaps best exemplifies the interaction of consumerism, slavery, and freedom. In a conversation marred by frustration, Johnson asked,

They say slavery was wrong but what 'bout hard times? Dat is de worse kind of slavery, I thinks. All dis hollerin' 'round 'bout freedom they has, shucks, all dat kind of talk ain't nothin'. When you has work and some money in your pocket so you can go to de store and buy some meat and bread, then you has de best freedom there is, don't tell me.[51]

Apologists might point to Johnson's narrative and argue for the essential moral and material soundness of slavery. Such a conclusion, however, confuses slavery in her statement with its legacy. Inherent in Johnson's rant is a critique, not of emancipation itself, but its unfulfilled promise. Freedom, as emancipated slaves and their progeny would come to realize, entailed more than a removal of the shackles that had once bound them. In describing the work they performed for their masters, bondpeople expressed a republican desire for independence and the free use and disposal of the fruits of their labor. As participants in the internal economy, they harbored a classically liberal desire for freedom of contract. In the years following emancipation, they realized that freedom encompassed both of these ideologies, although its precise meaning was a source of contest in American life into the twentieth century.

---

[49] Claim of Peter Miller, Chatham County, Georgia, SCC; Claim of Charles Warner, Liberty County, Georgia, SCC; Claim of William Gilmore, Liberty County, Georgia, SCC; Claim of William LeCounte, Liberty County, Georgia, SCC.

[50] Testimony of James Stacey in claim of Edmund Bacon, Liberty County, Georgia, SCC.

[51] Rawick, *American Slave*, 2, pt. 1: 185; *Ibid.*, 3, pt. 3: 51.

In *Roll, Jordan, Roll*, Eugene Genovese argued that bondpeople in the American South "learned how to value their own land and to work for themselves but not how to defend and expand their interests in vigorous marketplace competition."[52] Genovese, however, only examined the productive capacities of slaves' participation in the internal economy. With the steady expansion of American markets, black and white southerners patronized local stores and exchanged with each other the consumer goods such a burgeoning economy offered. All segments of society struggled to define themselves using this expanding vocabulary of market and consumer culture, but African Americans and, particularly black slaves, also faced restrictions on spending designed to preserve slaveholder hegemony. Yet enslaved consumers adapted to shifting frameworks of management and moralism established by white southerners and developed strategies to acquire material goods in the manner they chose. They did not always succeed, but in their capacity as consumer and consumable, slaves understood – perhaps better than their masters – the risks and realities of marketplace exchange.

[52] Eugene D. Genovese, *Roll, Jordan, Roll: The World The Slaves Made* (New York: Pantheon Books, 1974), 539.

Conclusion

> But, tell me, Faustus, shall I have thy soul?
> And I will be thy slave, and wait on thee,
> And give thee more than thou has wit to ask.[1]

Across three generations and more, countless masters and slaves posed the question Mephistopheles asked and made their choice. Faustus's reward of riches and power was blighted by the knowledge that earthly abundance was fleeting; twenty-four years on he would be dragged down to hell and torn limb from limb. Whatever gratification they found in the temporary comforts of material exchange, masters knew and slaves surmised, there could be no lasting solace: the same fate, in one form or another, must befall all who worship Mammon.

Tens of thousands of individual transactions dot the documentary record of the Old South. In these scratched ciphers, practical prescriptions, and righteous recollections, we see snapshots, not just of local economic exchange or the banality of slave life, but of inexorable political struggle. Indeed, in most of the transactions this book has described, we see only the point of collision, that moment when goods, cash, or promises passed from hand to hand. The goal of this book has been both to understand the way forces accumulated, focused, and arrived at the point of contest and to trace the repercussions that echoed outward, reaching far out from the moment of talk and trade in which they began.

Consider James Towns, the Georgia planter who established a "pay day" for his slaves at the end of the year. We may imagine him sitting at a desk or table, his bondpeople appearing before him one by one. He glances up at the expectant man nervously awaiting his judgment, then looks down again, finding his

---

[1] Christopher Marlowe, *The Tragical History of Doctor Faustus*, in *The Complete Plays*, ed. J. B. Steane (London: Penguin, 1969), 280 (Act 1, Scene 5, Lines 44–46).

name amid the columns on the page. Are the "silver" coins in which he pays him and his fellows totaled and stacked near to hand, or does he reach into a sack, carefully and deliberately counting coin on the table? We cannot know. Thinking back to earlier days, weeks, or months, we can see Towns waking early and making his way to the local bank, exchanging a note for a bagful of silver. Amid holiday pleasantries, he made his request. Trading a knowing smile with the clerk, did Towns say that the silver was for his slaves? Or did he keep his plans to himself, avoiding the scrutiny that might attend explanation? Finally, we might conjure images of the moments immediately following judgment and payment, when his slave cast a smile, turning away, the jingle of coin hanging in the air. What satisfaction does Towns feel at that moment, imagining the tobacco or molasses his man might enjoy, or the fine hat he might parade a few days hence as a result of this largesse? Or is the aftermath of that transaction more grim, another end-of-the-year reckoning Towns can little afford?

We might think, too, about the other side of such transactions – Henry, Richard Eppes's tippling tidewater slave, for example. Eppes paid Henry $1 for not drinking whiskey over the course of 1852 – that is what the record tells us. We can paint the scene. It is a chilly, damp day, and Eppes keeps his remarks short – this much we know, too, from his diary. Eppes calls Henry forward before his bond kin, ceremoniously placing a crisp note in his hand. With a nod and a "thank you, Massa," Henry backs away, finding his place among the group once again. His take exceeds theirs, we know, and so do they. We can confirm little else about that trade: why Henry was singled out, when the deal was struck, whether Henry actually managed to abstain, or whether his master simply missed demon rum's mark. We don't know what he did with that dollar. Did he share the wealth with his fellows? Did he hide it under lock and key, reserving it for some future purchase? Or did Henry take that dollar – the very money he earned for his temperate behavior – and sneak off to drain a dram, chuckling heartily at master's naiveté?

And what about Sophie, the slave to whom her master, Auguste Genty, had become so "greatly attached" that he put off fulfilling his promise to free her year after year? We know that she "anxiously" expected her freedom and may envision her laying in bed at night, planning a life in which labor's reward belonged to her alone. How crushed she must have felt to hear of South Carolina's decision to restrict manumissions in 1820. Imagine the scene months later, her master's petition to the legislature – his last chance and hers for legal emancipation – denied. How does he break the news? We can see him calling her to the drawing room. With a curtsy, she complies, heart in throat, awaiting the words she has so longed to hear. They are not forthcoming. Is his voice strong and soothing, dismissing disappointment and offering sanctified security in perpetual bondage? Or does he shift uncomfortably, afraid to look Sophie in the eye, mastery flickering, acutely aware that he has let her down? We cannot know whether Sophie lets out a gasp of dismay, whether her eyes flash with anger, or if she simply stands in stony silence, her master's words washing over her. What does she think of this man who has failed so utterly to keep his promise to give her this most precious gift?

Again, we cannot know. Between evidence and imagination, the objective and the subjective, the gap remains vast and ultimately unbridgeable. Slavery's deepest secrets remain hidden. Arjun Appadurai has made this point plain, arguing that "[p]olitics (in the broad sense of relations, assumptions, and contests pertaining to power) is what links value and exchange in the social life of commodities. In the mundane, day-to-day, small-scale exchanges of things in ordinary life, this fact is not visible, for exchange has the routine and conventionalized look of all customary behavior."[2] Translated, we might say, a man may gain the world and lose his own soul – although we might never know it. Even in the increasingly mundane moments of southern exchange, we cannot forget that whatever else grew up on the threshold between master and slave, the dynamic core was constant struggle. It would be wrong to think that neither slaves nor masters understood the complexity and political import of this exchange. Even though they might not have fathomed the multivalent meanings of the ties transactions built and severed, both sides saw them as at once enticing and deeply worrisome.

Emancipation may have seemed no more than a dream for the enslaved. Yet markers of freedom assumed tangibility in the vast array of material goods available to slaves who spent money fulfilling more immediate needs and desires. Why should we imagine that the world of commerce would do any less, in that tortured place and time, than it does in our world today? Appetites, whetted by the enticing sensuality of masters' and markets' bounty, transfixed and transformed daily life. Slaves' fetishization of selves and surroundings diverged from masters' provisioned prescriptions. The ability to spend money, to make choices, to taste a material world outside of the one designated for the slave thus served as a powerful threat to slaveholders' hegemony.

Slaveholders saw the danger. As closely as they tried to script slave lives, they knew, markets were messy. Outside agents and material dreams encroached on the carefully-tended ties they had woven between slave and master. South Carolina planter Charles Cotesworth Pinckney admitted as much in 1837: "There is but one valid objection to this system; it gives trouble." Yet, he beckoned, "is not the object attained worth that trouble?"

My own experience of twenty years, and that of my predecessors for double that period, satisfy me, that in addition to the advantages already stated, it strengthens the bond of union between the master and his people. The sacrifice of our own time and attention

---

[2] Arjun Appadurai, "Introduction: Commodities and the Politics of Value," in *The Social Life of Things: Commodities in Cultural Perspective*, ed. Arjun Appadurai (New York: Cambridge University Press, 1986), 57. See also Frank Trentmann's discussion of the history and historiography of the "Politics of Everyday Life" in *The Oxford Handbook of the History of Consumption*, ed. Frank Trentmann (New York: Oxford University Press, 2012), 521–547.

to promote their comfort, is not in vain. They are susceptible of gratitude for favors repeatedly bestowed; and this one does not come under the doubtful head of privileges and indulgences that encourage idleness and discontent. It brings the reward of their surplus industry within the reach, and removes or diminishes the temptation to that illicit traffic which is the opprobrium of legislation.[3]

Here, in Pinckney's warming words, we see all that slaveholders strove for. A hunger for profit drove planters onward, but no wealth could ensure mastery. "The bond of union between the master and his people," perfect power, was the aim. That pursuit of this ideal risked all made its achievement, however partial, all the more precious. Yet strategizing masters proved too clever by half. Every aspect of the conscious schemes they spun ensnared them in dilemmas moral and practical, rarely finding resolution and perpetually undermining the peace and order slaveholders strove so desperately to create.

Whips and chains are but the most visible historical markers of chattel slavery. And, as historians from Kenneth Stampp to Walter Johnson have rightly emphasized, neither masters nor their "people" ever forgot what a "peculiar species of property" enslaved men and women truly were.[4] But to argue that the principle of property ownership dominated the master-slave relation underplays the gross cruelty of this most devilish – and human – of systems. More important than the whip's searing slash was the snap that hung in the air long after human flesh had scarred over. It was in that time and place that slaveowners did their most sinister work. Mastery meant manipulation, not just of material matters, but of emotional ties too. Slaveholders solidified their rule by cultivating a culture of mutual interest, enticing men and women with promises of gains most immediate. What bondpeople offered – and withheld – in return was mastery itself. Human drama, full of anger and affection, resentment and regard, played out daily as rulers and ruled negotiated this perilous terrain.

Property accumulation and paternalism both flourished amid expanding market culture. Far from resisting the incursions of trade, slaveholders embraced them, though warily, and as Eugene Genovese and others have argued, "on their own terms." Scorning unruly, divisive, and worrisome free labor, they used new market opportunities to bolster precapitalist social order. As this book has demonstrated, the increasing availability of cash and goods served planter purposes as well as the lash, although that political course came with significant costs. Time and again, the same weapons slaveholders wielded to scheme, manipulate, and repress were taken up by bondpeople to challenge masters' hold upon them. Payoffs backfired on both sides and the consequence was fracture, heartache, and redoubled contradictions.

---

[3] C. C. Pinckney, "The Traffic of Bond with Free," *Southern Agriculturist, and Register of Rural Affairs* 10 (1837): 283.

[4] Kenneth M. Stampp, *The Peculiar Institution: Slavery in the Ante-bellum South* (New York: Vintage Books, 1956); Walter Johnson, *Soul by Soul: Life Inside the Antebellum Slave Market* (Cambridge: Harvard University Press, 1999), esp. 19–44.

Caveat emptor, masters and slaves came to know with a bitter depth of understanding the legal maxim cannot begin to convey. Both sides cultivated and exploited spending opportunities to advance their interests. In the end, though, neither nearly reached their heart's desire, double bound as they were within a corrupting web of paternalist expectation. Some on each side drew back from this devil's bargain, but the lure of Faustian freedom mesmerized most, as it does today. Only in 1865 was the integument burst asunder.[5] Freedom's bell tolled and the twisted world planters and slaves had built was borne away.

---

[5] Karl Marx, *Capital: A Critique of Political Economy* (Moscow: Progress Publishers, 1977), 1: 715.

Note on Sources

Eric Hobsbawm has compared grassroots history to the "trace of the ancient plough," explaining that, although seemingly lost to time, "in a certain light, and seen at a certain angle, the shadows of long-forgotten ridge and furrow can still be seen." Getting at the mindset of a largely illiterate people is a difficult task and one that, as Hobsbawm has noted, can only be achieved through careful and imaginative querying of a vast array of sources. As Hobsbawm argued, "We cannot be positivists, believing that the questions and the answers arise naturally out of the study of the material." Such a philosophical model underlay the consideration of sources in this project. Hence, this book draws on a variety of perspectives and resources, ranging from tracts drawn from annals of planter prescriptive literature to court and claims records to the more intimate reminiscences of ex-slaves in WPA narratives.[1]

Slave life and culture did not evolve in isolation and the records of white southerners are crucial to understanding the opportunities and constraints faced by enslaved people on a day-to-day basis. Like Genovese's work, *Masters, Slaves, and Exchange: Power's Purchase in the Old South* tells the story of hegemonic struggle, sorting out the ideology, language, and tools of power in the Old South. The evidence used to tell this story reflects the wide discussion and consternation that marked ruling class discourse. Debates over slave management played out in the pages of southern agricultural and commercial journals such as the *Southern Cultivator, Southern Agriculturist, De Bow's Review*, and published treatises. Slaves' market activity, as described by contributors to these publications, emerges simultaneously as threat to

---

[1] Eric J. Hobsbawm, *On History* (New York: New Press, 1997), 209, 205. For a discussion of scholars' struggle to find, contextualize, and make sense of "voices" in the history of slavery, see Kathleen M. Hilliard, "Finding Slave Voices," in *The Oxford Handbook of Slavery in the Americas*, eds. Robert L. Paquette and Mark M. Smith (New York: Oxford University Press, 2010), 685–701.

plantation discipline, incentive and reward for industrious behavior, and evidence marshaled in defense of the material welfare of the enslaved.[2] Planter journals and diaries reveal similarly conflicting messages and anxiety. Taken together, these "white" sources-E support the complex and shifting material, moral, and management framework within and against which slaves engaged in the consumer process.

Petitions to southern state legislatures likewise provide a useful glimpse into the mindset of the master class, reflecting the wariness many whites felt toward slaves with money to spend. Between 1800 and 1860, over 1500 petitions regarding slavery were submitted to North Carolina, South Carolina, and Virginia legislatures. These documents describe slaves selling crops and labor, hiring time, and spending money on alcohol, weaponry, and games of chance. Just as importantly, the petitions reveal ambivalence and debate among members of the white community as they attempted to regulate exchange. But these petitions reveal more than white concerns – slaves (through the pen of white advocates) and free blacks petitioned the legislatures as well, especially on matters of property and manumission. These petitions indicate that the purchase of oneself was often a perilous undertaking and hence document the striking limitations facing enslaved consumers.[3]

Information gleaned from interviews of ex-slaves by employees of the Works Progress Administration in the 1930s is valuable for its insights on the mundane details of everyday life. For the purposes of this study, the narratives are particularly useful for commentary on the material and, notably, consumer landscape of antebellum slaves. In addition to general questions about the type, quantity, and quality of provisions, interviewers asked specific questions about slave spending. Among these queries:

> Did you ever earn any money?
> How?
> What did you buy with this money?[4]

---

[2] For a survey of management strategies outlined in southern prescriptive literature, see James O. Breeden, ed., *Advice Among Masters: The Ideal in Slave Management in the Old South* (Westport, CT: Greenwood Press, 1980).

[3] Loren Schweninger, ed., *Race, Slavery and Free Blacks: Series 1, Petitions to Southern Legislatures, 1777–1867* (Bethesda, MD: University Publications of America, 1998). Few legislative petitions from Georgia exist and thus were not included in Schweninger's collection. For an overview of Schweninger's edited collection of petitions, see Schweninger, *The Southern Debate over Slavery: Volume 1, Petitions to Southern Legislatures, 1778–1864* (Urbana: University of Illinois Press, 2001), xxv–xxxvii.

[4] "Supplementary Instructions #9-E to the American Guide Manual," Administrative Files, 22 April 1937, in *Slave Narratives: A Folk History of Slavery in the United States From Interviews with Former Slaves*, xx-xxii, Born in Slavery: Slave Narratives from the Federal Writers' Project, 1936–1938, American Memory, Library of Congress, http://lcweb2.loc.gov/mss/mesn/001/001.pdf.

The criticisms of WPA records are well-known, among them that, seven decades after emancipation, time had likely taken its toll on the memory of ex-slaves and that white interviewers might have influenced and/or overtly altered slave testimony as a means of portraying a more rosy picture of life on the plantation. Taken collectively, however, the narratives from Georgia, the Carolinas, and Virginia provide a crucial portrait of the material landscape established by the master and supplemented by the slave through his or her own earnings. Likewise, even though the memories of elderly ex-bondpeople might have been fuzzy about their experiences as the youngest members on the plantations, the narratives provide a unique chance to gauge spending opportunities by children as well as their first experiences with money.[5]

Although WPA narratives provide a useful glimpse into the lives of the enslaved, they sometimes frustrate the curious historian who desires a fuller account of thought processes and interpersonal relationships. Published narratives and memoirs by ex-slaves serve as useful elaborations of many themes that would later be broached by slaves in their interviews with the WPA. The style and content of these texts mirror the expectations of their northern middle-class audience. On one hand, the narratives reflect the market consciousness of the time, with special attention paid to the industry and thrift of the heroic slave. But the reform impulse that grew in tandem with market expansion in the North tinges these narratives, with most texts celebrating themes of domesticity, temperance, godliness, and overall consumptive propriety. Even though these were values likely held in high esteem by many members of the slave community, the texts' overt appeal to members of the benevolent empire is worth remembering.[6]

In 1866, as a means of reimbursing loyal United States citizens for property appropriated by Federal troops for military use during the Civil War, the federal government established the Southern Claims Commission. By 1880, 22,298 men and women filed petitions for lost property. Of the 5,004 claims allowed by commissioners, 602 were filed by ex-slaves freed before and during the war. Commissioners requested that petitioners answer a standard set

---

[5] For a useful discussion of the use of slave narratives as historical evidence, see Norman R. Yetman, "The Background of the Slave Narrative Collection," *American Quarterly* 19 (1967): 534–553; Yetman, "Ex-Slave Interviews and the Historiography of Slavery," *American Quarterly* 36 (1984): 181–210. Emily West has relied extensively on WPA narratives in her study of slave couples in antebellum South Carolina in which she engages in a thoughtful discussion of the rewards and drawbacks of WPA narratives as a source. See Emily West, *Chains of Love: Slave Couples in Antebellum South Carolina* (Urbana: University of Illinois Press, 2004), 5–8.

[6] For a discussion of the literary context of published slave narratives see West, *Chains of Love*, 8–9 and Jean Fagan Yellin, "Text and Contexts of Harriet Jacobs' *Incidents in the Life of a Slave Girl: Written by Herself*," in *The Slave's Narrative*, eds. Charles T. Davis and Henry Louis Gates, Jr. (New York: Oxford University Press, 1985), 262–282. Published northern travelers' narratives, also used in this project, similarly reflect much of this overt northern reform sentiment.

of queries regarding their loyalty to the union and the extent of their property ownership.[7] Among the questions asked:

> Did you own this property before or after you became free?
> When did you get it?
> How did you become owner, and from whom did you obtain it?
> Where did you get the means to pay for it?[8]

Black petitioners responded in some detail, anxious to convince dubious commissioners that, as chattel, they had been able to acquire property of some significance. This eagerness, it is worth noting, is one of the limitations of the use of SCC claims by historians. Some formerly enslaved men and women describing property lost between one and nineteen years prior surely exaggerated their claims, either of their own volition or at the urging of hired lawyers. On balance, however, the claims provide invaluable insight into specific methods of property acquisition in the antebellum South.

The claims reveal far more than information about property ownership, however. In all, 104 of the formerly-enslaved claimants had been freed prior to the start of the war. Upon interrogating a claimant of African descent, the commission first established his or her status prior to and during the conflict, asking, "Were you a slave or free at the beginning of the war?" and, more importantly for this project, "If ever a slave when did you become free?" In response, free blacks often described in detail not only their process of property accumulation, but also the material sacrifices and choices they made to save for and purchase the freedom of themselves or their families.[9]

Court records, particularly those that document trials of slaves and free blacks, are a useful resource for assessing patterns of black market consumption. The bulk of records used in this study is drawn from the Magistrates and Freeholders Courts in Anderson/Pendleton and Spartanburg Districts in upcountry South Carolina. Ideally, the study would draw records from a far

---

[7] Dylan C. Penningroth, *The Claims of Kinfolk: African American Property and Community in the Nineteenth-Century South* (Chapel Hill: University of North Carolina Press, 2003), 70–73. For a list of all African Americans with allowed claims, see Dylan C. Penningroth, "Claiming Kin and Property: African American Life before and after Emancipation" (Ph.D. diss., Johns Hopkins University, 1999), 308–328. For other work drawing heavily from SCC claims, see Philip D. Morgan, "The Ownership of Property by Slaves in the Mid-Nineteenth-Century Lowcountry," *Journal of Southern History* 49 (1983): 399–420; Dylan Penningroth, "Slavery, Freedom, and Social Claims to Property Among African Americans in Liberty County, Georgia, 1850–1880," *Journal of American History* 84 (1997): 405–435; Peggy G. Hargis, "For the Love of Place: Paternalism and Patronage in the Georgia Lowcountry, 1865–1898," *Journal of Southern History* 70 (2004): 825–864.

[8] See "Appendix A" in Frank W. Klingberg's *The Southern Claims Commission* for all eighty questions established by the Claims Commission for loyalty and property interrogations. Klingberg, *Southern Claims Commission* (Berkeley: University of California Press, 1955), 218.

[9] Penningroth, *Claims of Kinfolk*, 70; Klingberg, *Southern Claims Commission*, 218.

more expansive area. Indeed, some records of slave trials exist from Georgia, North Carolina, and Virginia, but for the most part these cases are widely scattered, interspersed within collections of inferior court files. Few records of property crimes remain and, with only a few exceptions, include very little of the extensive and detailed witness indictments and depositions required, by law, in South Carolina's Magistrates and Freeholders Courts. Although we have no way of knowing whether or not the collection of cases is complete, the 588 case files from these two districts serve as a solid sample of property crimes for which slaves faced trial, giving a more detailed picture of the goods that might have been stolen and traded in a given community during the years 1819 to 1860.[10]

---

[10] The Library of Virginia has begun a project to catalogue county Commonwealth Causes. At the time this research was conducted, only Albemarle County had been indexed by name, date, and race. Hence, the Virginia court cases I utilize in this project derive from this region alone. For explorations of the operation and, often, the inequities of the slave courts, see William Cinque Henderson, "Spartan Slaves: A Documentary Account of Blacks on Trial in Spartanburg, South Carolina, 1830–1865" (Ph.D. diss., Northwestern University, 1978); Michael S. Hindus, "Black Justice Under White Law: Criminal Prosecutions of Blacks in Antebellum South Carolina," *Journal of American History* 63 (1976): 575–599; and Hindus, *Prison and Plantation: Crime, Justice, and Authority in Massachusetts and South Carolina, 1767–1878* (Chapel Hill: University of North Carolina Press, 1980). See also Ariela J. Gross, *Double Character: Slavery and Mastery in the Antebellum Southern Courtroom* (Princeton: Princeton University Press, 2000); Daniel J. Flanigan, "Criminal Procedure in Slave Trials in the Antebellum South," *Journal of Southern History* 40 (1974): 537–564; Philip J. Schwarz, *Twice Condemned: Slaves and the Criminal Laws of Virginia, 1705–1865* (Baton Rouge: Louisiana State University Press, 1988); J. Thomas Wren, "A 'Two-Fold Character': The Slave as Person and Property in Virginia Court Cases, 1800–1860," *Southern Studies* 24 (1985): 417–431; Betty Wood, "'Until He Shall Be Dead, Dead, Dead': The Judicial Treatment of Slaves in Eighteenth-Century Georgia," *Georgia Historical Quarterly* 71 (1987): 377–398; Roberta G. McPherson, "Georgia Slave Trials, 1837–1849," *American Journal of Legal History* 4 (1960): 364–377; John C. Edwards, "Slave Justice in Four Middle Georgia Counties," *Georgia Historical Quarterly* 57 (1973): 265–273; Robert Saunders, "Crime and Punishment in Early National America: Richmond, Virginia, 1784–1820," *Virginia Magazine of History and Biography* 86 (1978): 33–44.

Bibliography

Manuscript Collections

Chapel Hill, North Carolina

Southern Historical Collection, Louis Round Wilson Special Collections Library, University of North Carolina at Chapel Hill
  Alexander Robert Lawton Papers
  Ben Sparkman Plantation Journal
  David Gavin Diary
  Elliott and Gonzales Family Papers
  George J. Kollock Plantation Journals
  Jackson and Prince Family Papers
  James Hervey Greenlee Diary
  John Edwin Fripp Papers
  John Walker Plantation Journal
  Macay and McNeely Family Papers
  William D. Valentine Diaries

Charleston, South Carolina

South Carolina Historical Society
  Almira Coffin Letters
  Celestine Lowndes Writings
  Cheves and Middleton Collection
  Francis Withers Springfield Plantation Journal
  John B. Milikin Plantation Journal
  Manigault Family Papers
  Thomas Porcher Ravenel Papers

College Park, Maryland

National Archives and Records Administration
    Case Files, Southern Claims Commission, Records of the 3rd Auditor, Allowed
        Case Files, Records of the U.S. General Accounting Office, Record Group 217

Columbia, South Carolina

South Caroliniana Library, University of South Carolina
    Charles and Company Papers
     Ledger, 1856–1861, Charles, Milling, and Company
    Davison McDowell Papers
    Edward Spann Hammond Papers
    James Ritchie Sparkman Papers
    John Black Papers
     Slave Account Book, 1824–1827
    John O. Willson Papers
    Michael Gramling Plantation Book
    Miller-Furman-Dabbs Family Papers
    Recollections of Louisa Rebecca Hayne McCord
    Samuel Gourdin Gaillard Memoir
    Thomas Cassells Law Papers
    Thomas Family Papers

South Carolina Department of Archives and History
    Anderson/Pendleton District Trial Papers, Records of the Court of Magistrates
        and Freeholders
    Pickens District Trial Papers, Records of the Court of Magistrates and Freeholders
    Store Accounts of Stephen McCulley
    Spartanburg District Trial Papers, Records of the Court of Magistrates
        and Freeholders

Durham, North Carolina

David M. Rubenstein Rare Book and Manuscript Library, Duke University
    James Burchell Richardson Papers
    Keating Simons Ball Plantation Journal
    McDonald Furman Papers

Morrow, Georgia

Georgia Department of Archives and History
    Audas and Rogers Store Account Books, Daybook, 1826
    [Coweta County] Store Account Books, 1829–1831
    Henry Freeman Store Account Book, 1822–1823
    James Morris Store Account Books, 1820–1830
    Morris and Freeman Store Account Book, 1847–1857
    Noel Burton Knight Journal, 1848–1849
    Sasnett and Smith Store Daybook, 1824
    W. L. Cleveland Store Account Books, 1830–1831

Raleigh, North Carolina

North Carolina Office of Archives and History
  Isham Edwards Accounts
    Ledger, 1821–1828
  McNeely, Young, and Company Daybooks, 1858–1859
  Richwine and Harrison Daybooks, 1853–1858
  Thomas Ballance Ledger, 1846
  [Valleytown Store Ledger], North Carolina Store, 1850–1871

Richmond, Virginia

Library of Virginia
  Albemarle County Commonwealth Causes
  Ledger and Account Book, 1825–1828, Frederick County Court Records,
    Local Government Records Collection

Virginia Historical Society
  Asa Dupuy Dickinson Letter
  B. C. Rousseau Account Book, 1855–1857
  Bagby and Gresham Account Book, 1841–1851
  Blanton Family Papers
  Eppes Family Papers
  Harrison Family Papers
  Holland Family Papers
  Keith Family Papers
  Mason Family Papers
  Payne Family Papers
  Richard Eggleston Hardaway Account Book, 1835–1864

Savannah, Georgia

Georgia Historical Society
  Couper and Wylly Family Papers
  Gilbert Isaac Germond [Overseer] Plantation Journal

Contemporary Journals

  De Bow's Review
  The Emancipator
  Farmer and Planter
  Farmers' Register
  Knickerbocker, or New-York Monthly Magazine
  New-England Magazine
  Southern Agriculturist, and Register of Rural Affairs
  Southern Agriculturist, Horticulturist, and Register of Rural Affairs
  Southern Cabinet
  Southern Cultivator
  Southern Planter

Contemporary Newspapers

Camden (SC) Commercial Courier
Charleston (SC) Courier
Charleston (SC) Mercury
Columbia (SC) Telescope
Daily Chronicle and Sentinel (Augusta, GA)
Daily Morning News (Savannah, GA)
Fayetteville (NC) Observer
Mountaineer (Greenville, SC)
Raleigh Register, and North-Carolina Gazette
Richmond (VA) Daily Whig
Semi-Weekly Raleigh (NC) Register
South-Carolina Temperance Advocate and Register of Agriculture and General Literature (Columbia, SC)
Weekly Raleigh (NC) Register

Contemporary Accounts, Memoirs, and Commentary

Achates [Thomas Pinckney]. *Reflections, Occasioned by the Late Disturbances in Charleston*. Charleston, SC: A. E. Miller, 1822.

Adams, John Quincy. *Narrative of the Life of John Quincy Adams, When in Slavery, and Now as a Freeman*. Harrisburg, PA: Sieg, 1872.

Adams, Nehemiah. *A South-Side View of Slavery; or, Three Months at the South, in 1854*. Boston: T. R. Marvin and B. B. Mussey, 1854.

Aleckson, Sam. *Before the War, and After the Union. An Autobiography*. Boston: Gold Mind, 1929.

Alexander, James. *Early Charlottesville: Recollections of James Alexander, 1828–1874*. Edited by Mary Rawlings. Charlottesville, VA: The Michie Company, 1942.

American Anti-Slavery Society. *The American Anti-Slavery Almanac, for 1840*. New York and Boston: Published for the American Anti-Slavery Society, 1839.

Avirett, James Battle. *The Old Plantation: How We Lived in Great House and Cabin Before the War*. New York: F. Tennyson Neely, 1901.

Ball, Charles. *Fifty Years in Chains; or, the Life of an American Slave*. New York: H. Dayton, 1859.

   Slavery in the United States. A Narrative of the Life and Adventures of Charles Ball, a Black Man, Who Lived Forty Years in Maryland, South Carolina and Georgia, as a Slave Under Various Masters, and was One Year in the Navy with Commodore Barney, During the Late War. New York: John S. Taylor, 1837.

Bear, John W. *The Life and Travels of John W. Bear, "The Buckeye Blacksmith."* Baltimore: D. Binswanger, 1873.

Bierce, Lucius Verus. *Travels in the Southland, 1822–1823: The Travels of Lucius Verus Bierce*. Edited by George W. Knepper. Columbus: Ohio State University Press, 1966.

Bodichon, Barbara Leigh Smith. *An American Diary, 1857–1858*. Edited by Joseph W. Reed, Jr. London: Routledge and Kegan Paul, 1972.

Branham, Levi. *My Life and Travels*. Dalton, GA: A. J. Showalter, 1929.

Bremer, Fredrika. *America of the Fifties: Letters of Fredrika Bremer*. Edited by Adolph B. Benson. New York: The American-Scandinavian Foundation, 1924.

Brown, David. *The Planter: or, Thirteen Years in the South.* Philadelphia: H. Hooker, 1853.

Brown, Henry Box and Charles Stearns. *Narrative of Henry Box Brown, Who Escaped from Slavery, Enclosed in a Box 3 Feet Long and 2 Wide. Written from a Statement of Facts Made by Himself. With Remarks Upon the Remedy for Slavery.* Boston: Brown and Stearns, 1849.

Brown, John. *Slave Life in Georgia: A Narrative of the Life, Sufferings, and Escape of John Brown, a Fugitive Slave, Now in England.* Edited by Louis Alexis Chamerovzow. London: [W. M. Watts], 1855.

Buckingham, J[ames] S. *The Slave States of America.* 2 vols. London: Fisher, Son, 1842.

Burge, Dolly Lunt. *The Diary of Dolly Lunt Burge, 1848–1879.* Edited by Christine Jacobson Carter. Athens: University of Georgia Press, 1997.

Burwell, Letitia M. *A Girl's Life in Virginia Before the War.* New York: Frederick A. Stokes, 1895.

Bushman, Claudia L., ed. *In Old Virginia: Slavery, Farming, and Society in the Journal of John Walker.* Baltimore: Johns Hopkins University Press, 2002.

Clay, Thomas S. *Detail of a Plan for the Moral Improvement of Negroes on Plantations.* n.p.: Georgia Presbytery, 1833.

Clifton, James M, ed. *Life and Labor on Argyle Island: Letters and Documents of a Savannah River Rice Plantation, 1833–1867.* Savannah, GA: The Beehive Press, 1978.

Clinkscales, J. G. *On the Old Plantation: Reminiscences of His Childhood.* Spartanburg, SC: Band and White, 1916.

Craft, William. *Running a Thousand Miles for Freedom; or, the Escape of William and Ellen Craft from Slavery.* London: William Tweedie, 1860.

Davis, Esther S. *Memories of Mulberry.* Brooklyn, NY: Eagle Press, 1913.

Drew, Benjamin. *A North-Side View of Slavery. The Refugee; or, The Narratives of Fugitive Slaves in Canada. Related by Themselves, with an Account of the History and Condition of the Colored Population of Upper Canada.* Boston: John P. Jewett, 1856.

Easterby, J. H., ed. *The South Carolina Rice Plantation as Revealed in the Papers of Robert F. W. Allston.* Columbia: University of South Carolina Press, 2004.

Elliott, E. N., ed. *Cotton is King, and Pro-Slavery Arguments: Comprising the Writings of Hammond, Harper, Christy, Stringfellow, Hodge, Bledsoe, and Cartwright, on this Important Subject.* Augusta, GA: Pritchard, Abbott, and Loomis, 1860.

Fedric, Francis. *Slave Life in Virginia and Kentucky; or, Fifty Years of Slavery in the Southern States of America.* London: Wertheim, Macintosh, and Hunt, 1863.

Floyd, Silas Xavier. *Life of Charles T. Walker, D.D. ("The Black Spurgeon.") Pastor Mt. Olivet Baptist Church, New York City.* Nashville: National Baptist Publishing Board, 1902.

French, Austa Malinda. *Slavery in South Carolina and the Ex-Slaves: or, The Port Royal Mission.* New York: Winchell M. French, 1862.

Gilman, Caroline Howard. *Recollections of a Southern Matron.* New York: Harper and Brothers, 1838.

Grandy, Moses. *Narrative of the Life of Moses Grandy; Late a Slave in the United States of America.* London: C. Gilpin, 1843.

Grimes, William. *Life of William Grimes, the Runaway Slave. Written by Himself.* New York: s.n., 1825.

Hall, Margaret Hunter. *The Aristocratic Journey; Being the Outspoken Letters of Mrs. Basil Hall Written during a Fourteen Months' Sojourn in America, 1827–1828.* Edited by Una Pope-Hennessey. New York: Putnam, 1931.

Hampton, Ann Fripp, ed. *A Divided Heart: Letters of Sally Baxter Hampton, 1853–1862.* Spartanburg, SC: Reprint Company, 1980.

Harland, Marion. *Marion Harland's Autobiography: The Story of a Long Life.* New York: Harper and Brothers, 1910.

Hawkins, William G. *Lunsford Lane; or, Another Helper from North Carolina.* Boston: Crosby and Nichols, 1863.

Howe, Samuel G. *Report to the Freedmen's Inquiry Commission, 1864: The Refugees from Slavery in Canada West.* 1864. Reprint, New York: Arno Press, 1969.

Hundley, Daniel R. *Social Relations in our Southern States.* New York: Henry B. Price, 1860.

Ingraham, John Holt. *The South-West, By a Yankee.* 2 vols. New York: Harper and Brothers, 1835.

Jackson, John Andrew. *The Experience of a Slave in South Carolina.* London: Passmore and Alabaster, 1862.

Jacobs, Harriet A. *Incidents in the Life of a Slave Girl. Written by Herself.* Edited by Lydia Maria Francis Child. Boston: Printed for Author, 1861.

Jones, Charles Colcock. *The Religious Instruction of the Negroes in the United States.* Savannah, GA: Thomas Purse, 1842.

Jones, Friday. *Days of Bondage. Autobiography of Friday Jones. Being a Brief Narrative of His Trials and Tribulations in Slavery.* Washington, DC: Commercial, 1883.

Jones, Thomas H. *Experience and Personal Narrative of Uncle Tom Jones; Who Was for Forty Years a Slave. Also the Surprising Adventures of Wild Tom, of the Island Retreat, a Fugitive from South Carolina.* Boston: H. B. Skinner, n.d.

   The Experience of Thomas H. Jones, Who was a Slave for Forty-Three Years. Boston: Bazin and Chandler, 1862.

Keckley, Elizabeth. *Behind the Scenes, or, Thirty Years a Slave, and Four Years in the White House.* New York: G. W. Carleton, 1868.

Kemble, Frances Anne. *Journal of a Residence on a Georgian Plantation in 1838–1839.* New York: Harper and Brothers, 1863.

LeConte, Joseph. *The Autobiography of Joseph Leconte.* Edited by William D. Armes. New York: D. Appleton, 1903.

Lowery, Irving E. *Life on the Old Plantation in Ante-Bellum Days.* Columbia, SC: The State, 1911.

Mallard, Robert Q. *Plantation Life before Emancipation.* Richmond, VA: Whittet and Shepperson, 1892.

Marlowe, Christopher. *The Complete Plays.* Edited by J. B. Steane. London: Penguin, 1969.

McKim, James Miller. *The Freedmen of South Carolina: An Address Delivered by J. Miller M'Kim, in Samson Hall, July 9th, 1862; Together with a Letter from the Same to Stephen Colwell, Esq., Chairman of the Port Royal Relief Committee.* Philadelphia: Willis P. Hazard, 1862.

[Mell, Patrick H.]. *Slavery. A Treatise Showing that Slavery is Neither a Moral, Political, Nor Social Evil.* Penfield, GA: Benjamin Brantley, 1844.

Murray, Charles A. *Travels in North America during the years 1834, 1835, and 1836: including a summer residence with the Pawnee tribe of Indians in the remote prairies of the Missouri, and a visit to Cuba and the Azore Islands.* 2 vols. London: Richard Bentley, 1839.

Nott, Josiah Clark, George R. Gliddon, Samuel George Morton, Louis Agassiz, William Usher, and Henry S. Patterson. *Types of Mankind: Or, Ethnological Researches, Based Upon the Ancient Monuments, Paintings, Sculptures, and Crania of Races, and Upon Their Natural, Geographical, Philological and Biblical History.* Philadelphia: Lippincott, Grambo, 1854.

Olmsted, Frederick Law. *The Cotton Kingdom: A Traveller's Observations on Cotton and Slavery in the American Slave States, 1853–1861.* 1953. Reprint, New York: Da Capo Press, 1996.

A Journey in the Backcountry. New York: Mason Brothers, 1860.

A Journey in the Seaboard Slave States, with Remarks on Their Economy. London: Sampson Low, Son, 1856.

Journeys and Explorations in the Cotton Kingdom. A Traveller's Observations on Cotton and Slavery in the American Slave States. 2 volumes. London: Sampson Low, Son, 1861.

O'Neall, John Belton, ed. *The Negro Law of South Carolina.* Columbia, SC: John G. Bowman, 1848.

Parker, Allen. *Recollections of Slavery Times.* Worcester, MA: Charles W. Burbank, 1895.

Parsons, Charles Grandison. *Inside View of Slavery: or a Tour Among the Planters.* Boston: J. P. Jewett, 1855.

Perdue, Charles L., III, Thomas E. Barden, and Robert K. Phillips, eds. *Weevils in the Wheat: Interviews with Virginia Ex-Slaves.* Charlottesville: University of Virginia Press, 1976.

Pinckney, Charles Cotesworth. *An Address Delivered in Charleston, before the Agricultural Society of South-Carolina, at its Anniversary Meeting, on Tuesday, the 18th August, 1829.* Charleston, SC: A. E. Miller, 1829.

Proceedings of the Meeting in Charleston, S.C., May 13–15, 1845, on the Religious Instruction of Negroes, Together with the Report of the Committee, and the Address to the Public. Charleston, SC: B. Jenkins, 1845.

Randolph, Peter. *From Slave Cabin to the Pulpit. The Autobiography of Rev. Peter Randolph: The Southern Question Illustrated and Sketches of Slave Life.* Boston: James H. Earle, 1893.

Rawick, George P., ed. *The American Slave: A Composite Autobiography.* 41 volumes. Westport, CT: Greenwood Press, 1972–1978.

Redpath, James. *The Roving Editor, or Talks with Slaves in the Southern States.* Edited by John R. McKivigan. 1859. Reprint, University Park, PA: Pennsylvania State University Press, 1996.

Rice, William, ed. *Reports of Cases at Law Argued and Determined in the Court of Appeals; Court of Errors of South Carolina from December, 1838, to May, 1839, Both Inclusive.* Charleston, SC: Burges and James, 1839.

Robinson, William H. *From Log Cabin to the Pulpit, or, Fifteen Years in Slavery.* Eau Claire, WI: James H. Tifft, 1913.

Roos, Rosalie. *Travels in America, 1851–1855.* Translated and edited by Carl L. Anderson. Carbondale: Southern Illinois University Press, 1982.

Rosengarten, Theodore, ed. *Tombee: Portrait of a Cotton Planter.* New York: William Morrow, 1986.

Ruffin, Edward. *Agricultural, Geological, and Descriptive Sketches of Lower North Carolina, and the Similar Adjacent Lands*. Raleigh, NC: The Institution for the Deaf and Dumb and the Blind, 1861.

  The Political Economy of Slavery; or the Institution Considered in Regard to its Influence on Public Wealth and the General Welfare. Washington, DC: L. Towers, 1857.

Schweninger, Loren, ed. *Race, Slavery, and Free Blacks: Series 1, Petitions to Southern Legislatures, 1777–1867*. Bethesda, MD: University Publications of America, 1998.

Seabury, Caroline. *The Diary of Caroline Seabury, 1854–63*. Edited by Suzanne L. Bunkers. Madison: University of Wisconsin Press, 1991.

Shippee, Lester B., ed. *Bishop Whipple's Southern Diary, 1843–1844*. New York: Da Capo Press, 1968.

Simpson, John Hawkins. *Horrors of the Virginian Slave Trade and of the Slave-Rearing Plantations. The True Story of Dinah, an Escaped Virginian Slave, Now in London, on Whose Body Are Eleven Scars Left by Tortures Which Were Inflicted by Her Master, Her Own Father. Together with Extracts from the Laws of Virginia, Showing That Against These Barbarities the Law Gives Not the Smallest Protection to the Slave, But the Reverse*. London: A. W. Bennett, 1863.

Smith, James Lindsay. *Autobiography of James L. Smith, Including, Also, Reminiscences of Slave Life, Recollections of the War, Education of Freedmen, Causes of the Exodus, etc*. Norwich, CT: Press of the Bulletin Company, 1881.

A South-Carolinian [Edwin C. Holland], ed. *A Refutation of the Calumnies Circulated against the Southern and Western States Respecting the Institution and Existence of Slavery Among Them. To which is added, a Minute and Particular Account of the Actual State and Condition of the Negro Population. Together with Historical Notices of All the Insurrections that Have Taken Place Since the Settlement of the Country*. Charleston, SC: A. E. Miller, 1822.

A Southern Farmer, *Plantation and Farm: Instruction, Regulation, Record, Inventory, and Account Book*. Richmond, VA: J. W. Randolph, 1852.

Steward, Austin. *Twenty-Two Years a Slave, and Forty Years a Freeman; Embracing a Correspondence of Several Years, While President of Wilberforce Colony, London, Canada West*. Rochester, NY: William Alling, 1857.

Stroyer, Jacob. *My Life in the South*. Salem, MA: Salem Observer Book and Job Print, 1885.

  Sketches of My Life in the South. Part I. Salem, MA: Salem Press, 1879.

Thomas, Ella Gertrude Clanton. *The Secret Eye: The Journal of Ella Gertrude Clanton Thomas, 1848–1889*. Edited by Virginia Ingraham Burr. Chapel Hill: University of North Carolina Press, 1990.

Thomson, William. *A Tradesman's Travels, in the United States and Canada, in the Years 1840, 41, and 42*. Edinburgh: Oliver and Boyd, 1842.

Warren, Edward. *A Doctor's Experience in Three Continents*. Baltimore: Cushings and Bailey, 1885.

Washington, Booker T. *An Autobiography: The Story of My Life and Work*. Toronto: J. L. Nichols, 1901.

  Up From Slavery: An Autobiography. Garden City, NY: Doubleday, 1900.

Williams, Isaac D. and William Ferguson Goldie. *Sunshine and Shadow of Slave Life. Reminiscences as told by Isaac D. Williams to "Tege."* East Saginaw: Evening News Binding and Printing House, 1885.

Secondary Sources

Abelson, Elaine S. *When Ladies Go A-Thieving: Middle Class Shoplifters in the Victorian Department Store*. New York: Oxford University Press, 1989.

Anderson, James D. "Aunt Jemima in Dialectics: Genovese on Slave Culture." *Journal of Negro History* 61 (1976): 99–114.

Appadurai, Arjun, ed. *The Social Life of Things: Commodities in Cultural Perspective*. New York: Cambridge University Press, 1986.

Aptheker, Herbert. *American Negro Slave Revolts*. New York: Columbia University Press, 1943.

Atherton, Lewis E. *The Southern Country Store, 1800–1860*. 1949. Reprint, Westport, CT: Greenwood Press, 1968.

Ayers, Edward L. *Vengeance and Justice: Crime and Punishment in the Nineteenth-Century American South*. New York: Oxford University Press, 1984.

Barnes, L. Diane, Brian Schoen, and Frank Towers, eds. *The Old South's Modern Worlds: Slavery, Region, and Nation in the Age of Progress*. New York: Oxford University Press, 2011.

Baumol, William J. "Entrepreneurship: Productive, Unproductive, and Destructive." *Journal of Political Economy* 98 (1990): 893–921.

Benson, John. *The Rise of Consumer Society in Britain, 1880–1980*. New York: Longman, 1994.

Berlin, Ira. *Slaves without Masters: The Free Negro in the Antebellum South*. New York: Oxford University Press, 1974.

Berlin, Ira and Philip D. Morgan. *Cultivation and Culture: Labor and the Shaping of Slave Life in the Americas*. Charlottesville: University Press of Virginia, 1993.

The Slaves' Economy: Independent Production by Slaves in the Americas. London: Frank Cass, 1991.

Berry, Daina Ramey. *Swing the Sickle for the Harvest Is Ripe: Gender and Slavery in Antebellum Georgia*. Urbana: University of Illinois Press, 2007.

Bigham, Shauna and Robert E. May, "The Time O' All Times? Masters, Slaves, and Christmas in the Old South," *Journal of the Early Republic* 18 (1998): 263–288.

Blassingame, John W. *The Slave Community: Plantation Life in the Antebellum South*. New York: Oxford University Press, 1972.

Bogger, Tommy L. *Free Blacks in Norfolk, Virginia, 1790–1860: The Darker Side of Freedom*. Charlottesville: University Press of Virginia, 1997.

Bourdieu, Pierre. *Distinction: A Social Critique of the Judgement of Taste*. Translated by Richard Nice. Cambridge, MA: Harvard University Press, 1984.

Bowman, Shearer Davis. "Conditional Unionism and Slavery in Virginia, 1860–61: The Case of Dr. Richard Eppes." *Virginia Magazine of History and Biography* 96 (1988): 31–54.

Brana-Shute, Rosemary and Randy J. Sparks, eds. *Paths to Freedom: Manumission in the Atlantic World*. Columbia: University of South Carolina Press, 2009.

Breeden, James O., ed. *Advice Among Masters: The Ideal in Plantation Management in the Old South*. Westport, CT: Greenwood Press, 1980.

Breen, Timothy H. "Horses and Gentlemen: The Cultural Significance of Gambling among the Gentry of Virginia." *William and Mary Quarterly*, 3rd Series, 34 (1977): 239–257.

The Marketplace of Revolution: How Consumer Politics Shaped American Independence. New York: Oxford University Press, 2004.

Brewer, John and Roy Porter. *Consumption and the World of Goods.* New York: Routledge, 1993.

Buchanan, Thomas C. *Black Life on the Mississippi: Slaves, Free Blacks, and the Western Steamboat World.* Chapel Hill: University of North Carolina Press, 2004.

Bushman, Richard L. *The Refinement of America: Persons, Houses, Cities.* New York: Vintage Books, 1992.

Byrne, Frank J. *Becoming Bourgeois: Merchant Culture in the South.* Lexington: University Press of Kentucky, 2006.

Camp, Stephanie M. H. *Closer to Freedom: Enslaved Women and Everyday Resistance in the Plantation South.* Chapel Hill: University of North Carolina Press, 2004.

Campbell, Stanley W. *The Slave Catchers: Enforcement of the Fugitive Slave Law, 1850–1860.* Chapel Hill: University of North Carolina Press, 1968.

Carrier, James G. *Gifts and Commodities: Exchange and Western Capitalism since 1700.* London: Routledge, 1995.

Clark, Christopher. *The Roots of Rural Capitalism: Western Massachusetts, 1780–1860.* (Ithaca, NY: Cornell University Press, 1990).

Cohen, Patricia Cline. *A Calculating People: The Spread of Numeracy in Early America.* 1982. Reprint, New York: Routledge, 1999.

Cornelius, Janet Duitsman. *When I Can Read My Title Clear: Literacy, Slavery, and Religion in the Antebellum South.* Columbia: University of South Carolina Press, 1991.

Crowley, John E. *The Invention of Comfort: Sensibilities and Design in Early Modern Britain and Early America.* Baltimore: The Johns Hopkins University Press, 2001.

Danesh, Abol Hassan. *The Informal Economy: A Research Guide.* New York: Garland, 1991.

David, Paul A., Herbert G. Gutman, Richard Sutch, Peter Temin, and Gavin Wright, eds. *Reckoning with Slavery: A Critical Study in the Quantitative History of American Negro Slavery.* New York: Oxford University Press, 1976.

Davis, Charles T. and Henry Louis Gates, Jr., eds. *The Slave's Narrative.* New York: Oxford University Press, 1985.

Densmore, Christopher. "Understanding and Using Early Nineteenth Century Account Books." *Midwestern Archivist* 5 (1980): 5–19.

Dorson, Richard M., ed. *American Negro Folktales.* Greenwich, CT: Fawcett, 1956.

Eaton, Clement. *The Waning of the Old South Civilization.* Athens: University of Georgia Press, 1968.

Edwards, John C. "Slave Justice in Four Middle Georgia Counties." *Georgia Historical Quarterly* 57 (1973): 265–273.

Egerton, Douglas R. "Slaves to the Marketplace: Economic Liberty and Black Rebelliousness in the Atlantic World." *Journal of the Early Republic* 26 (2006): 617–639.

Elkins, Stanley M. *Slavery: A Problem in American Institutional and Intellectual Life.* 3rd ed., rev. Chicago: University of Chicago Press, 1976.

Fede, Andrew. *Roadblocks to Freedom: Slavery and Manumission in the United States South.* New Orleans: Quid Pro Books, 2011.

Fehrenbacher, Don E. and Ward M. McAfee. *The Slaveholding Republic: An Account of the United States Government's Relations to Slavery.* New York: Oxford University Press, 2001.

Finkelman, Paul, ed. *Slavery and the Law*. Madison, WI: Madison House, 1997.

Flanigan, Daniel J. "Criminal Procedure in Slave Trials in the Antebellum South." *Journal of Southern History* 40 (1974): 537–564.

Fogel, Robert William and Stanley L. Engerman. *Time on the Cross: The Economics of American Negro Slavery*. Boston: Little, Brown, 1974.

Ford, Lacy K. *Deliver Us from Evil: The Slavery Question in the Old South*. New York: Oxford University Press, 2009.

Forret, Jeff. "Conflict and the 'Slave Community': Violence among Slaves in Upcountry South Carolina." *Journal of Southern History* 74 (2008): 551–588.

Race Relations at the Margins: Slaves and Poor Whites in the Antebellum Southern Countryside. Baton Rouge: Louisiana State University Press, 2006.

"Slaves, Poor Whites, and the Underground Economy of the Rural Carolinas." *Journal of Southern History* 70 (2004): 783–824.

Fox-Genovese, Elizabeth. "The Many Faces of Moral Economy: A Contribution to a Debate." *Past and Present* 58 (1973): 161–168.

Franklin, John Hope. *The Free Negro in North Carolina, 1790–1860*. 1943. Reprint, Chapel Hill: University of North Carolina Press, 1995.

Franklin, John Hope and Loren Schweninger. *Runaway Slaves: Rebels on the Plantation*. New York: Oxford University Press, 1999.

Fredrickson, George M. *The Black Image in the White Mind: The Debate on Afro-American Character and Destiny, 1817–1914*. New York: Harper and Row, 1971.

Frow, John. *Time and Commodity Culture: Essays in Cultural Theory and Postmodernity*. New York: Oxford University Press, 1997.

Geertz, Clifford. *The Interpretation of Cultures*. New York: Basic Books, 1973.

Genovese, Eugene D. *In Red and Black: Marxian Explorations in Southern and Afro-American History*. New York: Pantheon Books, 1968.

The Political Economy of Slavery: Studies in the Economy and Society of the Slave South. 2nd ed. Middletown, CT: Wesleyan University Press, 1989.

Roll, Jordan, Roll: The World the Slaves Made. New York: Pantheon Books, 1974.

The Slaveholders' Dilemma: Freedom and Progress in Southern Conservative Thought, 1820–1860. Columbia: University of South Carolina Press, 1991.

Genovese, Eugene D. and Elizabeth Fox-Genovese. *Fatal Self-Deception: Slaveholding Paternalism in the Old South*. New York: Cambridge University Press, 2011.

"The Political Crisis of Social History: A Marxian Perspective." *Journal of Social History* 10 (1976): 205–220.

Glickman, Lawrence, ed. *Consumer Society in American History: A Reader*. Ithaca, NY: Cornell University Press, 1999.

Goffman, Erving. *Relations in Public: Microstudies of the Public Order*. New York: Basic Books, 1971.

Gramsci, Antonio. *Selections from the Prison Notebooks of Antonio Gramsci*. Edited by Quintin Hoare and Geoffrey Nowell-Smith. New York: International Publishers, 1971.

Greenberg, Kenneth S. *Honor and Slavery: Lies, Duels, Noses, Masks, Dressing as a Woman, Gifts, Strangers, Humanitarianism, Death, Slave Rebellions, the Proslavery Argument, Baseball, Hunting, and Gambling in the Old South*. Princeton: Princeton University Press, 1996.

Gregory, Christopher A. *Gifts and Commodities*. London: Academic Press, 1982.

Gross, Ariela J. *Double Character: Slavery and Mastery in the Antebellum Southern Courtroom*. Princeton, NJ: Princeton University Press, 2000.

Guillory, James Denny. "The Pro-Slavery Arguments of Dr. Samuel A. Cartwright." *Louisiana History* 9 (1968): 209–227.

Gutman, Herbert G. *Slavery and the Numbers Game: A Critique of Time on the Cross*. Urbana: University of Illinois Press, 1975.

Hadden, Sally E. *Slave Patrols: Law and Violence in Virginia and the Carolinas*. Cambridge, MA: Harvard University Press, 2001.

Hargis, Peggy G. "For the Love of Place: Paternalism and Patronage in the Georgia Lowcountry, 1865–1898." *Journal of Southern History* 70 (2004): 825–864.

Henderson, William Cinque. "Spartan Slaves: A Documentary Account of Blacks on Trial in Spartanburg, South Carolina, 1830–1865." Ph.D. diss., Northwestern University, 1978.

Hilliard, Kathleen M. "Spending in Black and White: Race, Slavery, and Consumer Values in the Old South." Ph.D. diss., University of South Carolina, 2006.

Hilliard, Sam Bowers. *Hog Meat and Hoecake: Food Supply in the Old South, 1840–1860*. Carbondale: Southern Illinois University Press, 1972.

Hindus, Michael. "Black Justice under White Law: Criminal Prosecutions of Blacks in Antebellum South Carolina." *Journal of American History* 63 (1976): 575–599.

   Prison and Plantation: Crime, Justice, and Authority in Massachusetts and South Carolina, 1767–1878. Chapel Hill: University of North Carolina Press, 1980.

Hobsbawm, Eric J. *On History*. New York: The New Press, 1997.

Hodes, Martha. *White Women, Black Men: Illicit Sex in the Nineteenth-Century South*. New Haven, CT: Yale University Press, 1997.

Horowitz, Daniel. *The Morality of Spending: Attitudes toward the Consumer Society in America, 1875–1940*. Baltimore: Johns Hopkins University Press, 1985.

Hudson, Larry E., Jr., ed. *Working toward Freedom: Slave Society and Domestic Economy in the American South*. Rochester, NY: University of Rochester Press, 1994.

Hunt, Lynn, ed. *The New Cultural History*. Berkeley: University of California Press, 1989.

Huston, James L. "The American Revolutionaries, the Political Economy of Aristocracy, and the American Concept of the Distribution of Wealth." *American Historical Review* 98 (1993): 1079–1105.

Inscoe, John C. "Carolina Slave Names: An Index to Acculturation." *Journal of Southern History* 49 (1983): 527–554.

Jaffee, David. "Peddlers of Progress and the Transformation of the Rural North, 1760–1860." *Journal of American History* 78 (1991): 511–535.

   A New Nation of Goods: The Material Culture of Early America. Philadelphia: University of Pennsylvania Press, 2010.

Johnson, Paul. *Saving and Spending: The Working Class Economy in Britain, 1870–1939*. New York: Oxford University Press, 1985.

Johnson, Walter. "A Nettlesome Classic Turns Twenty-Five." *Common-Place* 1, no. 4 (2001). http://www.common-place.org/vol-01/no-04/reviews/johnson.shtml.

   Soul by Soul: Life Inside the Antebellum Slave Market. Cambridge, MA: Harvard University Press, 1999.

Joyner, Charles. *Down by the Riverside: A South Carolina Slave Community*. Urbana: University of Illinois Press, 1984.

Kaye, Anthony E. *Joining Places: Slave Neighborhoods in the Old South*. Chapel Hill: University of North Carolina Press, 2007.

Kelley, Robin D. G. *Race Rebels: Culture, Politics, and the Black Working Class*. New York: The Free Press, 1994.

King, Lovalerie. *Race, Theft, and Ethics: Property Matters in African American Literature*. Baton Rouge: Louisiana State University Press, 2007.

Klebaner, Benjamin Joseph. "American Manumission Laws and the Responsibility for Supporting Slaves." *Virginia Magazine of History and Biography* 63 (1955): 443–453.

Klingberg, Frank W. *The Southern Claims Commission*. Berkeley: University of California Press, 1955.

Kolchin, Peter. "Eugene D. Genovese: Historian of Slavery." *Radical History Review* 88 (2004): 52–67.

———. "Reevaluating the Antebellum Slave Community: A Comparative Perspective." *Journal of American History* 70 (1983): 579–601.

Koverman, Jill Beute, ed. *"I made this jar...": The Life and Works of the Enslaved African-American Potter, Dave*. Columbia: McKissick Museum, University of South Carolina, 1998.

Lemire, Beverly. "Peddling Fashion: Salesmen, Pawnbrokers, Taylors, Thieves and the Second-hand Clothes Trade in England, c. 1700–1800." *Textile History* 22 (1991): 67–82.

———. "The Theft of Clothes and Popular Consumerism in Early Modern England." *Journal of Social History* 24 (1990): 255–276.

Levine, Lawrence. *Black Culture and Black Consciousness: Afro-American Folk Thought from Slavery to Freedom*. New York: Oxford University Press, 1977.

Lichtenstein, Alex. "'That disposition to theft, with which they have been branded': Moral Economy, Slave Management, and the Law." *Journal of Social History* 21 (1988): 413–440.

Lockley, Timothy James. *Lines in the Sand: Race and Class in Lowcountry Georgia, 1750–1860*. Athens: University of Georgia Press, 2001.

———. "Trading Encounters between Non-Elite Whites and African Americans in Savannah, 1790–1860." *Journal of Southern History* 66 (2000): 25–48.

MacMillan, Dougald. "John Kuners." *Journal of American Folklore* 39 (1926): 53–57.

Mallios, Seth. *The Deadly Politics of Giving: Exchange and Violence at Acajan, Roanoke, and Jamestown*. Tuscaloosa: University of Alabama Press, 2006.

Martin, Ann Smart. *Buying into the World of Goods: Early Consumers in Backcountry Virginia*. Baltimore: Johns Hopkins University Press, 2008.

———. "Buying into the World of Goods: Eighteenth-Century Consumerism and the Retail Trade from London to the Virginia Frontier." Ph.D. diss., College of William and Mary, 1993.

Martin, Jonathan D. *Divided Mastery: Slave Hiring in the American South*. Cambridge, MA: Harvard University Press, 2004.

Marx, Karl. *Capital: A Critique of Political Economy*. 3 vols. Moscow: Progress Publishers, 1977.

———. *Grundrisse: Foundations of the Critique of Political Economy*. Translated and edited by Martin Nicolaus. New York: Penguin, 1993.

Mauss, Marcel. *The Gift: The Form and Reason for Exchange in Archaic Societies*. Translated by W. D. Halls. New York: W. W. Norton, 1990.

McCracken, Grant. *Culture and Consumption: New Approaches to the Symbolic Character of Consumer Goods and Activities*. Bloomington: Indiana University Press, 1990.

McDonald, Roderick A. *The Economy and Material Culture of Slaves: Goods and Chattels on the Sugar Plantations of Jamaica and Louisiana.* Baton Rouge: Louisiana State University Press, 1993.

McDonnell, Lawrence T. "Money Knows No Master: Market Relations and the American Slave Community." In *Developing Dixie: Modernization in a Traditional Society,* edited by Winfred B. Moore, Jr., Joseph F. Tripp, and Lyon G. Tyler, Jr., 31–44. New York: Greenwood Press, 1988.

———. "Work, Culture, and Society in the Slave South, 1790–1861." In *Black and White Cultural Interaction in the Antebellum South,* edited by Ted Ownby, 125–148. Jackson: University Press of Mississippi, 1993.

McPherson, Robert G. "Georgia Slave Trials, 1837–1849." *The American Journal of Legal History* 4 (1960): 364–377.

Mintz, Sidney W. "Caribbean Marketplaces and Caribbean History." *Nova Americana* 1 (1980–81): 333–344.

———. *Caribbean Transformations.* New York: Columbia University Press, 1974.

———. "The Jamaican Internal Marketing Pattern: Some Notes and Hypotheses." *Social and Economic Studies* 4 (1955): 95–103.

Mintz, Sidney W. and Douglas G. Hall. "The Origins of the Jamaican Internal Marketing System." *Yale University Publications in Anthropology* 57 (1960): 3–26.

Morgan, Philip D. "The Ownership of Property by Slaves in the Mid-Nineteenth-Century Lowcountry." *Journal of Southern History* 49 (1983): 399–420.

———. *Slave Counterpoint: Black Culture in the Eighteenth-Century Chesapeake and Lowcountry, 1740–1790.* Chapel Hill: University of North Carolina Press, 1998.

———. "Work and Culture: The Task System and the World of Lowcountry Blacks, 1700–1800." *William and Mary Quarterly* 3rd ser., 39 (1982): 563–599.

Morris, Christopher. *Becoming Southern: The Evolution of a Way of Life, Warren County and Vicksburg, Mississippi, 1770–1860.* New York: Oxford University Press, 1995.

Morris, Thomas. *Southern Slavery and the Law, 1619–1860.* Chapel Hill: University of North Carolina Press, 1996.

Muir, Edward. *Ritual in Early Modern Europe.* New York: Cambridge University Press, 1997.

Nicholls, Michael L. "'In the Light of Human Beings': Richard Eppes and His Island Plantation Code of Laws." *Virginia Magazine of History and Biography* 89 (1981): 67–78.

Nissenbaum, Stephen. *The Battle for Christmas: A Cultural History of America's Most Cherished Holiday.* New York: Vintage Books, 1996.

Oakes, James. "From Republicanism to Liberalism: Ideological Change and the Crisis of the Old South." *American Quarterly* 37 (1985): 551–571.

———. *The Ruling Race: A History of American Slaveholders.* New York: Alfred A. Knopf, 1982.

———. *Slavery and Freedom: An Interpretation of the Old South.* New York: Alfred A. Knopf, 1990.

Olwell, Robert. *Masters, Slaves, and Subjects: The Culture of Power in the South Carolina Lowcountry, 1740–1790.* Ithaca, NY: Cornell University Press, 1998.

Otnes, Cele and Richard F. Beltramini, eds., *Gift Giving: A Research Anthology.* Bowling Green: Bowling Green State University Popular Press, 1996.

Ownby, Ted. *American Dreams in Mississippi: Consumers, Poverty, and Culture, 1830–1998*. Chapel Hill: University of North Carolina Press, 1999.

Painter, Nell Irvin. *Creating Black Americans: African-American History and Its Meanings, 1619 to the Present*. New York: Oxford University Press, 2006.

Paquette, Robert L. and Mark M. Smith, eds. *The Oxford Handbook of Slavery in the Americas*. New York: Oxford University Press, 2010.

Penningroth, Dylan C. "Claiming Kin and Property: African American Life before and after Emancipation." Ph.D. diss., Johns Hopkins University, 1999.

The Claims of Kinfolk: African American Property and Community in the Nineteenth-Century South. Chapel Hill: University of North Carolina Press, 2003.

"Slavery, Freedom, and Social Claims to Property in Liberty County, Georgia, 1850–1880." *Journal of American History* 84 (1997): 405–435.

Phillips, Ulrich B. *American Negro Slavery: A Survey of the Supply, Employment and Control of Negro Labor As Determined by the Plantation Regime*. 1918. Reprint, Baton Rouge: Louisiana State University Press, 1966.

Phillips, Ulrich B., ed. *Plantation and Frontier, 1649–1863*. 2 vols. 1909. Reprint, New York: Burt Franklin, 1969.

Quist, John W. *Restless Visionaries: The Social Roots of Antebellum Reform in Alabama and Michigan*. Baton Rouge: Louisiana State University Press, 1998.

Radin, Margaret Jane. *Contested Commodities*. Cambridge, MA: Harvard University Press, 1996.

Roediger, David R. *The Wages of Whiteness: Race and the Making of the American Working Class*. New York: Verso Books, 1991.

Working Toward Whiteness: How America's Immigrants Became White. New York: Basic Books, 2005.

Rorabaugh, W. J. *The Alcoholic Republic: An American Tradition*. New York: Oxford University Press, 1979.

Rothman, Joshua D. *Notorious in the Neighborhood: Sex and Families across the Color Line in Virginia, 1787–1861*. Chapel Hill: University of North Carolina Press, 2003.

Russell, John Henderson. *The Free Negro in Virginia, 1619–1865*. 1913. Reprint, New York: Negro Universities Press, 1969.

Saunders, Robert. "Crime and Punishment in Early National America: Richmond, Virginia, 1784–1820." *Virginia Magazine of History and Biography* 86 (1978): 33–44.

Schwarz, Philip J. *Twice Condemned: Slaves and the Criminal Laws of Virginia, 1705–1765*. Baton Rouge: Louisiana State University Press, 1988.

Schweninger, Loren. *Black Property Owners in the South, 1790–1915*. Urbana: University of Illinois Press, 1990.

Schweninger, Loren, ed. *The Southern Debate over Slavery: Petitions to Southern Legislatures, 1778–1864*. Urbana: University of Illinois Press, 2001.

Schweninger, Loren, Robert Shelton, and Charles Smith, eds. *Race, Slavery, and Free Blacks: Petitions to Southern Legislatures, 1777–1867: A Guide to the Microfilm Edition*. Bethesda, MD: University Publications of America, 1999.

Scott, James C. *Weapons of the Weak: Everyday Forms of Peasant Resistance*. New Haven, CT: Yale University Press, 1985.

Singleton, Theresa A. "Slavery and Spatial Dialectics on Cuban Coffee Plantations." *World Archaeology* 33 (2001): 98–114.

Smith, Mark M. *How Race Is Made: Slavery, Segregation, and the Senses.* Chapel Hill: University of North Carolina Press, 2006.

 Mastered by the Clock: Time, Slavery, and Freedom in the American South. Chapel Hill: University of North Carolina Press, 1997.

Smith, Merril D., ed. *Sex and Sexuality in Early America.* New York: New York University Press, 1998.

 Sex without Consent: Rape and Sexual Coercion in America. New York: New York University Press, 2001.

Sobel, Mechal. *The World They Made Together: Black and White Values in Eighteenth-Century Virginia.* Princeton, NJ: Princeton University Press, 1987.

Sommerville, Diane Miller. "The Rape Myth in the Old South Reconsidered." *Journal of Southern History* 61 (1995): 481–518.

Stampp, Kenneth M. *The Peculiar Institution: Slavery in the Ante-Bellum South.* New York: Vintage Books, 1956.

Stanley, Amy Dru. *From Bondage to Contract: Wage Labor, Marriage, and the Market in the Age of Slave Emancipation.* New York: Cambridge University Press, 1998.

Stanton, William. *The Leopard's Spots: Scientific Attitudes toward Race in America, 1815–1859.* Chicago: University of Chicago Press, 1960.

Stearns, Peter N. "Stages of Consumerism: Recent Work on the Issues of Periodization." *Journal of Modern History* 69 (1997): 102–117.

Stuckey, Sterling. *Slave Culture: Nationalist Theory and the Foundations of Black America.* New York: Oxford University Press, 1987.

 "Through the Prism of Folklore: The Black Ethos in Slavery." *Massachusetts Review* 9 (1968): 417–437.

Sykes, Gresham M. and David Matza. "Techniques of Neutralization: A Theory of Delinquency." *American Sociological Review* 22 (1957): 664–670.

Taylor, Ian, Paul Walton, and Jock Young. *The New Criminology: For a Social Theory of Deviance.* New York: Routledge, 1973.

Thompson, E. P. *Customs in Common: Studies in Traditional Popular Culture.* New York: New Press, 1993.

Trentmann, Frank, ed. *Oxford Handbook of the History of Consumption.* New York: Oxford University Press, 2012.

Tyrrell, Ian R. "Drink and Temperance in the Antebellum South: An Overview and Interpretation." *Journal of Southern History* 48 (1982): 485–510.

Veblen, Thorstein. *The Theory of the Leisure Class: An Economic Study of Institutions.* 1899. Mineola, NY: Dover, 1994.

Venkatesh, Sudhir Alladi. *Off the Books: The Underground Economy of the Urban Poor.* Cambridge, MA: Harvard University Press, 2006.

Walker, Clarence E. *Deromanticizing Black History: Critical Essays and Reappraisals.* Knoxville: University of Tennessee Press, 1991.

Weiner, Annette B. *Inalienable Possessions: The Paradox of Keeping-While-Giving.* Berkeley: University of California Press, 1992.

West, Emily. *Chains of Love: Slave Couples in Antebellum South Carolina.* Urbana: University of Illinois Press, 2004.

 Family or Freedom: People of Color in Antebellum South Carolina. Lexington: University Press of Kentucky, 2012.

White, Shane and Graham White. "Slave Hair and African American Culture in the Eighteenth and Nineteenth Centuries." *Journal of Southern History* 61 (1995): 45–76.

Stylin': African American Expressive Culture from Its Beginnings to the Zoot Suit. Ithaca, NY: Cornell University Press, 1998.

Whitman, T. Stephen. *The Price of Freedom: Slavery and Manumission in Baltimore and Early National Maryland.* Lexington: University Press of Kentucky, 1997.

Wikramanayake, Marina. *A World in Shadow: The Free Black in Antebellum South Carolina.* Columbia: University of South Carolina Press, 1973.

Williams, Rosalind H. *Dream Worlds: Mass Consumption in Late Nineteenth-Century France.* Berkeley: University of California Press, 1982.

Wilson, Robert, III. "Early American Account Books: Interpretation, Cataloguing, and Use." Technical Leaflet 140, American Association for State and Local History. *History News* 36 (1981): 21–28.

Wood, Betty. "'Until He Shall Be Dead, Dead, Dead': The Judicial Treatment of Slaves in Eighteenth-Century Georgia." *Georgia Historical Quarterly* LXXI (1987): 377–398.

Women's Work, Men's Work: The Informal Slave Economies of Lowcountry Georgia. Athens: University of Georgia Press, 1995.

Wren, J. Thomas. "A 'Two-Fold Character': The Slave as Person and Property in Virginia Court Cases, 1800–1860." *Southern Studies* 24 (1985): 417–431.

Yates, Joshua J. and James Davison Hunter, eds. *Thrift and Thriving in America: Capitalism and Moral Order from the Puritans to the Present.* New York: Oxford University Press, 2011.

Yetman, Norman R. "The Background of the Slave Narrative Collection." *American Quarterly* 19 (1967): 534–553.

"Ex-Slave Interviews and the Historiography of Slavery." *American Quarterly* 36 (1984): 181–210.

Zakim, Michael. "The Business Clerk as Social Revolutionary; or, a Labor History of the Nonproducing Classes." *Journal of the Early Republic* 26 (2006): 563–603.

Ready-Made Democracy: A History of Men's Dress in the Early Republic, 1760–1860. Chicago: University of Chicago Press, 2003.

"Sartorial Ideologies: From Homespun to Ready-Made." *American Historical Review* 106 (2001): 1553–1586.

Zelizer, Vivian A. *The Social Meaning of Money: Pin Money, Paychecks, Poor Relief and Other Currencies.* New York: Basic Books, 1994.

Index